# TIME IN PRACTICE

# TIME IN PRACTICE

## ANALYTICAL PERSPECTIVES
## ON THE TIMES OF OUR LIVES

*Mary Lynne Ellis*

**KARNAC**

First published in 2008 by
Karnac Books Ltd
118 Finchley Road
London NW3 5HT

British Library Cataloguing in Publication Data

A.C.I.P. for this book is available from the British Library

ISBN-13: 978-1-85575-561-1

Edited, designed, and produced by Sheffield Typesetting
www.sheffieldtypesetting.com
e-mail: admin@ sheffieldtypesetting.com

www.karnacbooks.com

# CONTENTS

*For Noreen*

# ACKNOWLEDGEMENTS

I am very grateful to Keith Ellis and Myfanwy Rose Ellis for their support, their respect for diligence, and their courage to challenge. Niamh O'Connor's and Leonard Kelleher's thoughtful encouragement has been very important to me. Thank you, Katie, for your adventurous spirit.

Ide ní Laoghaire and Jane Aaron's friendship and advice have been enormously helpful to me. The support of friends and colleagues, particularly Hannah Cooke, Daphne Degotardi, Mercedes Nunez, and Heather Townsend, has also been very sustaining.

I especially want to thank Sally Berry for her incisiveness, imagination, and wisdom.

I am hugely grateful to Noreen O'Connor for her rigour, originality, and sensitivity. I very much appreciate the generosity of her critical reading of the manuscript.

Finally, I want to express my gratitude to my patients, supervisees, and students for all that I have learned from our times with one another.

## ABOUT THE AUTHOR

Mary Lynne Ellis is a psychoanalytic psychotherapist and art therapist in private practice in North London. She has an MA in Modern European Philosophy and has lectured and published widely on phenomenological perspectives of psychoanalysis. She is also a practising artist.

# Questions of time

*"If you live in time you want it to go fast. When you look back at it, it has gone too quickly. I often wish my life away".*

*"I am always a future person. Now I can't see beyond tomorrow. I can't see anything except what I have lost".*

T he words of these patients, spoken in their psychoanalytic sessions, highlight the ways in which experiences of time interweave our lives. This book argues for the crucial importance in the psychoanalytic relationship of an attentiveness to these temporal experiences in their conscious and their unconscious aspects. Although, as I show, psychoanalytic theorizing implicitly addresses this question, it is often not explicitly articulated. Freud's concepts of the unconscious, regression, displacement, condensation, and transference, for example, all rely on notions of time which remain unthematized. Heated debates between analysts as to what constitutes efficacy in psychoanalysis refer implicitly to time: the length and the frequency of the sessions, the length of the analysis, and breaks in the analysis (whether instigated by the analyst or the patient).

Articulations of time tend to use spatial metaphors and this is evident, as I show, in much psychoanalytic theorizing of subjectivity.

In this book, I emphasize instead the "intertemporality" of our subjectivities. This is not to deny that our notions of space and time are
enfolded within one another. This book aims to explore some of the
unexamined temporal assumptions which are built into psychoanalytic theorizing and to open out possibilities of new temporal perspectives for psychoanalytic practices.

In the first four chapters I identify the different implicit and explicit
theories of time in the texts of Freud, Jung, Klein, Lacan and Winnicott. I focus on their work since their heritage continues to be highly
influential on psychoanalytic theorizing and practices contemporaneously. This is transmitted through the psychoanalytic institutions
and organizations in the training, supervision, and personal analysis
of analysts. Embedded in the psychoanalytic tradition are assumptions about temporality (including the failure to acknowledge its
importance) which often remain unconscious and or unexamined on
the part of analysts and which are, nevertheless, operative in psychoanalytic work. Through my clinical examples I highlight why an
attunement to experiences of "lived time" in all three dimensions
matters in clinical practice.

A strong tendency to over-emphasize the importance of the past is
prevalent in psychoanalytic theorizing, with the exception of Jung's
and Lacan's work. This is not to dismiss the crucial importance of an
individual's shifting perceptions of their history, but rather to argue
for an attentiveness that is also inclusive of the present and the future
dimensions of their experiences. How individuals "live" time in all
three dimensions is pivotal to the analyses of subjectivity of philosophers writing from phenomenological, existential, and deconstructive perspectives, albeit with varying emphases. In later chapters
of the book I explore how modern European philosophical theories
of temporality (in particular, those of Merleau-Ponty, Foucault,
Levinas and Ricoeur) can contribute to an increased attentiveness to
individuals' lived experiences of time. My consideration of these is
interwoven with my reflections on Eva Hoffman's personal descriptions in her autobiographical work, *Lost In Translation* and also on
Thomas Mann's *The Magic Mountain*.

How can philosophy contribute anything to the rich and always
developing tradition? What is the value of its theorizing for psychoanalytic practices? These questions assume that, from Freud onwards,
psychoanalysts have eschewed philosophy as not being relevant to

interpretations of the complexities of unconscious experiences as they are expressed in the psychoanalytic relationship. However, throughout the writings of Freud, Jung, Winnicott, and Lacan the influence of philosophers is evident, although not always acknowledged. For example, Freud attended the seminars of Brentano, a German philosopher (1838–1913) who also taught Husserl, and Lacan debated publicly with Merleau-Ponty. Jung's work contains many references to Spinoza, Leibnitz, and others. Their interest in modern European philosophers arose because these writers were addressing the very concerns which preoccupy psychoanalysts, namely questions regarding the relations between mind and body, conscious and unconscious, subjectivity and temporality, language, feelings, and expression.

Many modern European philosophers, such as Merleau-Ponty and Foucault (see Chapters Five and Six), as well as Sartre, De Beauvoir, Wittgenstein and others, directly address the theorizing of psychoanalysts in their work. In France and Germany, a number of psychoanalysts and psychiatrists who were inspired by the work of phenomenological and existential thinkers (Heidegger in particular) developed "Daseins-Analyse". Debates and cross-fertilization between the disciplines of psychoanalysis is therefore not new. These exchanges continue to influence contemporary theorizing within in the fields of culture studies, literary criticism, and film studies. Within psychoanalysis a number of psychoanalytic trainings have integrated teaching in modern European philosophical thought alongside that of major figures in the psychoanalytic tradition.

The theme of time gathers together many questions which are central to both psychoanalytic and modern European philosophical thought. In this book I distinguish linear (chronological) time from "lived time", emphasizing that time is not an object which exists outside of or beyond us; it is a dimension of our being. Merleau-Ponty (1945), for example, argues that time *is* the subject. Hoffman's moving accounts of her shifting temporal experiences as a Polish refugee living in Canada from the age of thirteen, resonate with this notion of "lived time" and other conceptualizations of time in modern European philosophical texts. Through an elucidation of their thinking I show how these can extend analysts' sensitivity to unconscious and conscious experiences of lived time in the psychoanalytic relationship. As the book highlights, questions about time are intrinsic to those regarding memory and forgetting, embodiment, language, the continuity and/

or discontinuities of identities, the socio-historical specificity of the subject, the significance of death for us in our lived present, and of change. Contemporary psychoanalysts debate the question of whether engagement in the psychoanalytic relationship brings about changes and/or what is the value or meaning of such changes. The notion of psychotherapy as a "service" which requires increasingly extensive monitoring of its efficacy in achieving "goals" is becoming more and more pervasive. Such a view does not allow for the critical importance of the unfolding of unconscious desires and possibilities which may not be commensurate with the patient's initial hopes but may be, ultimately, much more significant for him/her. Throughout this book I return frequently to the theme of change, implicitly and explicitly. I argue for a non-normative conceptualization of change which is based on the analyst's commitment to exploring the unconscious speaking of individuals' suffering and on an attunement to the individual's creativity and the possibilities of their relationships in the future.

All of the chapters contain clinical vignettes through which I highlight the implications of my arguments for psychoanalytic practices. Chapter Seven, "States of Time", focuses particularly on examples of clinical work. The identities of the individuals I discuss are, of course, disguised for reasons of confidentiality. My aim is to highlight the diversity and specificity of people's conscious and unconscious experiences of time and to explore how these find expression within the context of the psychoanalytic relationship. Although the patient and the analyst are always "in time", albeit in different times from one another, the importance and the significance of temporal experiences, vary considerably within and between different psychoanalytic relationships. I address the question raised by Minkowski (1923) as to whether a problematic relation to time produces certain "symptoms" or whether these are the source of difficulties in relation to time. It is important to emphasize that my attentiveness to how these particular patients experienced time was only one aspect of my work with them. The value to them of my interpretations of their temporal experiences does not signify that their analyses were successful in all other respects.

In my presentation of the case vignettes and in the rest of the book, my aim is to emphasize the uniqueness and specificity of individuals' worlds. I thus challenge universalizing theories which preclude a recognition of this. The phenomenological method (see Chapters Five and Six for more elucidation of this), in contrast to such theorizing, emphasizes the importance of individual's *descriptions* of experiences, rather than explanations in terms of causes. An attention to language (verbal and non-verbal) and meaning is thus crucial to a phenomenological approach. My inclusion of quotations from Hoffman's autobiographical and Mann's fictional work highlights the power of language and how, as Merleau-Ponty argues, "the expression is indistinguishable from the thing expressed" (Merleau-Ponty, 1945, p. 151). As I discuss in Chapter One, the importance of language in the psychoanalytic relationship is intimated by Freud in his paper, "Constructions in Analysis" (1937d). In the final chapter I draw on the theorizing of Schafer, the analyst, and of Ricoeur, the phenomenological philosopher, to further explore the question of the role of language in analysis.

My interest in the question of language inevitably raises questions of the designation of the identities of the practitioner and the individual attending sessions for psychoanalytic work. After much reflection, I have decided to use the terms "analyst" and "patient" and to refer to their engagement in a "psychoanalytic relationship" for the purposes of "psychoanalytic work". A multiplicity of reasons and disagreements inform the different positions and alliances associated with the taking up of terms such as "psychoanalyst", "psychoanalytic psychotherapist", and "psychodynamic counsellor". A discussion of these is beyond the scope of this book. (This is not to dismiss the importance of any of the claims attached to these). In order to avoid any confusions which might arise from assumptions as to what may be implied through the use of any of the above identities, I assign the term "analyst" to all those practitioners whose practices are influenced by the theories of psychoanalysis and of analytical psychology, including arts therapists and arts psychotherapists. In referring to theories and practices (rather than the identity of the practitioner) I use the term "psychoanalytic", except in relation to Jungian theorizing and practices for which I use "analytic", as Jung does. Although the case vignettes I present are not of art therapeutic work, my hope is that practitioners in the various arts therapies can draw on the ideas in this book and develop them in relation to the dominant language of their particular mode, whether music, visual art, drama, or dance therapy.

I have never found any of the terms in psychoanalytic literature for the person who attends psychoanalytic sessions sufficiently
respectful of the courage and patience required for psychoanalytic
work. The impersonal term "client" implies that the individual
coming to analysis is in receipt of a service; it does not acknowledge that the work of the individual attending analysis brings to
the analyst unique challenges and discoveries. The term analysand,
while apparently more "open" can imply submission to an impersonal treatment procedure. It is for these reasons that, in this book I
have chosen to use the term "patient" (notwithstanding its medical
associations) because of its etymological roots in the Latin for both
"suffering" and "patience". Through this designation I wish to recognize the fact that people decide to engage with psychoanalytic
work in order to address profound states of pain, and also in recognition of the patience and determination required to sustain psychoanalytic work over time.

# CHAPTER ONE

# Freud's time: repeating or constructing?

A strange paradox runs throughout Freud's work: in his accounts of the vicissitudes of human subjectivity he refers to notions of temporality which operate as pivotal to his psychoanalysis, yet he rarely theorizes his concept of time. His early interpretations of the hysterical symptom as a symbolic expression of an earlier infantile conflict, as a fixation at an oral or Oedipal stage of development, hinge on a notion of subjectivity which is temporal: aspects of the person's present time are "fixated" or caught up in the time of the past. Freud's concepts of the unconscious, regression, displacement, condensation, transference all rely on particular, yet unthematized conceptions of time.

The crucial importance of these developmental conceptualizations highlight how significant temporality is in relation to psychoanalytic theorizing and practice (See also Green 2002). It is therefore surprising that Freud did not theorize temporality more explicitly, particularly given the discussions in European philosophy at that time, some of which Freud was aware. He had, for example, attended the seminars of Brentano, a German philosopher (1838–1913) who also taught Husserl. Husserl and other European philosophers such as Heidegger, both contemporaneous with Freud, regarded questions of temporality as crucial to questions of human subjectivity.

1

In this chapter I begin with discussions of two examples in which Freud does theorize time and to which he returns in later texts. They concern the question of how we develop our "abstract" (sequential) conception of time and also Freud's "discovery" that the unconscious is "timeless". Although briefly discussed by him, they are nevertheless important to consider as they point to some problematic positions held by Freud. They reveal the tensions between his appeals to science and rationality and those strands in his thinking which are concerned with the fluidity and non-linearity of what he theorized as unconscious experiences. In the later sections I shall go on to consider notions of temporality which are not explicitly thematized by Freud, but which implicitly underpin his theorizing in relation to memory, the transference relationship, the early development, and the death of the subject.

### Do we live abstract time?

Freud argues that our "abstract" conception of time, namely time as a succession of moments, derives from our experience of discontinuity in our perceptual system: the unconscious extends "feelers" through the medium of the perceptual system into the "external world" and quickly withdraws them in response to the excitations which are aroused (Freud, 1925a [1924], p. 231). We therefore conceive of time as a series of discrete present instances of "now", of objective points in time. Freud's conceptualization assumes a dualism: time is assumed to take its course independently of the subject, and "before" and "after" are conceived of as separate objective points in a series of "nows" (Freud, 1920g, pp. 299–300).

This view of time as a succession of moments was formulated originally by Aristotle (384–322 BC) in his work *Physics* and it continues to inform Western "common-sense" views of time in which instants are assumed to exist almost as entities. Freud's explanation of how we develop this conception of time arises from the particular socio-historical context of late 19th and early 20th century Vienna in which he lived as a white educated middle-class Jewish man. His recourse to biology is characteristic of Enlightenment thought, prevalent at that time, with its emphasis on "reason" (claimed to be ahistorical and acultural), and its privileging of "science" as the ideal form of knowledge. It was responsible for the major developments in science and technology during the late nineteenth and early twentieth century in Europe. As a neurologist Freud was particularly influenced by the work in mechanistic materialism, contemporaneous with his own (Fromm, 1970). His discipline was concerned with explaining all psychic processes in terms of physiological processes. In establishing the status of psychoanalysis as a serious discipline it was crucial for Freud to appeal to the interests of medicine through the discourse of science.

Although Enlightenment thinking was prevalent at the time of Freud's writing, it was, nevertheless being challenged by Modern European philosophers such as Husserl and Heidegger, who were contemporaneous with Freud. Distinguishing between chronological or calendar time and lived time, Heidegger (see Chapter Five) highlights the importance of the individuals' lived experience of time, i.e. historicity (see below) as human beings with a history. From within such a perspective, a notion of time as a succession of separate instants may be interpreted as one specific experience of time. As a "common-sense" view, it is likely to be transmitted to young children through language from very early on. According to the phenomenological psychoanalyst R. D. Laing (1959), drawing on Dooley (1941), an individual who lives time with an obsessive and conscious attention to time conceptualized as discrete moments is protecting himself from the risks associated with absorption in an activity. The "timelessness" of such absorption threatens obliteration and loss of identity (see Chapter Five for more discussion of this). It is interesting that Freud (1914g) himself, in "Remembering, Repeating and Working-Through", interprets those individuals who keep memories separate, and who break links between the past and the present, as suffering from obsessional neurosis.

## The timeless unconscious

In Freud's conception of the "timelessness" of the unconscious we are confronted once again with limitations which derive from his reliance on biology. Throughout his writing Freud claims that unconscious processes are "not ordered temporally ... time does not change them in any way and ... the idea of time cannot be applied to them" (Freud, 1920a, p. 28). Developing this, Freud argues that the wishful impulses arising from the id and impressions that have been repressed are "virtually immortal" and their effects on the individual remain unchanged (Freud, 1933a, p. 74). He stresses that his realization of the timelessness of the unconscious has profound philosophical implications but acknowledges that he is unable to develop his understanding of this any further.

What are the implications of Freud's view of the unconscious as atemporal? From one perspective, it is a very radical conception in its implicit recognition that subjectivity is not always located within linear or chronological time, and it allows for more fluidity in our understanding of individuals' lived experiences of time, both consciously and unconsciously. In our dreams, particularly, time is rarely chronological and linear; we shift effortlessly between the immediacy of childhood and that of adulthood, we experience the anticipation of impending horrors and the longings for possible pleasures in which past and future are conflated. Babies talk to us in highly articulated adult concepts, other dream characters die and come to life again. While we dream we do not think of the events of the dream as belonging to our conscious (or chronological) past or as pertaining to our conscious future; we "live" these events in the dream without such distinctions.

Freud's view of the unconscious as timeless, however, reveals some significant contradictions. In his theorizing of the drive (der Trieb as opposed to das Instinkt) as located "on the frontier between the mental and the somatic" (Freud, 1915c, p. 122) he appears to lean towards an integration of the socio-historical and cultural with the biological. However, he never fully relinquishes his reliance on Cartesian body-mind dualisms and the biologism on which his notion of the timelessness of the unconscious hinges. He describes the source of the drives as being "in an organ or part of the body" (Freud, 1915c, p. 123) and as exerting a "constant" force or pressure for which the drive seeks satisfaction (the timelessness of unconscious drives is related to this constancy). As Strachey (1957) points out, Freud (1915e) in his paper "The Unconscious" later differentiates even more clearly the instinct, which originates in the organism, and its psychical representative. This is already explicit in his discussion of the "Wolf Man" where he argues that there may be an "instinctive factor" ("*instinktiv*" as opposed to drive-related), which is "the nucleus of the unconscious, a primitive kind of mental activity" analogous to the "*instinctive* knowledge of animals" (Freud, 1918b [1914], p. 120). Developing this, Freud (1923b, p. 38) argues that repeated experiences of the ego over several generations are incorporated into the id and transmitted on to further generations phylogenetically; the portion of the id which the ego forms as the super-ego is therefore constituted through the restoration of numerous egos of previous generations and is inherited (see below for more discussion of this).

How can the unconscious be timeless if the drives can, nevertheless, be altered as Freud also claims: "what has belonged to the lowest part of the mental life of each of us is changed ... into what is highest in the human mind by our scale of values" (Freud, 1923b, p. 27). In 1915 he had expressed his cynicism as to how far drives can be transformed, arguing that "human nature consists of instinctual impulses which are of an elementary nature, which are similar in all men and which aim at the satisfaction of certain primal needs" (Freud, 1915b, p. 281) and that "the primitive mind is... imperishable" (Freud, 1915b, p. 286). It is important to acknowledge the sociohistorical context of Freud's remarks in this latter paper, "Thoughts for the Times on War and Death"; his theorizing is in part shaped by his despair at the brutality of the First World War and his desire to account for this (see below in my discussion of his notion of the death instinct). However, he does not modify this significantly, consistently maintaining until the end of this life that the unconscious is timeless.

This notion of the unconscious as "timeless" produces problems for Freud in his theorizing of "change" or "cure" in psychoanalysis. Reflecting on the length of an analysis he argues that the analyst should behave as "timelessly" as the unconscious itself (Freud, 1918b [1914], p. 10). It is clear from his subsequent remarks that, by this, he means open-ended and "lengthy" (p. 237) since this is likely to lead to a better prognosis for the patient, as well as a learning experience for the analyst. Freud (1937c) argues that the criteria for the termination of an analysis are the relief of symptoms, consciousness of previously repressed material, and a lessening of "resistance" such that a further recurrence of symptoms is unlikely. Through analysis unconscious drives are "tamed" by the ego, unless they are "excessively strong" (Freud, 1937c, p. 231). This implies that some drives *can* be modified through the controlling strength of the ego and that, therefore, they are changeable and are, implicitly, subject to the passage of time. Freud qualifies his claim, however, by suggesting that, if the drives are constitutionally strong, a fixation as a result of a trauma is more likely; furthermore some constitutional factors may not be amenable to treatment.

It is interesting to note how Freud acknowledges his own questions regarding his discoveries. He admits that he is unclear about the relation between the ego and the constitutional strength of the drive. Raising the question as to whether its strength is responsible for the modification of the ego he decides that since the ego itself has its own aetiology, this may not be the case. Freud concludes that "it must be acknowledged that our knowledge of these relations is as yet imperfect" (Freud, 1937c, p. 232). Avoiding pursuing these crucial contradictions further he suggests that the question of cure should engage with the obstacles to change rather than how it occurs.

Green attempts to clarify the contradictions in Freud's conception of the timelessness of the unconscious by claiming that "(w)hat Freud meant ... was that the "traces" of experiences related to sexuality, pleasure and desire, inscribed since earliest infancy, continue to be active outside consciousness, whatever other changes may affect sexuality proper or conscious psychic activity" (Green, 2002, p. 151). Green's project is to reinstate the importance of the concept of the drive since, he claims, they are the source of vitality and difference in the psychoanalytic relationship. His argument is unconvincing. The concept of the unconscious implies precisely that "traces of experience" are outside consciousness, but their unchangeability is not a necessary condition of this. Furthermore, Green's position implies that the drives can be known and universally identified as, for example, sexual or aggressive, regardless of the specific sociohistorical and linguistic context.

According to Merleau-Ponty, the French philosopher and phenomenologist, our emotions are inseparable from linguistic or gestural expression. He addresses the naturalism which he regards as integral to Freud's notion of the drive, arguing that it "is impossible to superimpose on man a lower layer of behaviour which one chooses to call "natural", followed by a manufactured cultural or spiritual world" (Merleau-Ponty, 1945, p. 189). Behaviours associated with, for example, anger or love are often different in different cultures and historical periods and, moreover, the differences in these correspond to a difference in the emotions themselves. He argues that "it is no more natural ...to shout in anger or to kiss in love than to call a table 'a 'table'. Feelings and passional conduct are invented like words" (Merleau-Ponty, 1962, p. 189). As Stein's (1980) account of the negotiation of cultural shifts indicates, aggression is not a natural instinct which arises from outside of language or of a particular time or culture and is then expressed or "represented" in a particular "higher" cultural form. Similarly, interpretations of what is erotic are shaped by the specificity of the socio-historical context. (See Chapter Six for further discussion of this).

Freud's notion of the unconscious as timeless has radical implications in its recognition that subjectivity is not lived within a linear, chronological time. Unconsciously and, often consciously, we slide and jump between past, present and future. Often we are driven to live aspects of the past as if they are our present, we may live in imagined futures instead of our present, or live in the present as if we have no past and no future as in psychosis. However, the problem lies in his notion of unconscious instincts as being "beyond time", unchangeable, and immortal. As the contemporary European philosopher Wood (1989) points out, it undermines the significance that Freud himself, in his theorizing of the transference and of the death instinct, attributes to repetition in its unconscious aspects.

Although contemporary psychoanalysts have criticized Freud's drive theory terms such as sexuality and aggression, their focus has tended to be on Freud's neglect of the role of the child's early object relations rather than on the problem of time and language. The psychoanalytic relationship is unavoidably embedded in languages of words, gestures, sounds, rhythms, and images. As an analyst I am curious about their particularity, their shaping of a unique world lived by the person who is talking to me in a moment in time which may be shared and/or unshared as our own lived temporalities shift and interweave. I listen in a present that moves between the patient's pasts, presents, and anticipated futures and my own. In attending to words, images, and gestures, conscious and unconscious, I am engaged in a poetic listening which would be profoundly restricted if I were to translate what is conveyed to me into a language of ahistorical wishful impulses; this would be to deny the particularity and uniqueness of a person's experience, which arises from a specific socio-historical context, even though it might satisfy the patient's demand to know or understand the causes of their distress.

## Freud's past times

In the sections which follow, it will be evident that Freud's contributions regarding the relation between time and memory implicitly contain a notion of time lived by subjects as historical human beings. Freud's detailed accounts regarding the complexity of memory are a rich source for reflection on the multiple relations taken up by an individual, consciously and unconsciously, in relation to their past and its emergence in the present.

Philosophers from the hermeneutic and phenomenological traditions in philosophy, from Dilthey and Husserl through Heidegger and Gadamer, use the concept of "historicity" to denote a person's lived experience of their past and present in anticipation of their future possibilities. This term, surprisingly, does not appear in psychoanalytic theorizing. However, it is a particularly relevant concept for analysts concerned with how individuals' past experiences shape their lived present and also their future expectations. The limitations of Freud's theorizing, as I shall show, lie both his neglect of the dimension of the future in an individual's lived experience and also the tension in his theorizing of developmental stages as linear and universal.

Freud's theorizing of the developmental stages reveals a paradox with regard to time and history. He (1933a) emphasizes the importance of the past in shaping individuals' subjectivities and argues that what is remarkable about the sexual drives is "their plasticity, their capacity for altering their aims, their replaceability" (Freud, 1933a, p. 97). He claims that heterosexuality is precariously established and "is not a self-evident fact … that is ultimately of a chemical nature", thereby "given" as natural (Freud, 1905d, note added 1915, p. 57). However, in his notion of "phylogenetic phantasies", Freud also views individuals' conscious and unconscious experiences through a lens of universality which simultaneously fixes time.

For Freud, every individual's past involves a negotiation of crucial developmental stages, which he designates the oral, the anal and the Oedipal. Sexual maturity is achieved through a successful negotiation of these in, as Freud poses it, their temporal linearity: the sexualized interest of the developing infant moves from the mouth to the anus and, finally, to the genitals. This culminates in the subject's taking up of a genital heterosexual position subsequent to a "normal" resolution of the Oedipus complex. Sexual maturity is allied to the capacity for heterosexual pleasure geared to reproduction. According to Freud, "mature" female sexual desire is passive. The girl moves from active "masculine" clitoral satisfaction to "passive" vaginal satisfaction following the successful resolution of her Oedipus complex. The boy's sexual desires are actively directed towards his mother and, although this phase is brought to a close, owing to the threat of castration, masculine sexual desire remains active. For Freud, the stages of male and female sexual development are universal, regardless of the particular socio-historical context.

According to Freud (1918b [1914]), phylogenetic phantasies, of which the Oedipus complex is the best known, are transmitted extralinguistically, independently of the socio-historical context. They are inherited "memories" of a historical reality prior to the child's own individual life history and they are drawn upon by the child in order to fill out gaps in his/her experience. These phantasies function as universal organising "categories" (Freud, 1918b [1914], p. 119) and override specific personal experiences. This is emphasized in his claim that "(e)very new arrival on this planet is faced by the task of mastering the Oedipus complex" (Freud, 1905d, note, p. 149). Freud argues that although different arrests of development may occur in relation to these phantasies and might give rise to different, "normal" and "abnormal" resolutions, the human subject cannot avoid negotiating them in one way or another. However, as Scarfone argues, there is a danger of attributing the status of a psychoanalytic theory to the patient's "subjective impression" that an event originates from "within" the patient or from an inherited past (Scarfone, 2005, pp. 37–38). As Wittgenstein (1967) indicates, the appeal of such mythological explanations to people is that they offer reassurance to people that what they are experiencing has happened before. There is an implication that the person does not have to take as much responsibility for their experiences. It is also interesting to note, in the light of Scarfone's warning, that Freud's claim that the Oedipus complex is universal is based on his hypothesis (through his self-analysis) that he must have seen his mother naked when he was two-and-a-half and on an overnight train with her. Freud deduced from this that he had been sexually aroused by this sight (see Webster, 1995, for more discussion of this).

The limitations of the notion of universal, phylogenetically transmitted phantasies as organizing experience is evident in Freud's interpretation of the "Wolf Man's" recollection of a childhood dream. A window at the foot of the child's bed suddenly opens out onto a huge walnut tree. It is night-time in winter. On the tree, six or seven white wolves with tails like foxes' sit, their ears pricked up, looking at the small boy. Terrified of being eaten by the wolves he awakes, screaming. Freud's interpretation of the dream extends over years of the wolf-man's analysis. In an almost obsessively painstaking account Freud traces the source of this powerful and imaginative dream back to the real or phantasized experience of the primal scene. He argues that this must have occurred at one and a half years old, and that sexual excitation led to the child's castration fears, symbolized by his terror of the wolves.

The poetry of the wolf man's dream and the richness of his associations ranging from memories of his relationships with his sister, nursery maid, nurse, governess and his parents to book illustrations, biblical stories and his fascination with the natural world of insects and animals, contract eventually to a single focus, namely the child's phantasies of the primal scene. Freud's question concerns the problem of whether the scene had been perceived by the child or whether it was a product of phantasy. Freud concludes that, if the child had observed the scene, his experience of it was, nevertheless, informed by an *"instinctive* ("instinktiv") knowledge" (Freud, 1918b [1914]), p. 120) equivalent to that pertaining to animals. This phantasy, like the Oedipus complex, is, for Freud, phylogenetically inherited. Freud does warn against ascribing phylogenetic status prematurely (an error for which he implicitly berates Jung), emphasizing that such an understanding can only be reached after exploration of what has been individually acquired in the the patient's past.

In the last section of "The Wolf Man", Freud claims that the treatment was successful. Yet subsequent reports (see Gardiner 1989) indicate that the patient continued to experience severe difficulties throughout his life and that he did himself challenge the view that Freud had cured him. This begs the question as to whether, in deriving his interpretations from a notion of temporality based on the assumption of the transmission of extra-linguistic phantasies across generations, Freud sufficiently attended to the uniqueness of the "Wolf Man's" lived experience as a historical human being, including the specificity of his language, visually (in dreams and metaphors) and verbally. Freud also did not explore his patient's explicitly stated desire to become an artist and the particular conscious and unconscious significance to him of his creativity. As I discuss in Chapter Two, for Jung, exploration of the individual's creativity as an expression of emerging, unconscious future possibilities is a crucial aspect of the psychoanalytic work.

Laplanche's challenge to Freud's notion of phylogenetically transmitted phantasies with his notion of "sexual messages" (Laplanche, 1992, p. 10) goes further in its acknowledgement of the role of intersubjectivity in the construction of sexualities. However, it is limited by his prioritization of the time of infancy as formative of sexuality. Laplanche argues that "erotic message(s)" are "implanted" verbally and non-verbally in the infant by his/her parents or carers (Laplanche, 1992, p. 10). According to Laplanche these messages are more extensive than, and are also contained in, occurrences of sexual abuse. They constitute a "one-way" communication because the adult (as "active") has more "knowledge" (conscious and unconscious) than the child who "passively" receives the enigmatic message posed by the adult (Laplanche, 1992, p. 10). Laplanche's position cuts across the dualisms of instinctual versus social or cultural and psyche versus soma. However, his certainty about the infant's "passivity" is unconvincing and does not give sufficient weight to the infant's lived history from birth onwards prior to the reception of these messages. Laplanche also does not take sufficiently into account the numerous other sexual messages transmitted to and actively engaged with by the subject throughout their infancy, childhood and adulthood. These messages are, furthermore, generated within and interpreted by the subject, consciously and unconsciously within specific and shifting social contexts.

Critiques of the concept of the Oedipus complex as universal by Fanon (1952) and O'Connor and Ryan (1993), by contrast, do address the specificity of the wider socio-historical and cultural contexts which produce such messages and to which individuals are exposed throughout their lives. Fanon, the black theorist, activist and psychiatrist who practiced psychoanalytically in Algeria, argues that in the French Antilles "97 per cent of the families cannot produce one

Oedipal neurosis" (Fanon, 1952, p. 152) and that every neurosis is culturally specific. O'Connor and Ryan (1993) emphasize how the continuing emphasis on the Oedipus complex as universal has been central to the maintenance and development of psychoanalytic theories which pathologize homosexuality. Although an increasing diversity of child-rearing arrangements have emerged, ranging from extended families, single-parent families, same-sex parent families, to families in which fathers are active co-parents or are the main carers of children, the consequences of these for psychoanalytic theorizing has not been sufficiently addressed. (For further discussion of this see Chapter Six). Such critiques continue to be met with resistance, particularly within psychoanalytic trainings, despite the increasing pressure (in the West) on mainstream psychoanalytic theorizing to examine its relevance and accessibility to people from a diversity of class and cultural backgrounds and different sexualities.

Freud's notion of phylogenetic phantasies raises significant questions for clinical practice. If psychoanalysts adhere to a notion of time which locates the sources of individuals' desires in a prehistorical past, in a complex which is claimed to exist for people across all time, they are likely to foreclose on the specific and shifting meanings sexualities might have for women and men. These meanings range across all three temporal dimensions. Conscious and unconscious experiences designated as sexual by an individual during the course of an analysis may point towards the future, reside in, or move through, the present as well as being shaped by the past. One or all of these dimensions of time might be present in each experience.

*Regression*

Freud's accounts of "regression" are interesting to consider since they reflect once again a tension between his biological and mechanistic analogies and his assurances that his investigations are "predominantly psychological in character" (Freud, 1900a, p. 6). In this initial explanation of regression he draws on the analogy of a telescope with a series of lens or systems through which excitations pass. He argues that, in waking life, stimuli at the perceptual and conscious end of the psychic apparatus produce excitations which normally proceed to motor activity. In sleep, where motor activity is restricted, ideas are, instead, transmitted backwards towards the perceptual end of the apparatus (which receives sensory impressions) and transformed into the sensory images from which they originated. Dreams are thus designated by Freud as "regressive" (Freud, 1900a, p. 542). Hallucinations in waking life as experienced in, for example, hysteria or paranoia occur, according to Freud, in the same way. His hypothesis of how regression occurs relies on a spatial analogy, namely the workings of the telescope. However, interestingly, Freud himself comments that the temporal sequence of the excitations might be equally relevant.

Expanding on his notion of regression Freud claims that "...the primitive stages can always be re-established" and that the biologically organic aspects of regression of the libido are "the most prominent" (Freud, 1920, p. 300). He describes regression as occurring when "external obstacles" (p. 298) impede libidinal impulses from achieving satisfaction. Fixation and regression are intrinsic to one another: the stronger the fixation, the more likely the occurrence of regression in the face of external obstacles. Freud specifies three forms of regression operative in the neuroses. These involve regression of the libido to attachments to primary sexual objects, as found in hysteria, regression of the libido to a fixation at an earlier stage of sexual development, as found in obsessional neurosis (anal-sadistic), and lastly, regression of the ego to earlier stages of development. Freud also theorizes the transference as a form of regression (see below).

Freud's concept of regression relies on mechanistic and biologistic explanations. Furthermore these are also rooted in a notion of development stages as universal (see below). However, his theorizing reveals a notion of time as "lived" and non-linear which differs radically from his Aristotelian account of the individual's "abstract concept" of time, namely as a linear series of discrete instants. The question, however, arises as to whether behaviour which may be described as "regressed" necessarily indicates an earlier difficulty or "fixation". This view is challenged by Jung (see Chapter Two) who argues, instead, that regression occurs in order to avoid a conflict in the present. Boss (1979), the existential analyst, also argues against Freud's interpretations, drawing on the example of a child who resumes bedwetting when a new sibling is born. He emphasizes the crucial importance of the child's *present* situation and their jealousy of the attention focused on the new baby. Boss's emphasis on the present, however, risks neglecting the specificity of the history of the child's relation to his/her family members prior to the birth of the sibling. Why does bedwetting become the child's unconscious choice for communicating distress? Cohn (1997) develops Boss's position in his argument that the past is not something we can "return" to; it is contained in our present, albeit disocciated from it. Cohn's view importantly highlights that the past experience can never be fully and completely replicated.

*Memory and forgetting*

Freud's paper, "Remembering, Repeating and Working-Through" provides some extremely useful phenomenological descriptions of various forms of memory and forgetting (Freud, 1914g). It reflects how far Freud allows for a diversity of interpretations of the notion of memory and of what we regard as, or fail to recognize as, "past". Aspects of his theorizing of memory are problematic with regard to their naturalism (see above). For example, he claims (Freud, 1914g, p. 149) that "internal acts" such as unconscious impulses, phantasies, "processes of reference", and thought-connections, which are "remembered" by the patient have never been truly forgotten (Freud, 1914g, p. 149). However, other aspects of his theorizing, such as his concept of "screen memories" and of "Nachträglichkeit" illuminate ways in which non-linear conceptions of time and memory operate unconsciously.

According to Freud everything that belongs to childhood and has been forgotten is retained in "screen memories". These memories "screen" (but do not destroy) other memories in the same way as the manifest memories of dreams represent the hidden dream thoughts. In his earlier paper "Screen Memories" he elaborates how screen memories can either be "positive" or "negative" (Freud, 1899a, p. 320), depending on whether they are similar to or opposite to the repressed thoughts or memories. They can also be memories of experiences which occurred prior to or following the events which they screen. Mitchell (2006) supports Freud's claim that all childhood memories are potentially accessible in analysis through an example of a patient of hers who can vividly remember the first time she stood up, aged nine to eleven months. She regards the memory as both "a mixture of a childhood experience and an unconscious fantasy" (Mitchell, 2006,

p. 103), interpreting it as a memory of an actual event, which is later embellished with fantasy.

Through his concept of "Nachträgligkeit" ("deferred action") Freud theorizes how memories of past events are revised and reshaped in the light of later experiences. For example, in the "Wolf Man", he argues that the "Wolf Man" had, as a boy aged one-and-a-half, seen his parents engaged in sexual intercourse (Freud, 1918b [1914]). However, his understanding of the act only became possible when he had reached the age of four, through a dream. Prior to this his observations were only impressions: he was not sufficiently mature to give significance to the actions he perceived.

In "Remembering, Repeating and Working-Through" Freud describes the multiple ways in which our subjectivities are shaped by conscious and unconscious memories, memories which have displaced other memories, memories which underlie other memories, by phantasies which are not memories (since they have never been "forgotten") and, in the case of obsessional neurosis, by an absence of connection between memories. In the transference, action replaces memory (see below for more discussion of this). These different interpretations of how memory works, including Freud's questions as to what it means to "forget", are an important contribution to expanding our sensitivity to individuals' differing relationships to the past.

The limitation of "Remembering, Repeating and Working Through" concerns Freud's emphasis on the importance of past time in the psychoanalytic method to the exclusion of the dimension of the future. Although Freud's concept of the drive implies that there is a future aim, Freud's focus is on how these aims or objects are determined by a person's past experiences. Fears in relation to the future as, for example, in the anxious anticipation of a terrible event, are also interpreted by him in terms of the past; they have their source in a memory of a time when something that was feared did actually happen.

Freud retains his conviction, from Breuer's work with hypnosis to his own emphasis on free association and the analysis of resistances, that the aim of psychoanalytic techniques has remained the same: "Descriptively speaking, it is to fill in gaps in memory; dynamically speaking, it is to overcome resistances due to repression" (Freud, 1914g, p. 148). The analyst must treat the patient's distress "as a present-day force", only to enable the patient's "reconciliation with repressed material" (Freud, 1914g, p. 152), and to transform the patient's compulsion to repeat, in the transference, into a "motive for remembering" (Freud, 1914g, p. 154). The problem with Freud's emphasis on the past dimension of lived subjectivity is further revealed in a critical exploration of his concept of the transference.

## The time of the transference

Although Freud states that the patient's "illness" must be treated "not as an event of the past, but as a present-day force" (Freud, 1914g, p. 151) his notion of the transference prioritizes the past dimension of time. He argues that in the transference "the patient does not *remember* anything of what he has forgotten and repressed, but *acts* it out. He repeats it not as a memory but as an action; he *repeats* it, without, of course, knowing that he is repeating it" (Freud, 1914g, pp. 150–153). Freud claims, somewhat unrealistically, that the patient is compelled to repeat *all* of his symptoms during the course of his treatment through the transference relationship.

Freud interprets negative transference as an expression of resistance to the psychoanalytic "treatment". The patient regresses to an (unconscious) fixation at an earlier stage of development which is lived out in the relationship with the analyst, impeding further progress. Freud stresses that although this dynamic does not occur exclusively in psychoanalytic treatment, it is an unavoidable feature of it: early infantile experiences are revived, and the analyst's desire to trace the unconscious libidinal paths is necessarily met with resistance. Freud delineates two forms of positive transference, one of which consists in conscious "friendly or affectionate feelings" (Freud, 1912b, p. 105) and the other, the erotic transference, which occurs when these feelings become linked to repressed primitive erotic impulses. The latter are drawn on, as in negative transference, in order to impede the psychoanalytic work and the bringing to consciousness of past memories as past.

Freud claims that all experiences of "being in love … reproduce(s) infantile prototypes" and that emotional connections to others in the form of trust, friendship, and sympathy, are "genetically linked to sexuality" and have their source in the sexual drive (Freud, 1915a[1914], p. 168). As I emphasize above, in relation to Freud's notion of the unconscious as timeless, this does not take into account the intersubjective specificity of these feelings and the role of language in their constitution.

Freud's conceptualization of the transference as the "compulsion to repeat" (Freud, 1914g, p. 151) also does not allow for its role in relation to the patient's anticipation of his/her future, whether as a refusal of the future (see Merleau-Ponty's case-example which I discuss in Chapter 5) or as an experimentation with future possibilities, as in Jung's theorizing (see Chapter 2). If analysts are not attuned to the specific ways in which their patients are oriented towards the future, there is a risk that patients' enmeshments in their past anxieties are prolonged. From my own clinical experience it is crucial that tentative, minute, and precarious attempts at possibilities other than repetition of the past are recognized by the analyst.

The following example illustrates the importance of an interpretation which addresses the patient's transference as a relation to their future. Jane telephoned me on the day before her session to cancel it. She had a week off work as holiday leave and felt she would prefer also not to come to her session (an early morning appointment); she would see me again the following week at her usual time. In her next session it emerged how important it was for Jane to cancel her session. It had taken her a lot of courage, she told me, since it felt to her that it was the first time she felt she had really said to someone that she did not want to do what they expected and that there was something else she would rather do. Her relation with her mother had been one in which she felt she had to meticulously anticipate and meet all her mother's needs. For her, unconsciously, if she did not do this, her mother's life would be at risk. Jane had been nervous of my response and had struggled with her wish to protect me. She was also excited that she had managed to choose to do what she herself wanted.

In the transference Jane was certainly re-enacting an aspect of her past relationship with her mother whom she perceived as fragile. However, more importantly, the analytical relationship allowed her a playground in which to experiment with new possibilities of future relationships which need not be completely controlled by her desire to please her mother. In "Remembering, Repeating and Working-Through" Freud uses the metaphor of the "playground" to describe the transference. However, his emphasis is on its relation to the past: it can "expand in almost complete freedom" and "display ... everything in the way of pathenogenic instincts that is hidden in the patient's mind", in order to become a "motive for remembering" (Freud, 1914g, p. 154). However, as the work with Jane illustrates, the transference may also offer a way of playing with new possibilities of future ways of relating.

### Freud's death

Freud's theorizing of individuals' responses to the death of another person in *Mourning and Melancholia* (1917e [1915]) contains a number of references to time, both explicitly and implicitly. Freud describes how both in mourning and in melancholia the individual withdraws their interest from the world and his/her capacity for a new love relationship is diminished. His account implies that an individual in mourning or in a melancholic state is unable to look towards the future. The love-object of the past, whether s/he is lost, has left, or died, is clung on to in the present until, after "great expense of time and cathectic energy" (Freud, 1917e [1915] p. 245), the tie can be relinquished. In melancholia this work is more complex: according to Freud, the individual's ego is experienced as impoverished, whereas in mourning it is the world which is perceived as depleted.

Freud attributes the individual's punitive and debasing attitude to his/her ego in melancholia to his/her unconscious ambivalence towards the lost object. He interprets the attacks which are directed against the subject as complaints against qualities in the lost object. Through narcissistically identifying with the latter, the subject attempts to preserve the love-relation. The conflict, which originates in the past relationship between the subject and the lost object, is converted into a split in the ego: that aspect which is identified with the lost object has become the target of criticism from the other aspect in the present.

Freud emphasizes that both mourning and melancholia require time: they both dissolve "after a certain time has elapsed" (Freud, 1917e[1915], p. 252) but "progress is long-drawn-out and gradual" (Freud, 1917e[1915], p. 256). It is in his reflections on how recovery from mourning is achieved that he refers to the perceived relation between the death of the other and one's own death. He suggests that, when the subject's memories of the dead person are met with the reality that they no longer exist, s/he is reminded of their own mortality.

Freud's theorizing of the subject's relation to their mortality focuses on his concept of the death instincts. These are aggressive instincts which, according to Freud, are in constant tension with the sexual or life-instincts. How far does Freud's theorizing of the death instinct acknowledge the impact of aging and death on our experience of our subjectivities? I have argued that Freud's theorizing of subjectivity is limited by his determinative emphasis on the individual's past experiences to the exclusion of their anticipation of the future. On the horizon of all our subjectivities is a knowledge that we will die, whether our response to this is one of acceptance or denial or one of a myriad of other possible responses. It is a part of our lives that can never be avoided and over which we ultimately have no control. Our knowledge that we are mortal has a major effect, consciously and unconsciously, on what we wish for, plan for, achieve, or lose. Although Freud, in his theorizing of the "death instinct", appears to incorporate very firmly the notion that we are going to die within his account of subjectivity, it is striking how little this concept takes account of the impact of the inescapable fact of our own death on our anticipation of the future.

It is in "Beyond the Pleasure Principle" that Freud (1920g) introduces his theory of the death instinct. In this paper Freud further develops his notion of the compulsion to repeat which he had begun to formulate in "Remembering, Repeating and Working Through" (1914g). There he describes how patients repeat repressed material in their relationship with him instead of being able to remember this material. In "Beyond the Pleasure Principle" Freud questions what makes people repeat experiences which are unpleasurable. For example, what is the purpose for a child who, in his mother's absence, repeatedly throws a wooden reel on a piece of string out of his view and then pulls it back gleefully making it reappear? Why would a child want to symbolically repeat the distressing experience of his mother's absence? He argues that in this case the pleasure derived from the activity outweighs the distress: the child may want to achieve a sense of mastery of something which is beyond his control, and this desire is linked to the child's pleasure in anticipating being an adult and also taking revenge on the adult who has failed him/her. However, Freud thinks such reasons do not account for why his adult patients are compelled to repeat unpleasurable past experiences in the transference from which, he claims, they cannot be deriving any pleasure at all.

Freud solves this problem by claiming that such repetition is derived from a desire to "restore an earlier state of things" which stems from "an inertia inherent in organic life" (Freud, 1920g, p. 36). Furthermore, all instincts, while appearing to be pointed in the direction of change and progress are, instead, seeking to return to a prior inanimate state from which the living "entity" initially emerged. Consequently, according to Freud, " 'the aim of all life is death' " (Freud, 1920g, p. 38). Self-preservative instincts exist only in order to ward off any forces which might return the "organism" to inorganic existence other than those which are immanent in the organism itself. These forces within the organism are what Freud designated the "death instincts". The death instincts are, furthermore, necessary in order to reduce the internal tensions produced in response to stimuli. As natural drives the death instincts are in constant conflict with libidinal drives.

In his theorizing of the death instinct Freud draws from findings in cellular biology to support his view. His account is consequently permeated with the language of "entities" and "organisms". In "The Economic Problem of Masochism" he takes this analogy further. For example, he describes how in multi-cellular organisms, "the libido meets the instinct of death, or destruction, which is dominant in them and which seeks to disintegrate the cellular organism and to conduct each separate unicellular organism into a state of inorganic stability" (Freud, 1924c, p. 163). In sado-masochism, the risk the death instinct poses to the subject is mitigated when it is channelled into the will for mastery over, and destruction of, another. A portion of it also serves the sexual function in the form of sadism, the remaining portion remaining within as the primary source of sadism.

The notion of death as an unavoidable occurrence on the horizon of every subject's life in the *future* and the effects of that on an individual is absent in Freud's theorizing. His emphasis is, instead, on why *past* conflicts are repeated in the present, in spite of providing no satisfaction for the subject. Furthermore, the drive towards death is theorized by Freud as a desire for a *return* to an earlier inorganic state. This is conceptualized in biologistic terms. The dimension of future time is once again eliminated in his account in favour of the past dimension. This is in stark contrast to Heidegger who wrote of death, shortly after Freud developed his theory of the death instinct, as a "Being-towards-the-end" (Heidegger, 1927, p. 303). Intrinsic to this "Being-towards-the-end" is a "Being *towards a possibility*" (Heidegger, 1927, p. 261) and involves anticipation of a "potentiality-for-Being", the "not-yet" (Heidegger, 1927, p. 289) of existence, and the possibility of individual, authentic existence. In being able to anticipate death one is "liberated in such a way that for the first time one can authentically understand and choose among the factical possibilities lying ahead of that possibility which is not to be outstripped" (Heidegger, 1927, p. 308). For more discussion of this, see Chapter Five.

Freud's accounts of how the death instinct is expressed in lived relationships focuses mainly on aggression and destruction towards others. This can be traced back to Freud's two impassioned essays, together entitled, "Thoughts for the Times in War and Death", written six months after the outbreak of the first World War. In these, Freud reflects on the destructiveness underlying "civilization" which has led to the cruelty and horrors of war, forcing people to face the reality of death: "Death will no longer be denied; we are forced to believe in it. People really die; and no longer one by one, but many, often tens of thousands, in a single day. And death is no longer any chance event ... the accumulation of death puts an end to any impression of chance" (Freud, 1915b, p. 291). At a time of war death has become almost solely associated for Freud with aggression towards others. He argues that deaths occurring in combat resemble the deaths perpetrated by "primaeval man" who killed without scruples, driven by hatred and the wish to annihilate. In the grief for the death of loved ones there is hidden hatred too, and it is this, according to Freud, that gave rise to the commandment, "thou shalt not kill". Freud sublates questions of ethical and political judgments regarding rights and justice under his own dominant concern with questions regarding biologistic dynamisms of aggression and destruction.

Freud's theorizing of the death instinct as primarily destructive thus arises from a particular socio-historical context, the time of the First World War. Although Freud invites the reader at the end of the second essay, "If you want to *endure* life, prepare yourself for death" (my italics, Freud, 1915b, p. 300), this text contains none of the hopefulness of Heidegger's (1927) later theorizing. Freud urges us to pay attention to the dangers of our destructive drives, while

Heidegger sees death as an opportunity to attend to our potential as human beings. (For further discussion of Heidegger's theorizing of death, see Chapter Five). Their very different interpretations of death highlight the diversity of associations with death which can arise in psychoanalytic sessions. They can arise from individuals' personal experiences of bereavement, the particular ways in which death is interpreted and mourned (or otherwise marked) within the particular cultural-historical period in which they live, phantasies derived from stories and myths, from familial discourses, and many other experiences. To assume that all thoughts of death are associated with aggression and destructiveness is to foreclose on the multiple possibilities of shifting meanings which every individual has in relation to his/her or another's death. These may be conscious or unconscious for the individual and they are extremely influential in shaping a person's orientation to the future.

One of the reasons for Freud's failure to take sufficiently into account the subject's awareness of their own mortality and the significance of this for their future life arises from his view that the unconscious cannot have any idea of its own death: "Our unconscious is just as inaccessible to the idea of our own death, as murderously minded towards the stranger, as divided or ambivalent towards the loved, as was man in earliest antiquity" (Freud, 1915b, p. 299). He does argue that the death of a loved one forced "primaeval man" to acknowledge that he would die too. There is no knowledge of this, however, in the unconscious. The fear of death therefore, according to Freud, arises from a sense of guilt, since there can be no unconscious conviction of one's imortality. He develops this idea further in his theorizing of the relation between death and anxiety in "Inhibitions, Symptoms and Anxiety". In this paper Freud argues that "the unconscious seems to contain nothing that could give any content to our concept of the annihilation of life" (Freud, 1926d [1925], p. 129). Since an individual cannot have directly experienced anything closely related to death, the fear of death must be interpreted as the fear of castration. Curiously Freud argues that experiences close to that of castration *have* been experienced when faeces have been removed from them in nappy-changing and on weaning! The main threat to the ego is that of separation from and abandonment by the protective super-ego. In melancholia the fear of death arises from feelings of persecution by the super-ego.

In none of these accounts does Freud argue convincingly why the human subject's experience of the fact of his/her own mortality, his/her lived experience of aging, illness, suffering, and the anticipation of death cannot also be experienced unconsciously. It is of course true that we can never know how we will die or what the experience, or non-experience, of death will be. This does not prevent us from having unconscious fantasies, wishes and thoughts in relation to the knowledge that we will die. These thoughts and fantasies will be connected to what has already been experienced in the subject's life, to their present, and also to their anticipation of the future. Although Freud may not have worked with combatants, his clinical practice in the early twentieth century was with patients who had a shorter life expectation and who, because antibiotics had not yet been developed, were more prone to serious illnesses. It is highly unlikely that their own experiences of bereavement and their own fears regarding their own death together with unconscious associations to this did not arise in their analyses.

One reason for this may lie in another crucial element which must be consistently addressed in any discussion of time and psychoanalysis, namely, the particular cultural and historical context from which theories arise. Freud's tone often implies an acultural objectivity (Ellis, 2000, p. 157); he argues that his theories arise from "various facts of analytic observation" (Freud, 1923b, p. 12). He does not acknowledge the extent to which concepts arise from within a specific historical context with its particular intellectual traditions and socio-cultural values. His theorizing of the death instinct was unavoidably affected by the hugely turbulent situation in which he was living in Europe. His refusal to consider that one might be unconsciously aware of one's own death may have been connected to an unconscious denial of his own anticipation of the terrible consequences for Jews during the rise of fascism in Germany.

## Time and language

Freud's work indicates possible directions for the development of a theorizing of the relation between time and language in the psychoanalytic relationship. Our interpretations of time are embedded in our language. The date or exact period of when something occurred in our lives can elude us, we may not be sure if we remembered something or we imagined it. The vividness of the language of our visual images in memories and dreams may force the datability of time to recede sharply. Some memories, as Freud's notion of screen memories indicates, can conceal other unwanted memories, others are understood only retrospectively. As we speak, new memories occur, others are reworked, fresh perspectives arise, and formerly clear memories fade as their significance shifts in our telling. Our hopes for the future intertwine with our pasts or, as I indicated in the case example of Jane, arise as new and unexpected possibilities in the present. We may talk of death as if it might arrive tomorrow or we speak as if we are immortal beings. All of these memories, phantasies and imaginings are articulated linguistically. Temporality is intrinsic to our speaking, to the shifting stories of our lives.

Our experience of our temporality does not rely on the concrete realities of dates, on precisely when something did or might occur. Freud's notion that "psychical reality" is distinct from material reality, that what we attribute to a concrete memory might be a phantasy, introduced the importance of attending to the stories of people's lives without being primarily concerned with objective historical truth (Freud, 1893a, p. 57). The shift occurred for Freud in his considerations of experiences of sexual abuse reported to him by his women patients. He initially argued that these seductions were the root of their hysterical symptoms, although it was the memory, rather than the event itself, which had traumatized the women. Freud began to question whether the event had taken place at the time they claimed and, furthermore, whether it had taken place at all. He postulated that alongside material reality there existed a psychic life of phantasy. The problem about his revised position is that it obscured the extent to which adults do sexually abuse children, and the necessity for social and political action in relation to the protection of children and young people.

In relation to psychoanalytic practices, Freud's emphasis on the specificity of individuals' experiences and the meanings attributed to these is important. This differs from the requirements of a legal perspective in which the question of exactly what physical contact took place is crucial, since proof of the abuse is required. Psychoanalytic work, by contrast, allows for time and attentiveness to the conscious and unconscious meanings of the abuse in the context of the individual's relationship with their abuser, their relationships with others prior to and following the experience of abuse, and to how an individual articulates or make sense of what has occurred. The telling and retelling (whether through verbal, visual, or gestural languages) of memories of the abusive relationship shift constantly with new revisions and new perspectives.

The relation between memories, construction, and recollection within the psychoanalytic relationship is explored by Freud (1937d) in "Constructions in Analysis". This paper reflects an interesting tension between Freud's view of "truth" and its relation to recollection and his acknowledgement of the significance of language and temporality in the psychoanalytic relationship. Freud's argument is concerned with the truth of the analyst's construction of an event in the patient's past. Since agreement or disagreement on the part of the patient might equally be forms of resistance, it can be difficult for the analyst to be certain of the construction's accuracy.

For Freud the search is for a "complete" and "trustworthy" picture of everything that the patient has repressed. (Freud, 1937d, p. 258). He argues that the psychoanalyst has an advantage over the archeologist as memories are always preserved somewhere, unlike historical artefacts which can be destroyed. He implies that there are fundamental memories which are unchangeable pieces of historical truth lying within the psyche, that is, if one looks beyond screen memories and other forms of defences. However, he also writes, almost as if in parentheses, that

> The time and manner in which he conveys his constructions to the person who is being analysed, as well as the explanations with which he accompanies them, constitute the link between the two portions of the work of analysis, between his own part and that of the patient. [Freud, 1937d, p. 259]

This statement highlights the importance of the relationship in which constructions take place. It is necessarily temporal since its efficacy when presented to the patient relies on its timing at a specific point in the relationship, namely *when* such a construction can be experienced as meaningful by the patient.

The work of analysis occurs *between* the analyst and the patient with the analyst offering a possible construction and the patient responding with a further, spontaneous association. For Freud, the production of an association analogous to the analyst's interpretation indicates confirmation of the correctness or "truth" of a construction, which corresponds to a preserved memory. However, what is understated by Freud is the importance of construction as an opening out of possibilities through language, in the sense that we always say more than we know. These constructions are meaningful between the patient and the analyst, but they are also contingent, "truths" or, rather, perspectives which hold at a particular moment in time but which can also shift over time, to be replaced by new stories from fresh angles.

The emergence of a fresh perspective within the psychoanalytic relationship which is accepted by the patient is attributed by Freud to its timing. He implies that the timing of an interpretation involves ascertaining that the patient is free of resistance at that moment and ready to absorb a piece of truth, an accurate construction of a past event. Yet, as Roy Schafer (1983, pp. 229–230) points out, resistance can itself be regarded as a "narrative strategy" on the part of the patient which can, itself, have multiple meanings. I expand further on the question of the relation between time and language in Chapter Eight.

The rightness in the timing of a construction or any other form of interpretation arises from a recognition that something meaningful at a specific moment within the transference relationship has been been crystallized. It is not because it turns out to be an accurate reflection of the past in any empirical or lasting sense. Even if the construction points to the past, its production relies on the taking up of a new position within time: it allows for a separation from the past and, as a new articulation of an experience, it also opens out to possibilities of new ways of speaking in the future.

### Concluding Freud's time

In this chapter I have highlighted the paradox in Freud's accounts of the subject's historicity. Although he rarely theorizes time as a concept, his work is saturated with implicit references to time as lived by individuals. His view of the unconscious as timeless emphasizes that the lived time of the subject is never chronological or linear, rather, a shifting between past and present dimensions. These shifts are evident within the transference relationship in psychoanalysis.

His accounts of memory and forgetting including his concepts of "regression", "nachträglichkeit", and "screen memories" enable us to be sensitive to the complexities of memory and how, as subjects, we position ourselves in relation to the past.

I have argued that his notion of the subject's history is limited by his theorizing of developmental stages as universal and based on biologistic explanations. This does not allow for the cultural specificity of individuals' lives with their diverse interpretations of sexualities, aggression and death. This is critically important for the development of psychoanalytic practices which are sensitive and relevant to individuals across different class and cultural backgrounds, and different sexualities.

A further limitation in Freud's work concerns his neglect of the dimension of the future in the subject's experience. Even death is conceived primarily in terms of destructive drives rather than a horizon towards which our lives are orientated in a complexity of ways, consciously and unconsciously. Freud's emphasis on past experiences as primarily shaping human subjectivities has implications for change in psychoanalysis and the question of how new experiences can arise for individuals in the psychoanalytic relationship which point to future possibilities of being.

I have indicated also how Freud's notions of "psychical reality" and "constructions" in psychoanalysis are an important contribution to the development of a theorizing of the relation between time and language. (See Chapter Eight for more discussion of this). These conceptions allow for the specificity of individuals' experiences as arising *in* time, not bound to a linear view of time, and for different interpretations of "memory". The constructions which arise between psychotherapist and patient in the psychoanalytic session involve an orientation to a future dimension.

# CHAPTER TWO

# Jung and the future unconscious

In contrast to Freud (and also Klein), Jung explicitly addresses questions of temporality throughout his work. Furthermore, challenging Freud's emphasis on the past he argues for the crucial importance for the analyst of distinguishing whether an unconscious expression is "historical", arising from the past, or "teleological", anticipating a future possibility. Jung's view of the subject as extending backwards and forwards through time appears to converge with a phenomenological view of temporality, which I discuss in Chapter Five. However, his notion of a "collective unconscious" introduces a crucial difference.

For Merleau-Ponty (1945), a phenomenologist, we are situated in a perceptual field which is run through with "retentions" and "protentions" (see Chapter Five). "Retention" refers to the transition of a present moment into the past, whilst remaining present, and "protention" refers to the overlap between the present and the impending future moment. Although past, present and future are distinguishable they are nevertheless embraced within a single flux which is present. Jung adds another layer in his conception of subjectivity: beneath the subject's personal history lies a deeper layer of inherited "a priori categories of possible functioning" (1930, p. 34, Vol. 16) in the form of the "archetypes" which influence our present and our future. He designates this the "collective unconscious".

In this chapter I argue that Jung's emphasis on the importance of all three temporal dimensions is a significant and crucial contribution to psychoanalytic practices which are concerned with possibilities for change and the importance of imagination rather than explanations in terms of the past. I critically discuss his notion of a collective unconscious as existing beyond the individual's lived history. Jung's theorising of synchronicity, which relies on the notion of the collective unconscious, is also explored. I also critically reflect on the problems of Jung's development of a psychology of nations in order to theorize cultural differences. I elucidate how Jung's view of death as having a multiplicity of meanings highlights the limitations of Freud's concept of the death instinct and its association with destruction.

*Past avoids present*

In his interpretations of neurosis Jung challenges Freud's earlier notion of neurosis as being caused by a fixation at an earlier stage of sexual development. He focuses on the present and asks what it is about the present conflicts and the context of the individual's relationships which have produced a regression to the past. He argues that if the source of a neurosis lay solely in the past its effects would be constantly present throughout a person's life. Furthermore, he claims, since all individuals, whether 'neurotic' or not, share similar fantasies and complexes, these cannot be regarded as causes of any particular neurosis. Jung cites the Oedipus Complex and its feminine equivalent, the Electra Complex, which he views as one of many archetypal configurations (see below for more discussion of this of Jung's theory of the "archetypes").

The notion of time underpinning Jung's theory of neurosis can be viewed as a reversal of Freud's: for Jung, the present can throw us back to the past while Freud focuses more on the past as producing our notion of the future. Jung argues that "a neurosis is more a psychosocial phenomenon than an illness ... it forces us to look upon the neurotic person as a sick system of social relationships" (Jung, 1935, p. 24). HIs emphasis on the specificity of present relationships is an important acknowledgement of the temporal context of experiences; we are not only the sum of our past experiences, we are continually affected by a constantly shifting present and by the temporalities of those with whom we relate.

According to Jung, a neurosis occurs at "the moment when a new psychological adjustment, that is, a new adaptation is demanded" (Jung, 1916, p. 246). He questions what it is in the present which the patient is not able or willing to accomplish since, he claims, it is the failure to adjust to a new situation which blocks the 'biological' libido and prevents it from being channeled in an appropriate way. This results in a regression to and an exaggeration of infantile fantasies. Neither these, nor any "fixation" to them (see Freud, Chapter One) are the cause of present experiences; regression to these fantasies is, instead, a way of avoiding present conflict. Any "bondage" to fantasies (Jung, 1913, p. 182), in the form of habitual regressive fantasizing, is secondary and arises in patients "as an excuse for running away from difficulties and shirking their duty" (Jung, 1913, p. 182).

Jung emphasizes that his interpretation of neurosis does not require a different analytic technique. The analyst must initially follow the patient's " 'false' track of regression" (Jung, 1913, p. 187) in order to discover where in the unconscious the libido has become attached. The aim of the analytical work is to reconnect this with the conscious mind, bringing it under the control of the will and once again available to the individual to face his/her responsibilities in the present. Too much attention to the past, Jung claims, prevents the libido from discovering new, more productive channels, allowing it to sink backwards. Moreover, these fantasies may be endless. If the analyst acknowledges instead the teleological value of the regression, namely its prospective role in the subject's orientation to a new future, it can in Jung's view, become "the basic condition for the act of creation" (Jung, 1913, p. 180). When the patient stops producing fantasies, symptomatic of regression, the libido is freed for new possibilities and for, as Jung emphasizes, "action, in the fulfillment of certain necessary obligations to life" (Jung, 1913, p. 189).

In his theorizing of the movement of libido Jung relies on a mechanistic explanation, derived from Freud. He describes the libido as a river which, on meeting an obstacle (a conflict in the present), becomes dammed up and flows back (regresses) into older channels, formed in the earlier development of the main river-bed and which have since dried up. Jung likens these to the "subsidiary streams" (Jung, 1913, p. 163) of infantile sexuality. When the obstruction is removed, the libido flows once again in the main stream. It appears from this metaphor that, in the face of conflict, there is an *automatic* regression of libido. This is not consistent with Jung's claims that the individual's regression has an intention, albeit unconscious, namely to avoid present conflict and responsibilities.

Although Jung derives the metaphor of the damned up river from Freud, his theorizing of the concept of "libido", is broader than Freud's to include love, not solely sexuality. He (1955, p. 127) argues that the oral and sexual are not separate components; libidinal energy begins as focused on the nutritive, in the baby's experience of sucking, and gradually, as the child matures, becomes sexual around the time of puberty. Jung (1955, p. 165) also argues that the latency period, as described by Freud, is the *beginning* of sexuality and that everything prior to this cannot be designated as sexual, just as (Jung's own metaphor) the tip of a hot iron can only be described in terms of light when it is visibly glowing.

Jung's argument for the analyst's alertness to the dangers of a fascination with past fantasies (on his/her own or the patient's part) is an acknowledgement of the importance of psychoanalytic work in enabling change. In contrast to the dominant interpretations in psychoanalytic practices which too readily assume that present experiences are caused by fixations at earlier stages of development, Jung's theorizing acknowledges the complexity of the context of an individual's present relationships and the subtleties of new possibilities unfolding for the future. His concept of subjectivity is implicitly one of fluidity, shifting between present, past and future. However, there is also a risk, as the following example shows, of Jung not paying sufficient attention to an individual's accounts of their past experiences.

Jung describes a woman who develops "acute hysteria" after finding herself running compulsively down the middle of the road ahead of a horse-drawn cab and collapsing with exhaustion. Jung argues that the woman's action was a form of regression: she had repeated and made use of an earlier trauma involving horses in order to disguise her unconscious intention, namely her desire to be carried to the home of a man to whom she was deeply attracted and whose wife, her best friend, had just left for a trip abroad. At her farewell party the patient had felt overwhelmed by her desire for this man and intense anxiety as to what might happen. Running ahead of the horses she had also felt a panic "as if something inescapable now had to happen" (Jung, 1913, p. 162).

Jung's attentiveness to the details in the woman's narrative regarding her present conflict is very evident. In encouraging the patient to amplify the details in her description he enables the emergence of the conscious and unconscious meanings of her experience. He recognises that the repetition of her past trauma had a purpose, namely as an avoidance of her own conflictual attraction for her friend's husband. However, his account also neglects important aspects of the patient's experience of her past. For example, he briefly mentions that many of the young woman's earliest fantasies involved feelings of "horror, aversion, disgust, love, and ecstasy" (Jung, 1913, p. 131) in relation to her father. Jung claims, without qualifying this, that these are not derived from any traumatic experience (such as sexual abuse). Furthermore, his concern is focused on the activity, rather than the content, of the fantasizing which he describes as "introverted" and significant only as creations whose purpose is the avoidance of the present. Jung does not explore the links between these specific fantasies and the woman's experience of her attraction to men. Such links need not (and should not) imply a causal explanation in any empirical sense, nor necessarily signify a neglect of the woman's present circumstances. They might have allowed a more specific understanding of the immense fears bound up with her attraction to the man and also of how these may have resonated with her previous conscious and unconscious experiences of her father. (The question of their "reality" in any objective sense may or may not be important, depending on the individual; however, consciously and/or unconsciously these are conceived of as a meaningful part of the subject's individuality.) Such understanding may enable the emergence of a new relation to men.

## The time of the transference

In contrast to Freud, Jung (1946) does not regard the establishing of the transference as essential; it is one of a number of therapeutic aspects in the analytic work. He stresses that it only has any value if it is spontaneous and, importantly, warns against the tendencies he perceives amongst analysts to "enforce" it (Jung, 1946, p. 172). Furthermore, Jung emphasizes the originality of the analytical relationship: it is "a bond, a combination resting on mutual unconsciousness" (Jung, 1946, p. 178) and it confronts the analyst with that which his academic knowledge can never prepare him for. He alerts the analyst to the dangers of routine interpretations, arguing that "every new case that requires thorough treatment is pioneer work" (Jung, 1946, p. 178).

Jung's earlier conceptualizations of the transference contain a tension between his recognition of its creative aspects and his recourse to biologistic explanations of its role in psychoanalytic work. Jung draws on Freud's definition of the transference as a process whereby the patient transfers on to the analyst the sexual fantasies that were attached to the "memory-images" (Jung, 1913, p. 190) of the parents. He develops Freud's conceptualization further in his crucial acknowledgenent of its importance as enabling the individual to move beyond his/her immediate family, a task s/he has not yet sufficiently achieved. From early on his work Jung theorizes the transference relationship as enabling an orientation to the future as well as signifying a tie to the past. However, perhaps because of the early influence of Freud, Jung supports his claim with an argument from the biological sciences: the intensity of the relationship between patient and analyst is of "great biological value" (Jung, 1913, p. 190) as a "bridge" for the libido between the patient's past familial fantasies and a more "objective" view of the analyst. Jung appears to retract on this position in his last work, in which he is explicit about the limitations of science as an explanation for human experience: "(s)cience works with concepts … which are far too general to do justice to the subjective variety of an individual life" (Jung, 1961, p. 17).

In his development of his theorizing of the transference Jung places a strong emphasis on the importance of attending to its multiple meanings: it may be a "genuine" or "pathological" expression of an instinct, it may be associated with the Adlerian concept of "the will to power", it might signify a regression of the libido in the face of present conflicts, or a reactivation of the "incest archetype" of the collective unconscious (Jung, 1946, p. 179) (See my discussion of Jung's concept of the archetypes below). He stresses that this is not an exhaustive list and these different meanings are also present for individuals with varying intensity. While recognizing that the incestuous element of the transference contains extremely secret and painful feelings, Jung acknowledges that this also contains very positive aspects; it simultaneously involves "the most sacred feelings which go to make up the indescribable and inexplicable wealth of human relationships and give them their compelling power" (Jung,

1946, p. 179). These offer the patient important resources for the development of intimate relationships in the future.

Jung recognizes the value of dreams as revealing the unconscious transference aspects of the patient's relationship to the analyst in the present. He is also explicit about the effects of the transference relationship on the analyst: they are both engaged in the "paradoxical blend ... of trust and fear, of hope and doubt, of attraction and repulsion" which initially characterizes the analytical relationship (Jung, 1946, p. 182). The relationship changes both the analyst and the patient. His stress on the importance of the analyst's own analysis in ensuring against identifications which may prevent the patient from resolving the transference, is underpinned by an acknowledgement of the intersubjectivity of time. The relationship is temporal; it includes the shifting times of the analyst and of the patient, consciously and unconsciously, across all three dimensions. Jung argues that past unresolved issues on the part of the analyst are likely to impinge more strongly as the transference resolves and the patient's questions are increasingly directed towards the future. He warns against the temptation for the inexperienced analyst to give direction and advice at this critical point.

*Imagination and future-time*

Jung's theorizing of the transference critically departs from Freud's. In addition to acknowledging its relation to the past, Jung is also, importantly, attentive to its value for experimentation with future possibilities of relating: such acknowledgement of the importance of the future dimension of time is rare within the psychoanalytic tradition. Although Klein's accounts of anxiety (see Chapter Three) and Freud's notion of drives as having aims hinge on a recognition that human subjects have a notion of the future, consciously and unconsciously, the psychoanalytic focus is, as I have highlighted, on the past. However, a patient's relation to the future, whether in the form of escapism, or as signifying the possibility of the lifting of a grey veil of depression, is implicitly present, consciously or unconsciously, in a variety of ways, whether or not it is addressed by the analyst.

Throughout his work Jung pays close attention to the future dimension in individuals' conscious and unconscious experiences of their subjectivity. He characterizes the unconscious as being like Janus, facing two ways. It has a historical aspect, pointing towards the past, and an anticipatory aspect pointing towards the future. Jung stresses that it is important for the analyst to decide "whether an autonomous manifestation of the unconscious should be interpreted as an effect (and therefore historical) or as an aim (and therefore teleological and anticipatory)" (Jung, 1939, p. 280). He explicitly addresses how individuals are oriented to their futures with all their hopes, fears, desires, and intentions in a myriad of ways which shift according to the present context.

Jung claims that conscious and unconscious preoccupation with the future is intensified towards the end of an analysis. This assumption does not, however, sufficiently take into account the possibility that an individual may begin analysis partly because they are overly focused on the future; in this case, the end of analysis may bring a lessening of this preoccupation. As one patient said regretfully about her life, "There is always such a huge mountain ahead of me to climb ... I am always goal-oriented, I can't enjoy the presentness of the present". As Jung argues in relation to regression, such orientation to the future was, for this patient, an avoidance of conflicts in the present which were also connected with her relationships in the past.

Jung's recognition of the significance of the future in relation to the possibilities for creativity and imagination in the individual's life and in the analytic work is a crucially important and original contribution to psychoanalytic theorizing. He stridently criticizes Freud's notion of the unconscious for its denigration of its creative potential. According to Jung, the "slime" which is met with in regression contains "not merely incompatible and rejected remnants of everyday life, or inconvenient and objectionable animal tendencies, but also *germs of new life and vital possibilities for the future*" (Jung, 1928, pp. 34–35, my italics). Challenging Freud's view of dreams as "imaginary fulfilments of repressed wishes" designated by him as sexual, Jung argues that they instead "contain ineluctable truths, philosophical pronouncements, illusions, wild fantasies, memories, plans, anticipations, irrational experiences, even telepathic visions" (Jung, 1934, p. 147). Jung (1961) also expresses his regret at (European) culture's exaggerated fear of the risks of imagination.

In "The aims of psychotherapy", Jung is explicit regarding the importance of creativity and its relation to future change in the

analytic work. He stresses the value of dreams as containing unconscious "inklings of possibilities" (Jung, 1931, p. 43), and a crucial
aspect of the analytic work involves discovering the creative potential of fantasy in the individual's life. He stresses that "all the works
of man have their origin in creative imagination" (Jung, 1931, p. 45)
and it is this which frees individuals to play. He emphasizes the
importance of experimentation and the achievement of a state of
"fluidity, change, and growth, where nothing is fixed and hopelessly
petrified" (Jung, 1931, p. 46).

In addition to attending to patients' dreams Jung also encouraged his patients to explore unconscious symbols through painting
between the analytic sessions. The activity of artwork allows, he
argues, a more detailed study of the unconscious image and it also
enables the growth of the patient's independence. He differentiates
the artwork produced in the context of the analytical relationship
from professional or public art, stressing its importance as producing a "living effect" on the patient (p. 48): "by painting himself he
gives shape to himself" (p. 49).

Through my training and experience as an art therapist it is
evident to me how crucially important exploration of their artwork
is to some patients in the way in which Jung describes. This may be
either throughout or at different periods within the psychoanalytic
work, whether produced in or between the sessions. Differently to
speech, the artwork is permanent and can be returned to at different
times, both during and when the psychoanalytic work ends. Jung
emphasizes the content of the artwork and the symbolic value of the
images. Phenomenological theorizing (see Chapters Five, Six, and
Eight) contributes an additional perspective, namely that of the significance of artwork as a gestural language. Every mark and every
brushstroke carries the individual's historicity within it and like a
poem, a musical composition, or a novel, it is "a being in which the
expression is indistinguishable from the thing expressed" (Merleau-
Ponty, 1945, p. 151). Experimentation in a visual language can enable
conscious and unconscious articulation of possibilities for the future
(as well as the present and the past) which may be unimaginable in
words.

These may be creative possibilities but, as Jung argues, it is
important to be alert to anticipatory images or dream thoughts
which contain warnings. He illustrates his claim with an example of

a dream of one of his patients who was a mountaineer. The patient dreams of climbing higher and higher up a mountain with increasing elation and desire to climb in this way for ever. He does so, until he is mounting empty air and wakes in a state of bliss. For Jung the dream indicates an anticipation of the possibility of the patient's death on a mountain and he advises him, on his next ascent, to take two guides with him. The patient laughs at his advice and, three months later, accompanied by a younger friend and without any guides, falls to his death.

Jung does not claim that the dream was a prediction or form of precognition but, rather a warning about a future possibility which the patient could not admit into his conscious awareness. According to Jung, this event, just like every crisis, had a "long unconscious history" (Jung, 1964, p. 36). However, he acknowledges, this does not mean we can rely on dreams to warn us; often they do not. Jung's interpretation in this example is a literal one. It is likely, given his view of symbols as unconscious and indefinite aspects of experience, that Jung would have interpreted a similar dream to another patient (who was not a mountain climber) more metaphorically, in relation to the risks of denying limits. Jung's example highlights the impor-tance of an attentiveness to the direction in which dream symbols appear to be pointing and the limitations of assuming that they are primarily associated with the past.

*Collective time*

Jung's theorizing of the "collective unconscious" is extremely signifi-cant in relation to his conception of the individual's historicity. He argues that Freud's personalistic view of the unconscious is restrictive and pessimistic in its reduction of human beings to "a very private *affaire scandaleuse*" (Jung, 1930, p. 35). In 1913 Jung had dreamt of descending into a cave, which was situated beneath a cellar, containing pieces of ancient pottery and bones, including two skulls. Departing from Freud's interpretation of this aspect of the dream as signifying Jung's death wish, Jung theorizes that, instead, the cave symbolized the existence of a deeper portion of the psyche, the contents of which he designates as "archetypes". Unlike the contents of the "personal unconscious", these have not been forgotten or repressed, since they have never been conscious. The archetypes are, according to Jung, "inherited possibilities of ... ideas" and are, as such "*a priori* categories of possible functioning" (Jung, 1930, p. 34). As "inborn and universally present formal elements" (Jung, 1936–37, p. 44), they are also, Jung claims, timeless. Although Jung's original conception of the collective unconscious is derived from his dream, Jung stresses that its existence is "an empirical matter" (Jung, 1936–37, p. 44).

Jung claims that the archetypes are neither transmitted in the form of representations nor can they be encompassed by the notion of instinct. Their content is only evident when it becomes conscious in the form of imagery (visual symbols). Jung claims that archetypal images appear in dreams, in the delusions of people who are in psychotic states, and in myths and fairy tales across the world. Examples of these include symbols of the mother and father (not the individual's own, but a "collective" image), the hero, the eternal child, the hermit, the animus and the anima (the "male" side of a woman's personality and the "female" side of a man's). Extending back through the times of our ancestors and beyond personal, lived time, according to Jung, archetypes unconsciously influence our present and our future. Although derived from our (inherited) past, Jung claims that archetypes can also be anticipatory, pointing to emerging possibilities of being. He also views them as an essential feature of the transference relationship, claiming, for example, that a strong resistance in the patient to resolving the transference may indicate that its source is in the archetypes. Resolution might entail a disconnection from these and be experienced as a profound loss.

Although Jung argues that "possibilities" of ideas are inherited, rather than the ideas or representations of them, his examples are very specific. At times he claims that these ideas appear differently in different cultures (see below in my discussion of Jung's theorizing of cultural differences); at other times Jung implies through his examples that the images themselves are universal. The problems arising from this are particularly evident in a consideration of archetypical interpretations in relation to gender. In his reflections on the meaning of the myth of Demeter and Kore Jung claims that these figures represent archetypal extensions of feminine consciousness: "every woman extends backwards into her mother and forwards into her daughter ... a woman lives earlier as a mother, later as a daughter" (Jung, 1941, p. 188). According to Jung this is significant in relation to temporality; a woman's experience of her life as stretching back across several generations and forward into the future allows her a glimpse of immortality, of being "outside time" (Jung, 1941, p. 188). Her consciousness of this flow of life enables a sense of "wholeness", countering the isolation of individuality. In Jung's view this is the aim of rituals associated with the archetypes.

Jung's interpretation does not take into account the specific social expectations associated with femininity and masculinity which may be transmitted, through processes of identification, from one generation to the next. The imagery of Demeter and Kore's relationship bears a striking similarity to Eichenbaum and Orbach's claim that "a woman's first child is her mother" (Eichenbaum and Orbach, 1983, p. 57). Their interpretation is, by contrast, rooted in an analysis of male-female power relations in our patriarchal society and the expectation on women to become mothers and carers (See Chapter Six). Such theorizing, which takes into account the specific socio-historical context, addresses how femininity is constructed "in time". A recognition of these, in contrast to a notion of femininity which is claimed to exist "outside time", opens out a multiplicity of other identifications for men and women and to which they may find access through the psychoanalytic relationship.

In his theorizing of the archetypes of the "anima" and "animus", the respective unconscious "feminine" and "unconscious" masculine aspects of men and women, Jung attributes very specific and somewhat stereotyped qualities to these. The anima is associated with the maternal, with eros, with loyalty, solace and seduction, the animus with the paternal, with logos, with power and aggression. It is unclear how far these sufficiently allow for the very individual (including the specific socio-historical and cultural) associations a patient may have to, for example, masculinity or femininity, consciously and/or unconsciously. It is interesting that, although Jung conceptualizes the archetypes as universal, he also implies that "compensation", or "resistance", to them is also universal. For example, in relation to the Oedipus complex, he argues that this is an archetypical configuration, but he criticizes Freud for not recognizing that, with it, "there is already given the contrary, namely the resistance against it" (Jung, 1957, p. 276).

Jung argues that the concept of the "collective unconscious" can enable individuals to extend beyond the limitations of their personal concerns into a sense of commonality which, he implies, might be reassuring. However, I think that, more importantly, Jung's non-reductive approach can enable a recognition of the interplay between unconscious aspects of being manifest in the lived present as conflictual, paradoxical, contradictory, ambiguous, and creatively potent, without the necessity for clarity as to their specific relation to the individual's past. Rationalistic or deterministic explanations in terms of early childhood experiences risk cutting across more creative amplification of the dynamics between these. This does not constitute a claim that these unconscious aspects are inherited, as Jung theorizes, since, in my view, exploration of their complexity is limited if these are assumed to be ahistorical and acultural.

### Ahistoricism and cultural differences

Although Jung's concept of the collective unconscious emphasizes universality, he does acknowledge that there are cultural differences and that these are an aspect of a person's individuality. However, in his conceptualization of these as inherited in the form of a national psychology, Jung does not take into account the socio-historical, economic, and political factors which contingently shape cultural identities (Samuels, 1993). Samuels cogently traces the overlap between Jung's assumption of the existence of a specific Jewish psychology and the racial ideology of National Socialism in Germany in the 1930s and 1940s. According to Jung, Jewish analysts such as Freud and Adler, failed to acknowledge cultural differences because, as Jews, they were without land, and therefore without "cultural forms" (Samuels, 1993, p. 318). Samuels highlights how Jung's concern with "what a Jew *is*, rather than on what being a Jew is like" echoes the way in which he had "define(d) the psychological attributes of the two sexes" (Samuels, 1993, p. 315).

In his theorizing of cultural differences as innate, Jung does not allow for the mobility of cultural identifications, depending on the particular socio-historical and political context, and for individuals' own definitions of their cultural identities, which may shift over time. Jung also does not consider the way in which certain identifications and patterns of relationships which appear to be similar are transmitted linguistically (verbally and non-verbally) from one generation to the next. Such transmission is both conscious and unconscious. For example, as I describe in Chapter Six, Fletchman-Smith

(2002) argues that patterns of intimacy, which she identifies as having been operative at the time of slavery, can be identified in couple relationships contemporaneously, one and a half centuries later. Her account does not rely on a notion of an inherited black psychology (see Chapter Six). It is likely that the dynamics of intimate relationships are reproduced and transmitted within familial relationships, passing from parents to children and thus on to subsequent generations. It is unnecessary to explain this occurrence in terms of a racially or culturally innate characteristics or patterns of relating.

## Synchronicity

Jung's theorizing of "synchronicity" hinges on his concept of the collective unconscious and his reflections on it include specific references to time. Jung searches for an explanation for connections between events which cannot be explained causally. He argues that time and space do not exist as entities in themselves; the simultaneity of events indicates a point where there is no time at all. Space and time are psychic concepts created by the conscious mind, necessary for describing bodies in motion and that this is the reason for Kant's view of them as *a priori* categories (Kant, 1787). Jung concludes that synchronicity is an acausal connecting principle which may be added to the triad of space, time, and causality. This principle is rooted in the existence of an *a priori* knowledge of an occurrence which is, at the time, both unknowable and inexplicable.

As examples of synchronicity Jung describes how over two days a series of fishes, both dead or alive, or in the form of images or symbols, appears during his daily activities and in the material of his patients. On another occasion a flying beetle flies against the window of his consulting room just as a patient is recounting a dream of a golden scarab. A patient who noticed a gathering of birds on the death of her mother and her grandmother becomes acutely anxious at seeing a flock of birds arrive when her husband collapses, dying from heart disease.

Following a series of experiments involving the transmission of images on cards between two subjects in separate rooms, Jung hypothesizes that the dreamer of the golden scarab and the patient's wife who became anxious at seeing the flocks of birds must have had an unconscious, prior, knowledge of later events. He attributes this knowledge to the existence of archetypes and argues that the collective unconscious is a microcosm which contains "the images of all creation" (Jung, 1952, p. 494). However, these *a priori* unconscious archetypal patterns of being do not only exist within human beings but also within other animate (such as the flying beetle and the birds in the examples) and even in inanimate existents. He draws on a number of pre-Enlightenment thinkers, including the ancient Chinese philosopher, Lao-tzu, and the Greek philosopher, Plato, and argues for the notion of a "World Soul" (Jung, 1952, p. 494). Jung conceptualizes this as an acausal and meaningful "orderedness" (Jung, 1952, p. 456) in which psychic and physical processes are equivalent. Awareness of this soul does not depend on the senses (hence the ability of people in comas to perceive events around them) but on an underlying stratum, an unconscious sympathetic system which is "transcerebral" (Jung, 1952, p. 131) Jung also draws on physics and its discovery of discontinuity to support his challenge to the dominance of causal explanations.

Shortly after I completed reading Jung's account of synchronicity an example of the kind he describes appeared in my own practice. I am certain that this kind of experience is familiar to, although little discussed, amongst other analysts. One of Jung's anecdotes concerns a woman who, in 1914, leaves a camera film to be developed which, owing to the outbreak of the war she does not manage to collect. Two years later she buys an apparently new film, takes it to be developed and, to her amazement, finds that the photographs contain the exact pictures, on which the new ones are super-imposed, that she had taken in 1914. An hour after I had read this a patient of mine, Suzanne, arrived and, after talking briefly about her sister's relationship with her father, she described how her brother had taken a photograph through the window of a tub of flowers her sister had recently planted up for her father. Although Suzanne had not yet seen the photograph herself, she had been told by her brother that an image of her deceased mother could be seen in it, hovering over the window-box. She herself was sceptical of this, assuming that it was an effect of light on the window, but also nervous as to the questions which might arise for her about life after death, should she also see this image.

The appearance of such a specific image, namely the layers of photographic imagery, in my reading just prior to Suzanne's arrival and then in her narrative seems to be more than a chance occurrence. Although I did not share my experience with Suzanne, she began to wonder herself whether we communicate unconsciously in very subtle, non-verbal, forms of language which affect one another subliminally. It is possible that Suzanne, in a particularly heightened sensitivity (this was her last session before the summer break), unconsciously picked up on what had just been of interest to me, although I had said nothing verbally about this. I am struck that both she and another patient with whom I have had experiences of this kind are both Catholics. Since imagery is extremely important in Catholicism, manifest in the paintings and sculptures of Catholic churches and the religious rituals associated with them, it may be that they both share a particular unconscious sensitivity to a non-verbal and possibly subliminally transmitted language of imagery.

My interpretation of what occurred with my patient does not, however, account for the equivalence of mental and physical processes and how the behaviour of other animate or inanimate beings can correspond with our own as in the appearance of the flying beetle to the dreamer of the scarab. It also does not account for how an experience can be transmitted with a simultaneity which defies all limitations of time and space. For example, another patient told me how she had been on a beach in Turkey talking to her partner about her sister who was ill, but not yet expected to die. In the course of the conversation she had found herself shifting from the present to the past tense. An hour later she phoned her family and was told that it had been at exactly that moment that her sister had died in her home in England.

Jung's notion of a world soul lying beyond space and time to which we all have access, albeit unconsciously, allows for the occurrence of such events. However, it is questionable, in the light of Jung's respect for the mysterious and irrational, whether we need such an overarching explanation to account for these diverse events. An acceptance of the limits of knowledge and explanation is crucial in psychoanalytic practices: there is much that affects us that we cannot control, and for which we are not responsible, and which cannot be rationally explained. Our own and others' mortality are obvious examples of this. The patient who had begun to speak of her sister in the past tense, just as she had died, felt delight that she had been, for whatever reason, so deeply attuned to her sister at the moment of her death, particularly as she had been deprived of the opportunity of being with her physically. The notion that there is a soul-world to which we all have access through our universal sharing of archetypal patterns would have not made her experience any more meaningful. Rather, it may have blunted the richness and uniqueness of her particular experience.

## *Times of life*

The significance for individuals of different stages of life from adolescence onwards is rarely considered in psychoanalytic theorizing, with the exception of, for example, Huet (1997), and Junkers (2004) (Ed.). This is largely due to its emphasis on an individual's early life and its neglect of the specificity of the present context in relation to the certainty of death in the future. Jung, by contrast, emphasizes that each stage of an individual's life has a very particular meaning. He designates these "the childish stage", the period of "youth" (from just after puberty to thirty-five or forty years) old, "middle life", and old age (Jung, 1931, pp. 390–398). His distinctions between stages are underpinned by his acknowledgement of human aging and the reality of mortality. Jung's contribution is somewhat limited by his assumption that there are universal characteristics which can be attributed to individuals at each of these stages, regardless of their specific historical and cultural background. However, his theorizing is a vital reminder to psychotherapists that different stages do produce different concerns.

For Jung, the first stage of life entails the growth of consciousness and, consequently, of continuity of memory and ego-identity. He describes how this occurs as early perceptions gradually become connected. Memories are formed, initially as isolated "islands" (Jung, 1931, p. 390), and these are perceived in an "objective" way: belonging to the ego, they are also separate from it. At this stage the child talks of him/herself, in the third person. As these 'contents' become more energetic, the child acquires a sense of ego-identity and begins to talk in the first person. For Jung, the growth of the ego is thus intricately connected with the accumulation of, and engagement with, memory.

Jung makes the striking claim that in *normal* development a child at this stage does not experience any conscious problems. He is explicit that "it is only the adult human being who can have doubts about himself and be at variance with himself" (Jung, 1931, p. 392). These begin to arise at puberty, the time of "psychic birth" with the emergence of sexuality and increased independence from parental figures. He claims that prior to this the child is subject only to instinctual impulses and that, even if these are opposed, this need not put the individual in conflict with him/herself. It is only when a second set of ego-contents emerges with equal intensity to the first that there may be an inner struggle.

Jung's notion of a "normal" early childhood as a conflict-free state is surprisingly idealized and at odds with his (1917) view that love inevitably involves problems and conflicts. It also contradicts his view of the Oedipus and Electra complexes as universal. Even if, as I argue, these particular complexes are not universal, they concern conflicts with regard to identity and desire, jealousy and competitiveness, and differing loyalties. Jung did work individually with children, such as an eight year old boy (Jung, 1949, p. 317) who was so frightened of other children (quite consciously) that he avoided them completely by staying at home with his mother whose relationship with his father he found intolerable. Given his experience of troubled children and the complexity of their relationships it is surprising that Jung could assume there might be a completely harmonious environment for any child. He was also very conscious of the struggles and pain he experienced in his own childhood which he vividly describes in *Memories, Dreams and Reflections* (Jung, 1963).

For Jung, the second stage of life begins at adolescence with its ambivalence of wanting to hold on to childhood, yet also stride into adulthood: Jung warns, "Whoever protects himself from what is new and strange and regresses to the past falls into the same neurotic condition as the man who identifies himself with the new and runs way from the past" (Jung, 1931, p. 393). Neither estrangement from the past nor flight into the future is productive; instead, it is the acceptance of this tension of opposites which can lead to an expanded consciousness. However, Jung stresses that the development of such a consciousness is inhibited by the demands of a society which values achievement over psychic development. Jung parallels the young adult's struggle to succeed with the child's struggle for an ego. The individual is changed by the process, through his/her identifications with the ideals and goals which have motivated him/her and the desire to preserve achievements indefinitely. This can lead individuals to either lose an important piece of their past or of their future, neglecting their full potential in their early adulthood. Jung's account of the cultural expectations which overvalue achievement may address the experience of many people in twentieth century Western culture but not necessarily in other cultures.

The influence of the historical context on Jung's theorizing is most evident in his account of what he designates the third stage of life. In his view, this period is most likely to produce difficulties such as depression which, he claims, appear earlier (at thirty-five to forty years) in women than in men (around forty) and he emphasizes the importance of psychological treatment in this third stage of life: "for the ageing person it is a duty and a necessity to devote serious attention to himself" (Jung, 1931, p. 399). He argues that "culture", as opposed to "nature" (the raising of children and the making of money) might be the purpose of this second half of life (Jung, 1931, p. 400). For some individuals, present interests are replaced by earlier ones or by new ones. The majority of individuals, Jung claims, are beset by a lack of tolerance and a refusal to relinquish their youth. This does not arise from a fear of death (this would be premature at this stage) but rather resembles the sun's decline in the afternoon, after reaching its highest point. This reversal, he argues, even changes bodily characteristics with older women taking on a more masculine appearance and role, and older men, more feminine ones.

The problems Jung attributes to individuals aged thirty-five to forty were characteristic of many white Europeans in the 1930s when there was a shorter life expectancy and when women were giving birth one, or even two, decades earlier than they do now. Opportunities for career development and change are now possible in the West at a much later age for both genders. Since women increasingly do not have to take sole responsibility for child rearing, their careers can continue to progress. Men are increasingly involved with the direct parenting of children. Jung's notion of a gender reversal which occurs as men and women age is therefore socially and historically specific. Women and men do not necessarily have to wait until they have fulfilled traditional gender roles before expressing other possibilities of existence; this depends on the particular context within which one lives. Jung's reliance on the Cartesian dualisms of nature/culture and male/female restrict his theorizing of the historical specificity of the stages he innovatively describes and analyzes.

Jung (1931) describes extreme old age, the fourth stage of life, as a descent into unconscious psychic events leading to the complete unconsciousness of death. He also claims that a belief in life after death is crucial therapeutically at this time as a sustaining goal. Jung's position changed, however, when he himself encountered old age. In an interview nine days before his eighty-fifth birthday, he addresses the feelings of loss and disappointment, and the risk of life becoming "stale" (Jung, 1960, p. 400). This can be assuaged through an "ever-deepening self-knowledge" (Jung, 1960, p. 401) of one's uniqueness in old age. He also emphasizes the importance of individuals discovering for themselves whether or not a belief in the after-life is helpful (see below for more discussion of this). He argues that a definite position is preferable to agnosticism: it contributes to life being more meaningful. Jung describes how, if an individual resists being carried along with the "universal current of instinctive mental behaviour" s/he may be opposed, but satisfaction may be gained from a recognition of one's ability to withstand the temptation to conform to "collective prejudices" (Jung, 1960, p. 402). The contradictions in Jung's comments regarding the individual and the collective are particularly interesting here. He appears, in his own old age, to be granting more status to an individuality which is less defined by the collective unconscious.

Jung does not address the specificity of the preoccupations of elderly people including the deaths of their partners, friends, and relatives, the negotiation of possibly three (or more) generations of family dynamics, and their experiences of their own and others illnesses. This is perhaps not surprising given Jung's designation of himself an "introvert" (Jung, 1955, p. 247). His acknowledgement of life as having different stages is valuable as a reminder to psychotherapists to be more attentive to an individual's relation to shifts in experiencing the different dimensions of their past, present and future in relation to the course of their whole life and their mortality. It is important, however, to acknowledge the cultural and historical specificity of attributes, goals and abilities associated with different ages. A Western notion of adolescence may, for example, differ radically from another culture's concept of the transition into adulthood.

In some cultures old age is associated with wisdom and leadership, in others with deterioration and frailty.

### Jung's death

In contrast to Freud and Klein, Jung focuses on our relation to death as a goal which lies ahead in all of our futures. Furthermore, rather than conceptualizing death as a finality, he regards it instead as a transition: "From the standpoint of psychotherapy it would … be desirable to think of death only as a transition, as part of a life process whose extent and duration are beyond our knowledge" (Jung, 1941, p. 402). Death is a life event which must be prepared for and it is transformative. In youth life is concerned with striving; and neurosis at that stage often involves a fear of such striving. In the second half of life an older person may, instead, shrink away from death.

Jung claims that the notion that there is life after death is symbolized in the collective unconscious. This claim highlights the limitations of the concept of the collective unconscious in that it arises from Jung's own Christian tradition; it is not a view shared by, for example, Jewish people. The notion of an after-life, of lived time extending beyond our bodily existence, may offer security to some people. It allows for the belief that the death of others in our lives is only a temporary separation. For others, however, the notion of an after-life about which we cannot have any scientific truth in advance may instead be perceived as threatening or, alternatively, unhelpful: a belief in the finiteness of existence may enable a heightened sensitivity to the value of the present.

Jung's particular focus on the spiritual dimensions of our existence highlights the importance for the analyst in being open to and respectful of a diversity of religious views, rituals and experiences, and the multiplicity of meanings these may have, even within one particular branch of one religious tradition. This may raise complex and challenging questions and carries the risk of too readily either accepting or pathologizing a particular belief-system. For example, if we do not believe in an after-life and we are listening to a patient who does so, and who also has difficulties with loss and separation, how do we interpret this? Do we interpret this belief as a defence and an avoidance of the present, or do we regard it as integral to the person's religious tradition, or as a necessary and, in Jung's terms, healthy way for them to cope with the idea of death?

In *Symbols of Transformation* Jung (1912) interprets death as having many meanings within the context of the notion of transformation and rebirth. These extend far beyond the associations of death with destructiveness in the form of aggression or a wish to return to a prior inorganic, inert state as Freud argues. Jung's numerous references to death are drawn from mythology, alchemy and case material. For example, he quotes an African legend in which death is attributed to the carelessness of an old woman. According to this myth there was a time when people were immortal and shed their skins regularly like snakes. The woman mistakenly put her old skin back on her and, consequently, died.

Many of Jung's interpretations of death are associated with aspects of the individual's relation to the mother archetype. According to Jung "it was from the mother that death came into the world in the first place" (Jung, 1912, p. 365). Death is the "Terrible Mother who "devours and destroys" if she insists on her children's continued dependence on her (Jung, 1912, p. 328). Killing this Great Mother archetype, Mother Nature, is also according to Jung, crucial in the individual's ("man's") struggles for separation from their mother. This is symbolized by the killing of animals in myths and dreams, which also enables the acquisition of some of the Great Mother's strength (Jung, 1912, p. 327). Separation from her can also involve returning to her womb, killing the mother from within, and being reborn (Jung, 1912, p. 211). The womb contains the waters of death, yet these are also the waters of life: "Those black waters of death are the water of life, for death with its cold embrace is the maternal womb, just as the sea devours the sun but brings it forth again" (Jung, 1912, p. 218). Jung suggests that a man's search for a mother in his lover stems from the desire to become child and to secure immortality (Jung, 1912, p. 332).

According to Jung, separation from the mother also demands self-sacrifice, the risking of one's own death. The neurotic is entrenched in attempts to avoid this risk but these, in themselves, constitute "partial suicide" (Jung, 1912, p. 110), a deadening of oneself as a futile attempt to avoid death. The struggles to climb higher as a way of avoiding mortality are also doomed (Jung, 1912, p. 111) as is the hope that passion, as a way of "rising above" oneself (Jung, 1912, p. 113), can eradicate death. Just as the tower of Babel stretching up into the sky crumbles, the individual can never escape his own mortality. Sacrifices of what is highly desired and valued, such as the killing of a first-born child or a domestic animal in stories and myths, are necessary for the renewal of life. Consciousness too has to sacrifice its powers to serve the interests of the unconscious, enabling a "release of energy" (Jung, 1912, p. 432). According to Jung, this act of sacrifice is also, symbolically, a fertilization of the mother: the archetypal hero regenerates himself through self-sacrifice and reentry into the mother. Jung views the crucifixion in this light. Christ is sacrificed on the the wooden cross which, as the tree of life, represents the mother. He pays in death for the original sin and enables a regeneration of life on a spiritual plane.

The frequency with which Jung associates death with the separation from the archetypal maternal imago deserves consideration. Since we cannot know for ourselves the experience of dying (see Heidegger, 1927, p. 281), we are likely to draw on past experiences of separation to inform our conscious and unconscious interpretations of death. It is not surprising that frequently in myths, religious imagery, and dreams, death may be associated with separation from the mother since, in most cultures, the biological mother continues to be the main carer of children. However, this is not universal and other parenting arrangements are likely to give rise to different struggles in relation to separation whether with a father, older sibling or another carer. Jung's associations rely on a biologistic interpretation: as birth-giver, a woman is associated with "nature" and fertility, and with the power to both give birth to life and also to take it away.

The breadth of Jung's interpretations of death, while limited by his assumption that these are "archetypal", do alert us to the richness and diversity of individuals' associations to death and its potential in relation to growth and change. They also challenge the Cartesian dualisms in Freud's theorizing of discrete life and death instincts. For Jung, to be human means to be constantly shifting between life and death. The connection between death and the possibility of life and growth is vividly illustrated in the following dream, but its meaning for the dreamer does not, as I show, require interpretations in terms of archetypes.

The dream begins with a conversation between Anna and two other women in the presence of a small boy in his home. Anna finds the conversation frustrating and repetitive. Suddenly the small boy gets up. He now looks about fourteen years old, and he is very angry. He says he has to go out. Anna asks him when he will be back, and she is concerned to acknowledge his need for independence, despite her own anxiety. He says that he will either be back by five o'clock or it will be much later. Anna realizes that she needs to accept this and trust the boy and not let her fears confine him. The dreams shifts and Anna is with an elderly woman and her sixty year old son, friends of hers who had lived together in a very symbiotic relationship until he died. In the dream they have a new cottage with a field edged with hedges. In one corner there is a gap in the hedge. In the space a beautiful, spreading oak tree is growing. Anna tells the elderly woman that she will take a photo of it for her to keep. In a final part of the dream Anna and her mother are dying of a terminal illness.

The dream is replete with references to time, age and death in relation to Anna's struggle to separate from her mother. She experiments with the possibility of independence through the figure of the boy, realizing even in the dream the importance of struggling with her own anxiety if this is to be achieved. At fourteen the boy is entering adolescence, the time at which tensions in relation to independence and separation are accentuated. Anna recalled how fraught this stage of her life was, particularly in relation to her mother who found her growing independence intolerable. The strength and beauty of the oak tree in the dream was very important to Anna: it signified that growth and expansion can be possible if sufficient separateness in relationships (the gap in the hedge) can be sustained. The mother and the son only found separation through the son's death. It seemed that the final image of her mother and herself dying from a terminal illness signified unconsciously the death of their particular symbiosis, a death which was required for the possibility of the new growth symbolized by the oak tree. I reflected on Anna's offer to take the photo of the oak tree and its connection with her creativity. Giving the photo to the old woman also expressed her wish that the woman (possibly representing her own mother) might accept and preserve an image in which growth and separation are linked. In Anna's relationship with her mother, separateness was, by contrast, associated with anxiety and rejection.

## *Conclusion*

Jung's explicit engagement with questions of time in the individual's conscious and unconscious experience is a vital contribution to psychoanalytic theorizing. Jung's subject spans all three dimensions of time. In addressing her/his current conflicts lived also in anticipation of the future, Jung is attentive to the creative possibilities and risks of change. His extensive interpretations of death enable us to be attuned to the particularity of its meaning (which also shifts) for each individual. It allows for the possibility of growth as well as loss and destruction.

I have also argued that there is a tension in Jung's theorizing of human temporality. He appears to allow for a mobility in the individual's experience between different temporal dimensions. Yet his concept of the collective unconscious ties the individual to a past which, Jung claims, stretches back across multiple previous generations. I have also reflected on the limitations of Jung's theorizing in addressing socio-historical and cultural specificity.

# CHAPTER THREE

# Klein: splitting the breast or split in time?

Aside from some brief references to time, contained mainly in footnotes, Klein rarely theorizes temporality. Similarly to Freud, she is concerned with how we develop a sequential conception of time. However, it is in her accounts of a patient's relation to the times of sessions that her recognition of the specific significance of lived time is most explicit. Her theorizing of infantile development thus reveals conceptions of time which underpin her theorizing of human subjectivity, but these are unacknowledged by her.

In this chapter I discuss the limitations of her emphasis on the importance of the past, although her concept of anxiety implicitly includes a notion of the future. I reflect on her over-valuation of spatial metaphors in her accounts of the mother/infant relationship and in her conception of splitting. My case study, "Janet's Time" illustrates the importance for the analyst in being attuned to the temporal dimensions of splitting as a defence. Through discussion of Klein's reflections on a painting by Kjar, a woman artist, I discuss the problem of her interpretation of creativity as "reparation"; this does not take into account the socio-historical context or the dimension of future time. I critically examine her notion of the death drive and her association, following Freud, of death with destruction. In my discussion of Kim's dream of death I highlight the limitations of this singular interpretation of death.

## Time's sequence

Klein, like Freud (1920g), prioritizes the theorizing of sequential time over other experiences of temporality. Her reflections on time appear just one year later than Freud's and it is likely that her considerations are inspired by his work. However, Klein's (1921) explanation of the origins of our concept of this departs radically from Freud's. She argues that it is the shift from intra-uterine to extra-uterine existence which enables the individual to conceptualize periodicity and notions of yesterday, today and tomorrow. Klein bases her claim on the analysis of just one case-example, her work with Fritz, who had two spells of analysis with her. Klein (1932) returns briefly to the importance of the sequence of time in her comments regarding the manner in which a child places her or his toys in space; she interprets this as indicating the time-order of their phantasies and experiences. However, she does not develop this thesis.

According to Klein, Fritz had been unable to grasp notions of "yesterday", "today" and "tomorrow" until the age of four and a half. In a footnote (Klein, 1921, p. 17) she mentions, without further comment, that at three years of age Fritz had run away from home and was found gazing into the window display of a watchmaker's shop. In a further footnote she interprets his comment "Mamma, doesn't the night always belong to the day before and early in the morning is a new day again?" as indicating that he has an improved conception of time. Klein also mentions that Fritz's acquisition of speech and ability to distinguish colour had been delayed.

According to Klein, Fritz's slowness to develop a notion of time as sequential is connected with his lack of interest in his life in the womb, both where and when he existed prior to birth. She writes that these questions were repressed in Fritz, who equated intra-uterine existence with sleep and death. This leads her to conclude that the shift from intra-uterine to extra-uterine existence, is "the prototype of all periodicity, is one of the roots of the concept of time and of orientation in time" (Klein, 1923, p. 110). Klein does not quote examples of Fritz's associations between life in the womb and sleep and death and there are contradictions in her account. In her report of his first analysis she describes how at four and three quarters he *was* asking questions about his life prior to his birth. Interestingly, despite his numerous attempts to find out how a baby is formed (from questions put to his mother, Klein, and his governess) in the mother's womb, he appears not to have been given any explanation of his conception and his father's role in this. Yet his refusal to accept the answers he is given is interpreted by Klein as his difficulty in accepting the fact of intra-uterine existence.

Even if, as Klein claims, Fritz did convey a lack of interest in his life in the womb, Klein does not provide sufficient argument as to why this might be the cause of his being unable to grasp conceptions of "today", "tomorrow", and "yesterday". It is more likely that his lack of interest in his life in his mother's womb might be a symptom of his not having a notion of sequential time (See Chapter Seven for further discussion of the way in which a symptom might arise from a problematic relation to temporality). Alternatively, an individual may have no interest in the question of when he was in the womb, yet may have developed a concept of periodicity through other experiences. Klein prioritizes the experience of birth over other moments either pre- or post-natally on the basis of just one case. Most significantly, Klein does not consider the role of language in the development of a notion of time as sequential. Since Fritz was, according to Klein, delayed in his acquisition of speech, it is possible that this might be connected with his particular inability to distinguish "today", "tomorrow" and "yesterday".

Although Klein's explanation of how we acquire a notion of chronological time differs from Freud's, it is nevertheless, similarly limited to a somewhat Aristotelian and naturalistic explanation of a single aspect of our relation to time, namely our experience of time passing (see Chapter One). Certainly, the importance of developing concepts of yesterday, today, and tomorrow should not be under-estimated. However, this is just one of many ways in which we experience time. In Klein's case studies, as I show in the following sections, she refers to other experiences of "lived" time which are not restricted to a notion of time as sequential. For example, she describes individuals' fears in relation to their mortality in the context of the Second World War and their connection with earlier terrors of annihilation. Their experience of temporality in these cases is not simply linear: present, past and future overlay each other, shifting in emphasis. Future time is, for many of those individuals, leaden with dread and acute anxiety that it may not come to exist as the next step in the sequence. In this context the notion of "tomorrow" is not neutral or objective.

### Session times

Klein's emphasis on the importance of a sequential conception of time for individuals contrasts with other accounts of her patients' many different lived experiences of time. In her reflections on the length of the psychoanalytic session she is sensitive to the very specific meanings this has for the patient. The patient's particular experience of time passing arises from the context of the transference relationship between the analyst and the patient (see more discussion of Klein's conception of transference below).

In contrast to Freud (1912b), Klein emphasizes the importance of ending sessions punctually, except in "exceptional circumstances" (Klein, 1961, p. 193). She is firm that it is not helpful to the patient to allow him/her to prolong sessions and that, from a pragmatic point of view, to do so would be very disruptive for the analyst's timetable. Like Freud, Klein did, however, see some of her patients outside session times in other contexts: for example, Fritz is the son of some relatives who live nearby. She does, however, question her decision to hold sessions in his family home. This experience had underlined for her the importance for the patient of his analysis being separated from the rest of his life.

In her account (1961) of her analysis of her ten year old patient Richard there are several references to his relation to the times of sessions. Richard is late for his sessions, he wants to change session times, and he is disappointed when his session ends. Klein acknowledges the unconscious significance of the patient's attitude to the times of his/her sessions and focuses on its meaning in the transference. She interprets Richard's lateness as "resistance" (Klein, 1961, p. 110) and also his regret at a session ending as his wanting Klein to himself (Klein, 1961, p. 458).

It is the patient's responses to the fixed time frame of the sessions which interest Klein. She does not argue, as later Object Relations theorists, that it serves the function of "containing", of providing secure boundaries necessary for regression or the expression of profound anxiety or aggression. This frame is, for Klein, for the convenience of the analyst, not specifically for the patient, and she is sensitive to the greed of patients who "try to take advantage of the analyst allowing them to stay longer" (Klein, 1961, p. 193).

Klein is refreshingly honest about the convenience of fixed session times to the psychoanalyst as well as its significance in the patient/ analyst relationship. Although she does not explicitly state it, her case-examples highlight her emphasis on the significance of time. The times of sessions are not abstract: how they are initially agreed upon, whether or not a patient sticks to them, and the reasons why, are all indicators of the patient's particular lived relation to time within his/ her relationship with the analyst. Klein focuses only on the patient's failure to keep to the arranged times. Should it not be equally open to interpretation if a patient is always on time and never requests a change in sessions? What might be the reasons why someone can never allow themselves to be late or express a wish to do something other than come to their analysis? As I argued in my presentation of Jane's desire to cancel her session in Chapter One, such a request might mark a positive shift in the analysis, symbolizing the loosening of compliant ways of relating on the patient's part.

## Klein's infantile past

I have argued that, despite Klein's emphasis on the importance of individuals' acquisition of a chronological notion of temporality, her interpretations of patients' responses to session times indicate that she is attentive to their conscious and unconscious lived experiences of temporality. In this section I argue that Klein, like Freud, is limited by her emphasis on the past dimension of time. In her theorizing, the time of the human subject shrinks even further back to the time of the infant driven by instincts and engaged in phantasies, projections, and introjections in relation to its primary objects, the mother and the father. The importance of this time in shaping subjectivity is stressed by her in her view of the criterion for the termination of an analysis, namely that "the conflicts and anxieties experienced during the first year of life have been sufficiently analyzed and worked through in the course of the treatment" (Klein, 1950, p. 44).

Klein's account of infantile development is founded on her claim, departing from Freud's, that the ego exists from birth and that the infant is engaged in object relations from the beginning of post-natal life. The infant's ego is fragile and constantly threatened with the possibility of annihilation by its own death instinct which, according to Klein is also present from birth. The positions designated by Klein as "paranoid-schizoid" and "depressive" respectively involve primitive defences against possible annihilation by the death instinct. In the former the baby fears for him/herself, and in the latter, his/her concerns are for the other. My reading of her accounts of early infantile development will highlight the extent of Klein's reliance on spatial metaphors: splits in the ego, feelings projected and introjected across the space between mother and baby. As I argue below, drawing on Scott, it is significant that Klein does not consider these defences as having temporal dimensions.

In her theorizing of the paranoid-schizoid position Klein claims that the hungry baby's destructive impulses (its death instinct) find expression in both oral and anally sadistic ways. Klein focuses particularly on the "phantasies" which, she claims, are the "mental expression of the activity of both the life and death instincts" (Klein, 1952b, p. 58). Initially the baby phantasises that s/he is incorporating the mother's breast or the mother herself. A split occurs whereby the mother's breast is experienced as persecutory, retaliatory towards the baby's aggressive impulses towards the breast. The loved, nourishing breast is protected from these destructive phantasies through idealization. Both the "good" and the "bad" breasts are introjected and then projected back on to the external world. External objects coloured by these projections are then reintrojected, reinforcing the nourishing or persecutory aspects of each. The strength of the introjected bad object is directly related to that of the introjected good object. For Klein, the establishment of a "good internal object" is crucial in mitigating persecutory anxiety in relation to the infant's death instinct and, therefore, for the integration of the ego. In order for the "good breast" to predominate, "external" circumstances, namely the "mother's smile, her hands, her voice, how she holds her/ him and attends to her/his needs" (Klein, 1952a, p. 64) are crucial. However, the influence of these also depend on constitutional factors, namely, the extent of aggressive and of libidinal impulses (the life and death instincts) present from birth.

In Klein's account of the "paranoid-schizoid" position, constituted by psychotic defences arising in the first four months of life, Klein distinguishes clearly between the "splitting", involved in these defences and "repression" (Klein, 1946). The ego and its object relationship are located within each piece of the rigidly divided split. These defences alter the structure of the ego, leading to states of disintegration (Klein, 1952a). In contrast "repression", Klein argues, drawing from Freud, involves a division between conscious and unconscious, with a degree of porosity between the two (if it is not excessive).

According to Klein, as the baby develops, his/her greed and sadistic phantasies strengthen. Not only does the infant want to consume the mother's breast but also to devour and scoop out her entire body and its contents. In the baby's phantasies the mother's body contains her babies, her faeces and, later, the father's penis. As anal sadistic impulses increase, the baby phantasises attacking the mother's body with unwanted, bad substances, excrements which are associated with "bad" parts of the self. (Klein does not explain how the baby "knows" that faeces are "bad".) The purpose is both to damage and to control the mother. The bad parts are split off and projected into the mother who is experienced as persecuting. This process, which has begun with the projection on to and the introjection of the breast, is the source of what Klein terms "projective identification". The object is imbued with and identified with the split-off, unwanted aspects of the infant's self.

As the child's phantasies come to include notions of the father's penis inside the mother, these are. according to Klein, elaborated and involve notions of intercourse, of breasts, penises and vaginas incorporating, devouring, biting, feeding, and controlling each other. These phantasies are the early roots of the Oedipus complex and a central, terrifying image for the infant is of the parents locked in sexual intercourse. Their relation is phantasized as aggressive and mutually destructive and the infant also feels violently aggressive towards both of them. The infant's phantasies involve both oral and genital desires in relation to the mother's breast and to the father's penis.

A shift into the "depressive position" (Klein, 1948, p. 35) occurs as the infant gradually integrates his/her loving and hating feelings, firstly in relation to "part-objects" (the mother's breast, and then the hands, faces, and genitals of both parents). This integration (at between the ages of three to six months), gives rise to "depressive" anxieties as the infant feels guilt for its destructive feelings towards the "object" s/he has also loved. This guilt evokes wishes for reparation, for healing the injured object. It intensifies as the infant's ego develops and s/he begins to establish relationships with the mother and father as "whole objects". The "depressive position", as I critically discuss below in relation to her interpretations of Ruth Kjar's artwork is, for Klein, associated with creativity. Creativity has its source, she claims, in infantile desires for reparation.

Klein argues against Freud's view of the time at which the super-ego develops. For him, the super-ego arises after the resolution of the Oedipus complex, at the age of four or five. Klein claimed that, instead, there is a conflict between the super-ego, which is innate, and the ego from birth. However, it is at the time of the depressive position (which, according to Klein, coincides with the early stages of the Oedipus complex) that the super-ego begins to appear as conscience. As a unity, it is derived from early introjected parental objects; she theorizes that if it is particularly harsh this is because it is underpinned by the sadism of introjected persecutory objects from the pregenital phases of infancy.

There is an unresolved tension between Klein's theorizing of the role of constitutional, biological factors and of the impact of the child's lived relationships with others on his/her subjectivity. As I argued in Chapter One in relation to Freud's theorizing, Klein's assumption of the existence of ahistorical, alinguistic drives and impulses does not sufficiently allow for different interpretations of aggression. The baby's aggressive phantasies are assumed to exist prior to, and independent of, a relational context in which, for example, frustration may arise.

The tensions and contradictions in Klein's position are highlighted in her argument against Freud's claim that the infant's relation to the breast is mainly derived from phylogenetic (i.e. inherited) phantasies and that this does not depend on their own early feeding experience. She counters this with her argument that people who have not been breast-fed experience a particularly intense longing for an "unobtainable object" (Klein, 1952b, p. 117). The original desire for and knowledge of the nipple is, however, viewed by Klein as instinctual and phylogenetically transmitted. This leads her to claim that bottle-feeding can never be experienced by the baby as offering the maximum satisfaction, even if s/he appears to readily accept it. Klein also assumes that the infant's oral- and anal-sadistic phantasies, and his/her mental representations of intercourse and parts of the body, including the nipple, the breast, and the father's penis, are phylogenenetically transmitted. They are thus conceived of as atemporal, since they exist prior to any lived relation to these aspects of the parents' bodies.

Although Klein occasionally acknowledges the importance of the mother's responses to her baby, she does not take into account how much these are shaped by prevailing socio-historical patterns of child-rearing, parental relationships and familial organization. Her interpretation of the meaning of not being breast-fed to individuals does not, for example, take into account the socio-historical and cultural meanings associated with this. These are likely to have been transmitted to them through language (verbally and non-verbally) leading to a retrospective, negative association to not having been breast-fed as infants.

Klein does not present any clear arguments as to why the early months of an infant's life are more influential than any later experiences. Foreclosing on challenges to her position she claims that her theorizing is objectively empirical in that it has been "derived by inference from material gained in the analyses of adults and children" and that it matches "observations familiar in psychiatric work" (Klein, 1946, p. 1). This is not sufficient justification for her attribution of universal status to experiences voiced by adults at a particular socio-historical time in Europe, nor her assumption that all of these have their source in the first year of life.

Klein's prioritising of the first year of life in her account of subjectivity begs the question as to how we can know what the experience of a baby is from an adult perspective. Klein (1946, p. 8) briefly acknowledges in a footnote that her account of projective identification is handicapped by the fact that the infants she describes do not yet think in words. In a later footnote the limitations of this are further revealed: the "pre-verbal emotions and phantasies" appear as " 'memories in feelings' " and require the words of the analyst to "put these into words" (Klein, 1957, p. 180). She fails to recognize the extensive implications that this might have for all of her theorizing of early infancy and the contradictions it highlights. She ascribes highly complex linguistic concepts to an infant and, at the same time, claims that these are extra-linguistic. How can such experiences exist outside language? I develop this question further in my discussion of Klein's relation to language in the section, "The Language of Klein's Time" below.

Klein's theorizing eliminates all possibility of the significance of later experiences to the individual and how these shift in priority throughout the subject's history according to different relational contexts. However, Klein's notion of "positions" nevertheless does challenge the linearity and a certain fixity implied in Freud's account of the developmental stages. "Positions" for Klein are, instead, "groupings of anxieties and defences" (Klein, 1952a, p. 93) and maturation involves an interplay between progression and regression, a shifting back and forth as different anxieties and their defences are aroused. Although she does theorize that these different positions tend to occur at certain ages in first months of the child's life, she emphasizes that these appear and reappear in the first few years of a child's life and also later on in adult life. Her theorizing of "positions", as opposed to developmental "stages", therefore allow for a greater diversity of specific configurations of anxieties and for greater complexity in interpretations as to how these are defended against.

### Time and splitting: Janet's time

As I have described above, the notion of "splitting" is central to Klein's account of early infantile development. In an interesting footnote Klein (1946, p. 6, note 1) refers to Dr. W. C. M. Scott's comments on her paper "Notes on Some Schizoid Mechanisms" (1946). Scott had suggested to her that the breaking in the continuity of experiences involves a temporal "splitting" rather than a "splitting" in spatial terms. Klein states that she fully agrees with this but does not elaborate this any further.

Scott's emphasis on time is important since any spatial separation of the baby from the mother or, in Klein's terms, "the breast", occurs within time. As Winnicott emphasizes (see Chapter Four), the duration of the separation, or the infant's experience of this, is likely to have a significant bearing on its tolerance of its feelings of frustration and anger in response to its hunger. The subsequent defences of "splitting" which Klein theorizes are also unavoidably located in time. It is thus surprising that the relevance of time would not have occurred to Klein if Scott had not pointed this out. It is also striking that, while in agreement with Scott, she affords his comments only a brief footnote.

The relation between temporality and splitting is highlighted in Janet's work in psychotherapy. A strong theme in the early years of her therapy concerned her fears, expressed in the form of furious rages, of being "trapped". Throughout her childhood as an only child her mother had been unpredictable, cruel and, at times, physically abusive, locking her in her room for hours if she disobeyed her. Time had felt endless to her in her pain and powerlessness. However, it was only after some years into her therapy that it became really possible to address the states of totalizing rage which gripped Janet and through which she attempted to freeze or paralyze me. Any interpretation in relation to her past, however gently suggested, was received as a brutal misunderstanding and a violent threat to her existence. At those times, for Janet, there was no past; any attempt at an interpretation in relation to a past experience, however gently suggested, was responded to with an annihilating attack. There was also no future, no end to this state. For Janet, this was the only reality in her life and it was forever. The present was all that existed; other dimensions of time were split off and unavailable.

Janet's experience resonates with Klein's accounts of schizoid states. However, while Klein's account uses spatial metaphors of projection and internalization, it was evident to me that, for Janet, her split state required interpretation in temporal terms. Janet did not have a notion of time passing, of change. In being trapped inside a feeling, she was partly repeating her experience of being locked, for her endlessly, in her bedroom as a child, or left alone in the house. But she was also killing time's movement, just as she tried to freeze me, to eliminate the unpredictability of the future, a future which was bound to bring the impingement on her of another's difference. I did not interpret this directly to Janet, other than to indicate that I did understand that she was caught in a feeling of something being endless. To offer a more complete interpretation would have been too intrusive: my perceptions offered from my viewpoint as an other who was beyond her control would have threatened to trap her even more and would have been met with further resistance.

As I have argued above, Klein's theorising is limited by her assumption that the paranoid-schizoid position originates in the first months of life and has to be negotiated universally by every infant. It was clear that Janet's later experience of being locked in her room, as she recalled it in her analysis, was extremely significant whether or not it resonated with any earlier experience. As a metaphor however, Klein's notion of the paranoid-schizoid position highlights the splits in Janet's experience. Yet, a reinterpretation of this in temporal, as opposed to purely spatial terms, was crucial in addressing Janet's lived experience of time, including its defensive aspects.

### Klein's future

Like Freud, Klein does not explicitly address the importance of the dimension of the future in the subject's lived experience of time. However, a notion of the future is integral to her theorizing of the death instinct, which I discuss in more detail below. In the paranoid-schizoid position the mechanisms of projection and introjection defend the baby from the risk of potential annihilation by the death instinct. As I have outlined, this becomes associated with the threats to the infant's existence from the internalized mother and father and, consequently, with fears of persecution. Klein therefore implicitly attributes to the infant a concept of the future, a future which is primarily associated with a sense of threat. This assumption precludes questions about the genesis of such a sense of future.

In her analysis of adults and children the threat of annihilation is interpreted in terms of early infantile anxieties. Klein's future time doubles back on itself as a loop which, while containing all three dimensions, reinstates the past as the most formative in every subject's life. Her theorizing of the depressive position relies on the infant having a notion of the future. This is integral to Klein's theorizing of the infant's wish to protect others from potential damage. However, her concept of the future, while here introducing a notion of creativity, again refers back to the past; the parental figures who have been attacked are restored.

This emphasis on the past continues to inform Kleinian theorizing. For example, Birksted-Breen, a contemporary Kleinian analyst, argues that unless the past remains "implicit", the analyst is "colluding with the patient in a malignantly denuded present" (Birksted-Breen, 2003, p. 1503). She does acknowledge that analysis produces a *"new creation of the past"*, leading to *"a modification of internal objects"* (Birksted-Breen, 2003, p. 1503). However, Birksted-Breen, along with Klein, does not offer any notion of a creativity which is not determined by the past. This forecloses on the possibility of a newness, involving discovery and surprise, an engagement with the unknowability and possibility of the future, which Jung's theorizing offers. I explore this notion further in my discussion of her interpretation of Ruth Kjar's artwork (see below).

## The time of the transference

For Klein, an analysis is successful only if "the infantile depressive position has been worked through, that is to say, that the whole gamut of love and hatred, anxiety, grief and guilt in relation to the primary objects has been experienced again and again" (Klein, 1950, p. 46). The lived relation between patient and analyst involves a constant shifting between the present and the past. Although the analyst attends to later experiences, these are interpreted in the light of the foundational first year of life. Klein's insistence on the importance of the first year of life runs through her theorizing of transference.

Klein claims that in the first months of life the relation is between two individuals exclusively. Phantasies relating to the father's penis then begin to interrupt this two-body relationship, initiating the Oedipus complex. Klein stresses that she extends her interpretations of the transference beyond the relation to the actual mother and father. She claims that although there are very few people in an infant's early life (we can assume she is describing the Western nuclear family) they are experienced as having numerous aspects which are imbued with the infant's denigrating and idealizing projections. Klein claims that it is because transferences have their source in infantile experiences that they can be extremely strong in the course of the analysis; the analyst represents those figures in their loved and hated positions as experienced in early infancy. She emphasizes that the patient is "bound" to draw on the very same defences as s/he did in the past in her/his relation to the analyst (Klein, 1952a, p. 55). Furthermore she interprets *all* of the patient's accounts of their everyday activities and relationships as defences against the anxieties evoked in the transference with regard to the patient's earliest relations with his/her "primal objects", including part-objects. Klein argues that it is "only by linking again and again ... later experiences with earlier ones and vice versa, it is only by consistently exploring their interplay, that present and past can come together in the patient's mind" (Klein, 1952a, p. 56).

Klein does warn of the possible defensive aspects of a patient's account of their past experiences: "'The patient may at times try to escape into the past rather than realizing that his emotions, anxieties, and phantasies are at the time operative in full strength and focused on the analyst" (1952a, p. 56, note 1). At other times the patient defends her/himself from re-experiencing the past. There is an implication here that the patient's relation to time itself arises from within a relational context, namely the lived relation between patient and analyst.

Klein's theorizing of the transference relationship is exceedingly limited. It is rooted in the problematic universalizing and speculative assumptions regarding infantile experience which I analyze above. Her focus on the past as exclusively shaping the present denies any recognition of the importance of the subject's relation to the future and how this may emerge transferentially and enable change. There is an omnipotent assumption that the relation with the analyst is the patient's main preoccupation in his/her descriptions of their experiences. This forecloses on the multiplicity of significances which such descriptions may have for the patient and which relate consciously and unconsciously to their past (ranging from the distant to the recent past), their present (including relationships with others as well as with their analyst) and their anticipation of the future.

### Creativity and temporality

The limitations underpinning Klein's theorizing of temporality are highlighted in a paper on creativity, "Infantile anxiety-situations reflected in a work of art and in the creative impulse" (1929) It is here that she introduces for the first time her concept of "reparation" in her interpretation of Ruth Kjar's urge to paint (Klein, 1929, p. 235). Klein draws on an article written by Kjar's friend, Karin Michaelis, who describes how Kjar began to make art. For many years Kjar had suffered from periods of suicidal depression which she experienced as an "empty space" within her which she could never fill (Klein, 1929, p. 232, quoting Michaelis, quoting Kjar's own words). When her brother-in-law (a famous artist) took away one of the many paintings of his which covered the walls of her home, Kjar felt acutely sad and consumed by the experience of the empty space which was left. Suddenly, however, she decided to purchase paints from her brother-in-law's art materials supplier and, for the first time ever, produced a painting with huge enthusiasm. The image which emerged was of a life-size naked black woman. From then on she continued to paint mainly portraits, including one of an elderly (white) woman, and also one of her mother as a powerful, challenging, and haughty (also white) woman. Her paintings, which she went on to exhibit, won much public acclaim.

Klein focuses on Kjar's portrait of the wrinkled and deteriorating old woman and on that of Kjar's mother. Klein interprets the former as deriving from Kjar's primary, sadistic wish (originating in the early stages of the girl's Oedipus complex) to "rob the mother's body of its contents, namely the father's penis, faeces, children" (Klein, 1929, p. 234) and to destroy her. The subsequent projection of this phantasy on to the mother produces anxiety in the girl that her own body will be "destroyed or mutilated" (Klein, 1929, p. 234) and this is intensified when the mother is absent. Klein connects Kjar's experience of an "empty space" with this anxiety. Klein views Kjar's painting of her mother as 'reparation', an expression of Kjar's desire to restore the mother whom she had destroyed in phantasy. She argues that "when the representation of destructive wishes is succeeded by an expression of reactive tendencies, we constantly find that drawing and painting are used as means to restore people" (Klein, 1929, p. 235).

Klein's account contains significant contradictions and omissions. If the motive to draw and paint itself originates, as she claims, in the infantile desire to make reparation, why does Klein differentiate between the *content* of two paintings in relation to the question of reparation? How can one be reparative and the other not if they are both, as creative expressions, motivated by the desire for reparation? In relation to temporality, it is particularly significant that Klein's view of creativity is so firmly secured in a notion of healing or repairing what has been phantasized about in the earliest months of an individual's life. Klein mentions that, according to Michaelis, Kjar had previously only expressed her creativity in relation to the arrangement of her home. She does not acknowledge the significance of Kjar's engagement with painting as a woman in the 1920s. (For an extensive analysis of women's relation to fine art practices historically I refer the reader to Parker and Pollock, 1981). Klein also does not comment at all on Kjar's first image (of the black woman), focusing instead on her portraits of white women.

The possible significance of the painting of the black woman for Kjar's entry into the discipline of what has been designated "fine art" unfolds if the socio-historical context is taken into account. Kjar's painting represented a courageous challenge to an artistic tradition which was dominated by men and to traditional expectations of gendered and racial femininity in the 1920s. In painting the naked black woman Kjar may have been unveiling an aspect of herself which she had experienced as "discriminated" against or disempowered, consciously and unconsciously, and which she could now reveal and celebrate without shame. Instead of signifying reparative wishes in relation to early object relations, the figure of the black woman may point towards the future, towards the possibility of living previously unacknowledged aspects of herself. Walton takes another view, namely that the painting of the black woman could represent a "masquerade" of "primitiveness" (Walton, 1997, p. 242). Its unconscious purpose would be to protect Kjar from a hostile response to her as a female artist since, as "primitive art" by an untrained artist, it would not threaten to compete with the art of Kjar's brother-in-law. The naked black women is therefore, according to Walton, a "kind of sacrifice within the gendered scene of power negotiations between a white woman and the white men whose retaliation she fears" (Walton, 1997, p. 241).

Klein's, Walton's and my own interpretations are all speculative to some extent since very few of Kjar's own words are recorded. However, they provide very vivid illustrations of divergent assumptions in relation to historicity and are therefore useful to compare. Klein's interpretations do not take into account the wider socio-historical context with its particular discourses in relation to race and gender which shape femininity from birth on. The life of Kjar as a newly emerging woman artist collapses into the life of the infant struggling to repair the damage done by her in her paranoid-schizoid phantasies. Such a perspective on temporality does not acknowledge the possibility of a radical break with the past in anticipation of the future (See Chapter Five for more discussion of this in the light of Foucault's theorizing).

Both Walton's and my own interpretations emphasize the socio-historical context. The time of the appearance of Kjar's figure of the naked black woman is not just an individual moment of an individual's history, it is located in a shared time, that of the socio-historical context, at a matrix of discourses in relation to race, gender and definitions of what constitutes fine art. Our interpretations differ in the extent to which we view Kjar's painting as a challenge to male-female power relations and in our understanding of what this means in temporal terms. My emphasis is on Kjar's unconscious undermining of traditional expectations of femininity and hinges on a notion of Kjar's (unconscious) anticipation of the future as possibility. Walton's focuses instead on the painting's role as placatory in relation to male power in the context of definitions of fine art. She argues that Kjar exploits power relations between white and black people in the present in order to protect herself from male artists' antagonism to her work.

My own interpretation does not exclude an interest in Kjar's earlier relationships. Throughout her life, Kjar would have been subject to discourses on femininity and creativity and their effects. These would have been communicated to her verbally and nonverbally from birth on. Her ability to be creative would have been shaped by, for example, how active and adventurous she was allowed to be from infancy on, how far she was expected to be attuned to or take care of others (See Orbach, 1982), how she experienced solitude, how loved she felt for her individuality, and how playful significant figures, including adults, siblings and peers, were with her. These relationships all occur within the context of particular socio-historically produced discourses on gender. Klein's interpretation of Kjar's creativity as a form of reparation in relation to early infantile destructive phantasies neglects the importance and complexity of a multiplicity of past experiences which are located at a specific historical time within a matrix of male-female and black-white power relations. As Walton (1997) points out, this does not depend on being raised in a mixed, black and white, culture.

### Klein's death

Klein (1948) agrees with Freud regarding the existence of life and death instincts. However she argues against his view that the unconscious cannot have a knowledge of its own death. She claims that the fear of death is, fundamentally, a fear of annihilation and it is a response to the death instinct. For Klein, if the death instinct exists there must also be a corresponding fear within the unconscious of its destructive possibilities. This cannot, she argues, be equated with the fear of castration, as Freud claimed. For him, the fear of death was derived from fears of the punitive super-ego. In Klein's view, conversely, the fear of annihilation and death underpins and shapes the child's experience of the super-ego since it is present from birth; it is the primary source of anxiety and it intensifies the persecutory fears evoked by the pain of that experience. The process of birth and the child's struggles with hunger in the first months of life are experienced as threats by the baby to its existence.

I have critically discussed (see above) Klein's theorizing of the baby's progression from the paranoid-schizoid to the depressive position, the analysis of which she emphasizes as critical for a successful psychoanalysis. It is in these accounts of early infantile development that Klein's theorizing of the subject's relation to their own death is evident. Her theorizing hinges on an assumption that the death instinct exists and is present from birth. In her view the baby is constantly struggling to protect itself from the destructiveness of its own aggression which Klein equates with the death instinct.

For Klein (1957) envy is closely associated with the death instinct and it is inherent in the subject. She defines envy as a wish to take away or spoil something desirable which is being enjoyed by another. It is both an oral-sadistic and an anal-sadistic expression of destructive impulses. Paranoia is, for Klein, also an expression of the death instinct deflected outwards. The strength of the death instinct is constitutional and there is a direct connection between its preponderance and the strength or weakness of the ego. Similarly, the impact of "external" experiences of birth and of feeding on the child depend on the strength of his/her death instinct. The work of mourning involves, for Klein, the re-establishment of the primary loved objects which are assumed to have been threatened or destroyed by the baby's destructive impulses.

Klein's accounts assume that the baby has an awareness, albeit unconsciously, of the possibility of his/her own death. It is unclear how the baby conceptualizes his/her fears of death if, as Klein seems to assume, knowledge of the death instinct lies outside language. It is also unclear why the concept of the death instinct is necessary as an explanation for the baby's rage and desperation. Why is not the unbearability of the extreme discomfort and helplessness experienced by the hungry infant sufficient to explain the baby's distress? Notions of annihilation and threats to survival are very sophisticated concepts for infants and young children. If these already existed unconsciously, it is unlikely that the extent of explanation needed by children up to the age of three or four when they lose relatives, pets or see other dead animals would be necessary. It seems likely that it is through those experiences that we acquire the knowledge that we will ourselves die and simultaneously absorb specific cultural and religious attitudes and beliefs about death.

For Klein, young children's and adults' fears of death in relation to "external" dangers such as air-raids, bombs and fires are intensified owing to the arousal of early infantile fears of death and annihilation. The actual danger may be denied as a manic defence against the extremity of those early anxieties. Those children who manage to remain relatively stable in the face of such dangers are able to do so, according to Klein, because of the "successful modification of early persecutory and depressive anxieties" (Klein, 1948, p. 40). Psychoanalysis in, for example, war-time, can bring about an alleviation of extreme anxieties if the earlier infantile anxieties are analyzed. Klein acknowledges the socio-historical context but, again, prioritizes the role of early infantile phantasies. This is in contrast to Jung's view of death as requiring acceptance and as transformative (see Chapter Two). Klein associates death with destruction and she assumes that this connection is universal. She does not address the effects of ordinary human aging and disease.

I have argued that Freud's view of death as destructive can be traced back to his writing about the horrors of the First World War (1915). Klein was undoubtedly influenced by his position and also by her direct experience of the socio-historical context in which she too lived, a time which spanned both world wars, the rise of Nazism and the horrific persecution and killing of Jews in the holocaust. In contrast, Jung, as a Swiss German Christian, was not living in a social context where he was at risk of his life as Jews were at that time and this is likely to have influenced his more optimistic view of death. In Klein's (1961) case-study of Richard during a four-month period in World War II, much of Richard's material is related to guns, bombs, battles, troops, and fleets. Richard was therefore growing up in a context in which death was associated primarily with violence and his notion of time included a strong possibility that he and/or his analyst, Klein, would have their futures obliterated as a consequence of the violence of war.

## Kim's dream of death

A dream recounted to me by Kim illustrates how we can have an unconscious knowledge of our own death. It also, significantly, opens up a plurality of meanings in relation to death which are not primarily concerned with destructiveness, the focus of Klein's interpretations of death.

> "I was in a tent with a woman called Lynne. When I came out of the tent I was abducted and killed. I saw my head and body being pulled apart, my stomach was slit and white stuff oozed out. All the parts of my body were being thrown into a cauldron. Lynne was there saying 'It's all good stuff, it mustn't be wasted.' Then I was holding a tiny child and slapping water on to its eyes for them to open. I felt such maternal, loving feelings for it".

Kim said that she was not alarmed at this dissection and associated it with her therapy (Lynne is, of course, a part of my name) and the possibility of recognizing and accepting her vulnerability. For Kim, her fear of her mortality had terrified her: it was associated with incompletion, imperfection and the unknown. This fear had, until some months into our work, been largely unconscious. She complained of its effects, which had gone on for many years: she felt driven to work obsessively and to drink alcohol excessively, and her body was in the grip of numerous psychosomatic symptoms. This dream, brought to me after several years of analysis, seemed to symbolize the possibility of acknowledging, with my encouragement in the transference, her own death. Instead of this being destructive it was, instead, productive. The realization of her own vulnerability allowed for new life, symbolized by the baby whom she could care for. Until then her unconscious fear of death had compelled her to drive herself to death.

Kim's work in her analysis exemplifies Klein's notion that we do have an unconscious knowledge of our own death. However, for Klein this knowledge is associated with the fear of annihilation. Certainly Kim's unconscious associations to death had been, earlier on in her therapy, with its destructive aspects. The dream above contrasts with these and marked a new stage in the analytic work: dying is associated with the possibility of new life, with sensitivity and vulnerability, and an ability to be in an alive relation to another. Kim's new association to death is reminiscent of Heidegger's view that our comprehension of our own death is of "being *towards a* possibility ... towards something possible" (Heidegger, 1927, p. 305).

Kim's dream highlights the importance of being attuned to the multiple possibilities of meanings associated with the certainty that, as human beings, we will one day die. Fear of annihilation may be a very prevalent unconscious association with death but there may be many other meanings for individuals at different times in their lives. For Klein, in contrast, our fears of death are always fears of annihilation, of not surviving and the development of the super-ego hinges on this: to oppose the demands of the super-ego is to risk death.

## *The language of Klein's time*

Klein's language is permeated with dualisms of internal/external, inner/outer, good/bad, love/hate, and phantasy/reality. In her accounts of infantile development she theorizes maturation as the ability to tolerate ambivalence; this becomes possible as the baby moves out of early schizoid states into the depressive position and the realization that the object that is loved and hated is the same. However, her own writing nevertheless reproduces the very dualisms which she designates as schizoid. Her theorizing of the internal world as so distinct from the external world has implications for the conception of temporality which underpins her work.

As I have outlined, for Klein, the crucial time of the individual's life is its first year. She does not give substantive arguments as to how we can know that a small baby phantasizes and what the content is. Yet her notion of how the history of the subject is shaped hinges on her conviction regarding the existence and meaning of these phantasies. Her theorizing is derived from older children and adults whose verbal and non-verbal communications she interprets within the framework of her pre-existing assumptions.

These assumptions arise from a notion of an inner world which exists independently from and prior to the external world. This is exemplified in her insistence that her small patient Richard's fears of his mother being kidnapped by a tramp symbolize his anxieties that his father will *hurt* his mother in sexual intercourse, that "when his parents went at bed at night something could happen between them with their genitals that would injure Mummy"

(Klein, 1961, p. 21). She describes Richard's surprise and fear in the face of this interpretation, which Klein understands as his response to not knowing the meaning of the word "genital". It does not seem to occur to her that, as well as being mystified by this term (not his own), Richard might be puzzled and upset by Klein's assumption that his fears of his mother being *kidnapped*, namely taken away, had been translated into a notion of her being *hurt* by his own father in bed.

In her introduction to the case of Richard, Klein claims that she makes "a point of using the words that the patient has used, and I find this has the effect both of diminishing resistance and of bringing back fully into his mind the material I am referring to" (Klein, 1961, p. 18). However, in the example of her interpretation of Richard's material Klein does not adhere to the specificity of his own language; her own associations link the tramp with Hitler and his hostility to the Austrians, which she interprets as indicating Richard's fears for her safety as an Austrian woman, and finally to his (earlier infantile) phantasy of his parents having intercourse. According to Klein this is a universal phantasy and it inaugurates the early Oedipus complex. Her interpretation of Richard's anxiety about a phantasized future event doubles back to his past, his "inner reality", fixed by the assumption of universality.

The opportunity for further exploration of the meaning of the tramp and his abduction of Richard's mother in relation to Richard's present and past experiences is therefore missed. If the tramp does represent Richard's father, why is he characterized in this way at the present time? Did Richard have a particular experience of his father in the past which evoked this association? Klein's splitting of inner and outer realities cuts across the historicity of the individual. This historicity includes the socio-historical context. It might be the case that certain aspects of the past are experienced by the individual as split off, distant or no longer relevant to his/her current experience of his/her identity. However, as I discussed in the section, "Time and splitting; Janet's time", Klein's reliance on spatial metaphors, as opposed to interpretations in temporal terms is inadequate to address the individual's lived experience of time and subtle shifts between all the temporal dimensions.

Klein claims that language is a "bridge to reality" (Klein, 1932, p. 14, note 1). Whether Klein is referring to her notion of inner or outer reality, her position indicates a split. How can we experience the world except through language, whether verbal or non-verbal? As Heidegger argues, to exist is to be "thrown into language" (Heidegger, 1927, pp. 160–211). Klein implicitly assumes that language names pre-existent realities and that it does not have any part in constructing them. In contrast to Freud's notions of "construction" and "psychical reality" (see Chapter One), Klein's assumption precludes the possibility of language as opening out contingent truths, or perspectives, which are constantly shifting and arise from within a specific temporal context; in psychoanalysis this context is the relationship between patient and analyst.

Klein does include in her notion of language the verbal and the non-verbal; it includes play, drawing and gesture, and her detailed case-studies of her work with children convey her detailed attention to all of these linguistic forms. However, she argues that the termination of an analysis cannot occur until the child has used speech "to its fullest capacity" (Klein, 1932, p. 14, note 1). Since speech is the dominant mode of communication between human subjects this might be a reasonable expectation. Yet it also begs the question as to whether the ambiguity of non-verbal language is too challenging to the dualisms in Klein's theorizing.

## Conclusion

For Klein, the temporality of adulthood has its source primarily in the time of the baby and its relation to the mother's breast. Her interpretations of anxiety in the face of phantasies of future annihilation point towards the past, to early infantile experiences. Although Klein's theorizing is restricted by its emphasis on this, her account contrasts with the linear temporality of Freud's notion of "stages of development"; it emphasizes instead a shifting *between* the depressive and schizoid positions and the phantasies which characterize them.

Although Klein specifically refers to language, she appears to views its role as naming pre-existent inner realities. This contrasts with Freud's notion of construction which allows, as I have argued, for the possibility of language as opening out contingent perspectives. Her dualistic notion of reality as either internal or external does not sufficiently address the lived historicity of the individual as s/he is positioned within a specific socio-historical context. As O'Connor points out, Klein does not take into account the extent of twentieth century century theorizing in hermeneutics which "systematically criticize divisions between thought and language, and spatial metaphors of 'inside' and 'outside' arising from that dualistic split" (O'Connor, 1990, p. 184).

In relation to the death drive, Klein argues against Freud that we do have an unconscious knowledge of our own death. However, her theorizing of the individual's relation to death is, as is Freud's, limited in her equation of death with destruction. It is likely that this arises from her experience of living through two world wars and it highlights that theorizing is always of its own time; it is never neutral or value-free.

# CHAPTER FOUR

# Winnicott and Lacan: more about time

B oth Winnicott and Lacan have been inspirational for the contemporary development of two radically divergent and increasingly popular strands of theorizing in British psychoanalysis. This chapter critically considers their theorizing in relation to the theme of time. I do not aim to make an explicit comparison; their differences are very evident. They do, however, share a recognition of the significance of time in human subjectivity which extends far beyond Freud's, Klein's and Lacan's.

## Winnicott: holding in time

### Mother in time

Temporality has central importance in Winnicott's understanding of subjectivity. The most significant time of the subject's life is, for him, the time of the early mother/infant relationship. Arguing against Freud and Klein's neglect of the role of the environment in the development of the infant, he emphasizes the provision of "good enough" mothering, and its crucial importance to the baby's sense of continuity. It is this that enables the infant to develop an integrated self with a past, present, and future" (Winnicott, 1971, p. 86).

In contrast to Klein's theorizing, Winnicott conceptualizes the infant's gradual separation from the mother in predominantly temporal, rather than spatial terms. It is possible that he was inspired by Scott's (1946) argument that splitting might be more appropriately conceived of in terms of time, which Klein (1946) briefly refers to and which I discuss in Chapter Two. Winnicott argues that initially there is "absolute dependence" (Winnicott, 1971, p. 87) on the immediacy and sensitivity of the mother's adaptation to his/her needs, such that the baby has the illusion of magical control. He refers explicitly to the importance of time being "kept going by the mother" (Winnicott, 1963a, p. 77) in the continuity of her holding of the baby. As the baby develops, the mother's failure to adapt precisely to his/her needs becomes vital to the growth of his/her independence. Food may be delayed but the baby becomes able to recognize noises that signify its preparation and the gap becomes bearable. It is at this stage (lasting from six months to two years) that the infant begins to be aware of its dependence; if the mother is absent for more than a certain time-span, his/her survival feels threatened and this gives rise to anxiety.

Winnicott emphasizes that the baby's ability to retain an 'internal" imago or memory of the caretaker is what sustains him/her through time. Language, in the form of explanation or reassurance can also (at a later time in the child's development) enable the duration to be bearable. If the mother is away longer than expected the imago fades, but can be repaired if she is not absent for too long. However, if the absence is too extended the infant is likely to be traumatised; defences become organized as a protection against a repetition of the acute anxiety generated. (Winnicott, 1971, p. 114).

As the baby becomes more independent from the mother, continuity through time is provided through the baby's relation to the "transitional object" (Winnicott's term for the soft toy, sound, word, mannerism, or the mother herself) which both symbolically stands for the mother and is (in reality) not the mother. The transitional object contains the past and the future: it is "related backwards in time to auto-erotic phenomena ... and also forwards to the first soft animal or doll and hard toys" (Winnicott, 1971, p. 16). It signifies the transition from a merged relation with the mother to one of separateness. Offering an "intermediate area of experience" (Winnicott, 1971, p. 15) it lays the ground for later cultural and religious experiences.

It forms the basis of the capacity to play and to create "which takes up space and time" (Winnicott, 1971, p. 59) and which, Winnicott argues, is intrinsic to healthy living. Its creative potential thus points forward into the future.

Winnicott's theorizing of the temporal dimensions of separation is important in its recognition of the specificity of the infant's frustration in relation to time (as opposed to the negotiation of the *space* between mother and baby, self and other, inner and outer, internal and external). As Priel, the relational psychoanalyst, also emphasizes, the individual's capacity to be alone is rooted in the "capacity to project from past to future ('it will return')" (Priel, 1997, p. 437). Winnicott's theorizing is also an important challenge to Klein's interpretation of aggression as a manifestation of the death drive and as hereditary. For Winnicott "the history of an individual baby cannot be written in terms of the baby alone. It must be written in terms also of the environmental provision which either meets dependence needs or fails to meet them" (Winnicott, 1971, p. 83). It is in his emphasis on the relation *between* the actual mother and the infant that the crucial importance of the time factor is so evident.

Winnicott lapses into an ahistoricism, however, in his references to the drive. Despite his emphasis on the environment and his critique of Freud's and Klein's notions of the drive (of the "death instinct" in particular), he resorts to it in contradictory and unexpected ways, arguing for example that theories which "bypass the importance" of the instincts are "unhelpful" (Winnicott, 1988, p. 36). He acknowledges that the Oedipus complex might take a particular form in the context of an insititution or where the parents are absent, but he does not question its universality. He regards the "maturational processes" (Winnicott, 1963h, p. 239) as "drives" but they depend on the facilitating environment. Winnicott does not clarify how it is possible to distinguish between what he designates as "instincts" (or "drives") and what is environmentally produced. For example he writes that "Instinct-drives lead to a ruthless usage of objects" (Winnicott, 1963a, p. 77) and that the mother's presence assists the baby in becoming "more and more bold in the experiencing of id-drives" (Winnicott, 1963a, p. 77). These assume that there are aspects of subjectivity which are timeless and ahistorical which is at odds with his emphasis that the history of the baby can never be about the baby alone. However, it is significant that Winnicott references Foucault in his book, *Playing and Reality*. Foucault (1976) launches a strong critique of Freud's notion of repression, arguing that what is claimed to be natural is itself a cultural construct. Bodies and sexualities are *produced* by specific socio-historical contexts (see Chapter Six below). It is likely that, had Winnicott lived longer, he would have developed a more extensive critique of the notion of drives and instincts, given the radical possibilities of his theorizing of the "facilitating environment" (Winnicott, 1963h, p. 239).

Winnicott's emphasis on the early months of the subject's life is an important acknowledgement of the vulnerability of the human infant and of his/her capacity for relationships which are not theorized as purely instinct driven. However, in prioritising this as universally the most formative, Winnicott risks underestimating the significance of the multiplicity of relationships of varying complexity which every individual is subject to and affected by throughout their life. This is exemplified in his insistence that psychosis always has its source in the earliest state of absolute dependence. Furthermore, it seems likely that the notion that infants are completely merged with their mothers or caretakers is a historically specific interpretation and is not universal. More recent research (Aitken and Trevarthen, 1997, and Stern 1998) suggests that infants are able to distinguish others as separate from themselves before the age of two months. Parker (1995) suggests that the notion of fusion between mother and baby may be a retrospective fantasy on the part of adults and that, furthermore, states of fusion in adults may not necessarily contain traces of infantile fusion. According to Benjamin it is crucial that we acknowledge the possibility of a "shared intersubjective third position" (Benjamin, 2006) between mother and infant, patient and analyst, which is not dependent on the intervention of the father or the Phallus, as Lacan claims (see below).

*Socio-historical time*

Winnicott leans towards a recognition of the wider historical context in his theorizing. For example, in *Playing and Reality* (1971) he refers to Mead's and Erikson's accounts of the historical and cultural specificity of maternal care and its shaping of individuals' defences, but he does not develop this. Furthermore, there is a subtle implication that there is one model for "good-enough" mothering which some cultures might be better at than others. He is clearly influenced by the dominant discourses on gender in 1950s Britain which equated femininity with motherhood, deeming the latter as "natural" for women. These were fuelling the political demand on women to return to their roles as wives and mothers after World War II (see Chapter Six). Winnicott does, however, occasionally recognize the mother as having other interests (personally and professionally) and the importance of their function in enabling the baby to separate. For Benjamin (1990), writing from a feminist perspective within a different socio-historical context, this is essential if the child is to develop a sense of his/her own individual subjectivity.

There are tensions and confusions in Winnicott's perspectives on gender. In a radical move for psychoanalytic writers at that time Winnicott refers to the father, if present at a very early stage of infantile development, as "another mother" (Winnicott, 1960, p. 142). However, this is within the context of the infant's perception of the father (as Winnicott interprets it) rather than an appreciation of the value of men being involved in the care of babies and children.

Contradictions are particularly evident in his development of his claim that there are "female" elements in boys and men, and "male" elements in girls and women (Winnicott, 1971, pp. 84–95). Despite his challenges to the dualisms of femininity as equated with passivity and masculinity with activity, and to assumptions that these should belong exclusively to one biological gender, he resorts to another pair of dualisms. He designates the "female" element as non-instinctual, relating in terms of identifications and "being" (Winnicott, 1971, p. 94) and the "male" element as instinctual, whether relating actively or passively to another. "Being" is transmitted through the female element of men and women, providing "continuity over generations" (Winnicott, 1971, p. 94). Winnicott states that creativity is shared by men and women yet that, "in another language", it belongs mainly to women and, "in yet another language", it is a masculine feature (Winnicott, 1971, p. 85) but he does not clarify this.

The limitations of Winnicott's attempts at a new theorizing of gender and sexuality are further thrown into sharp relief in his claim that bisexuality is a "less than optimal" expectation of sexual experience (Winnicott, 1971, p. 92). The logical outcome of his own arguments could imply the opposite. It is surprising, given Winnicott's emphasis on historical and environmental factors, that his thinking about gender remains so undeveloped and does not take into account its socio-historical specificity.

Winnicott briefly engages with the question of the socio-histori-cal specificity of concepts of normality and how particular social-cultural contexts are conducive to creativity. He acknowledges, for example, that for some cultures in some eras creativity would not be regarded as an expression of healthy living. His particular interest is in the relation between culture and tradition, acknowledging the importance of the transmission of narratives over six thousand years. He argues that it is only possible to be original on the basis of tradi-tion and he parallels the relation between the newness of creation and the past of tradition with the union and separateness between mother and baby. This raises the question as to how far identities can be assumed to always be continuous across past, present, and future.

## Self in time

For Winnicott, "continuity of being" is essential for the develop-ment of "inherited potential" (Winnicott, 1960, p. 54). This position contrasts with that of many modern and post-modern European philosophers, such as Foucault, some of whom were contempora-neous with Winnicott: they argue that identities are always partial, contextual, shifting, and discontinuous. For Winnicott an underly-ing continuity of being, facilitated by "good enough" mothering, enables the infant to tolerate both interruptions and also particular social demands, such as learning to say "thank you", for example. This continuity of being is closely connected with the developing of the "True Self" (Winnicott, 1960b, p. 140), a primary bodily alive-ness which becomes the source of spontaneity and individuality. It is unclear what Winnicott means when he refers to the "True Self" as hereditary. Is he referring simply to the "aliveness of the body tissues and the working of the body-functions"? (Winnicott, 1960b, p. 148). He concludes that "the True Self idea ... does no more than collect together the details of the experience of aliveness" (Winnicott, 1960b, p. 148) which, he implies in his account of the mother/infant relation, is always contextual.

Although originating in an Enlightenment view, Winnicott's "True Self" is, however, neither rational nor universal; it is closely associated with the capacity for play and originality within a relational context. In this sense, the "True Self" is fluid, not fixed, and not compulsively compliant. His notion of the importance of the continuity of being has been critically developed by analysts in the contemporary relational school who have been influenced by post-modernism. For example, Ryan (2000) argues that an illusion that the self is continuous is necessary in order for us to be independent enough to act in the world. He alerts us to the dangers of either a too rigid or a too fragmented self identity and poses the possibility of a "fine balance" (Ryan, 2000, p. 155) between the two (see also Chapter Five).

Perhaps the value of such an illusion varies according to the context. In my work with Ian it was his recognition that he was now, as a fifty-year old man, a different person than the young man he had been twenty years earlier. At that time he had decided to end his relationship with Carol; their sexual relationship had ended and he felt that her emotional difficulties were too much for him. They did, however, maintain a close friendship, despite living several hundred miles apart, and his marrying and having a child. Ten years later Carol committed suicide. In his analysis he constantly berated himself for not having stayed with her and taken care of her. One aspect of this was, the unbearability of his anger towards his ex-partner for killing herself and leaving him in a final way (see Freud (1917e[1915]), "Mourning and Melancholia") which we explored. However, more important to Ian was his recognition that he had been "a different person" at the time he left Carol. He was wondering why he could not "connect" to how he had felt when he decided to leave her; it was as if he was a different person. When I said to Ian explicitly, "But you *were* a different person then. We tend to think of ourselves as continuous, but you have changed hugely in your life. You could not have made the choices then that you are able to now", he was very visibly relieved, saying "that thought makes me feel better".

In my response to Ian's memory of himself I assumed some continuity with the past (this continuity is integral to the capacity to remember), but what was more crucial to Ian was the sharpness of my distinction between his sense of himself in the present and his memory of himself in the past. There was regret that he was not the person he is now, but it also alleviated his guilt. Winnicott's notion of the continuity of identity over time does not adequately allow for such marked shifts in experiences of in subjectivity. Ian's acknowledgement of discontinuity did not threaten fragmentation (as Winnicott's theorizing implies) but a recognition of how radically individuals can change through time. I discuss the question of continuity of identity in more detail in Chapter Five.

### Back and fore in time

Although Winnicott stresses the importance of a sense of self-continuity through time he does view the experience of time as non-linear, with subjectivity shifting between past, present, and future and back through previous generations. The development of the baby's subjectivity relies on the mother's own experiences as an infant since these inform her responses to her baby. The breakdown that is feared in the future is a breakdown that has already occurred in the past; the fear is derived from the person's need to remember. For Winnicott, to remember is to re-experience a past event. He claims that the breakdown always has its origins in early infancy, and that this is the reason that in psychotherapy the work is focused on the memory of a later reoccurrence of it, for example in early adolescence.

Winnicott's interpretation of the origins of what is feared in the future as being located in the past is, in my experience, often useful, and not only in relation to the fear of breakdown. A patient who feared that anything that she produced and of which she was proud would be attacked at some point in the future, traced this, through our work, back to her mother's frequent envious criticisms. Her fear connected her to her mother; to relinquish it signified an intolerable separation from her. Winnicott's assumption that all breakdowns have their origin in a breakdown in early infancy is, however, a generalization which denies the profoundly hurtful and confusing complexities of relationships which can arise later in the child's life.

Intrinsic to Winnicott's concept of regression is the notion of (albeit unconscious) hope for the future, He argues that it is not, as previously assumed, a regression to a fixation point of libidinal development, such as the oral, anal or genital phase. Such an interpretation neglects the fact that the baby depends on his/her environment. Regression is therefore a "regression to dependence" (Winnicott, 1959–1964, p. 128) and is an attempt at self-healing. It is the communication of a hope that the original failure (of parental care) will be re-experienced and that, this time, the appropriate care will be available, enabling new opportunities for development. The value of this interpretation is that it allows the analyst to be open to its creative possibilities and the subtleties of how these might emerge in the relationship with the patient. Winnicott is explicit that the role of the analyst is not to offer a corrective experience. It is the patient's use of the analyst's failure which is crucial. It is his experience of working with patients in regressed states which leads Winnicott to argue that more can be learned about infancy in this way than through infant observation, from mothers of infants, or from clinical assessments of people who are in psychotic states. This raises the question: what constitutes the actual history of a person, from whose perspective, and what is the role of narrative and construction? (see Chapters One and Eight).

Temporal distinctions are important in Winnicott's delineation between dreaming and fantasy. In a case example he describes a woman's shift from the "here-and-now fixity" (Winnicott, 1971, p. 42) of dissociated fantasying to the emergence of imaginative possibilities which enable her to plan creatively for her future. In fantasy there is immediacy: it is therefore a "dead end" (Winnicott, 1971, p. 43). Dreaming, with its layers of symbolism embodying past, present and future is, by contrast, "poetic". Winnicott emphasizes that creativity is not solely the domain of artists; it is a lived expression of growth and aliveness and is derived from the transitional object and play. He argues that schizoid people are "estranged from dream" and a state of "time-space integration" (Winnicott, 1971, p. 79) and this has its roots in early environmental failure.

In this same case study Winnicott touches on the nostalgia for the symptom that has been discarded which often arises in the course of psychoanalysis as an individual changes. The importance of change and of the future reappears throughout his writing. The freedom associated with the future can produce paralyzing anxiety, whether in relation to the unknown, or the fear of what may have to be destroyed for a change to be achieved, amongst many other possible meanings. Winnicott's emphasis on the imaginative value of play and creativity allows for tentative explorations of emerging possibilities, consciously and unconsciously, which may mitigate some of the fears associated with the future. These can arise in the language of speech, images, words, sounds or gestures, and offer a reflection of the resources which are becoming increasingly available to the individual. This differs both from Klein's view of creativity as reparation (see Chapter Three) and also (as Winnicott acknowledges) from her emphasis on the *content* of play as opposed to its function as an imaginative activity which implicitly points towards the future.

### The time of interpretations

Given Winnicott's recognition of non-linearity in the subject's temporal experience, it is surprising how clearly he distinguishes three specific phases in an analysis: beginning with ego-strength which relies on the analyst's support, followed by a long phase of experimentation in relation to ego independence, and finally, the achievement of an independent ego with its own individuality. These seem very sharply delineated and chronological which is at odds with Winnicott's reluctance to precisely date stages in infantile and child development and his sensitivity to the complexity and fluidity of temporalities. However, despite the alleged specificity of these stages it is evident that he is acutely sensitive to the very different and individual needs of patients and the need to "modify" psychoanalysis to respond to these. For Winnicott, the aim of psychoanalysis is to "verbalize the nascent conscious in terms of the transference" but he also argues that if "we are analysts practising something else that we deem to be appropriate to the occasion … why not?" (Winnicott, 1962a, p. 170).

Winnicott frequently refers to the timing of interpretations, namely *"the earliest possible moment at which the material makes it clear what to interpret"* (Winnicott, 1958c, p. 122). He appears here to emphasize the accuracy of the interpretation, offering advice regarding the necessity of "playing for time" if there is some uncertainty as to this. However, as an afterthought, he considers the question of the "quick and the slow (psychoanalysts)" and, as if to reassure, claims that accuracy is not as important to the patient as the analyst's willingness to help, through their identification with the patient's "need" (Winnicott, 1958c, p. 122). Winnicott's stress on this recognition reflects his consistent emphasis on the analyst's openness to the material.

Winnicott does not define the meaning of "interpretation"; he is, however, explicit that interpretations of the transference do not necessarily require relating the patient's experience to his/her past. This may be because he is spontaneously located more closely to a phenomenological approach which attends to descriptions in their shifting perspectives, rather than a concern with inductive, explanatory arguments regarding "psychic realities". In his case vignettes his verbal interpretations are illuminations of, or reflections on, what is unconscious or not yet verbalized on the part of the patient and refer to the past, present or future. Winnicott questions Klein's equation of "deep" with "early" in relation to interpretations of the past, arguing that "depth" in the sense of unconscious fantasy and psychic reality comes later in the infant's life (Winnicott, 1957, p. 112).

Throughout his discussions of the timing of the interpretations, it is the importance of the patient's time that is stressed. This is related to his conviction of the value of the patient's creativity: "The patient's creativity can be only too easily stolen by a therapist who knows too much" (Winnicott, 1971, p. 67). He warns of the risk of premature interpretations which might induce feelings of hopelessness or annihilation in the patient or interfere with the creative unfolding of the transference in the relationship between himself and the patient or with an opportunity for the patient to experience the analyst's survival in the face of the patient's fury. With one patient it is Winnicott's ability to hold back interpretations regarding his going away for a period which allows her to produce dreams of regression and dependence. To have "weighed in", he writes, would be to have been "a bad analyst making good interpretations" (Winnicott, 1963j, p. 252) and he suggests that this could be a danger for more experienced analysts who may think too quickly for their patients. Winnicott's warnings are not techniques; the timing of interpretations (or responses) is not a science and depends on the analyst's sensitivity to his/her relationship with his/her patient at any one particular moment. It also, crucially, involves the patience of the analyst, the analyst's ability to wait, to take time. For Winnicott, this may also involve offering extended sessions over a number of hours.

*Death*

Winnicott rarely refers to the actuality of the individual's own death in the future. His main concerns are with the death of another in the patient's life: either the mourning of an actual death or, more predominantly, the fantasised death of another. Throughout his writing he repudiates the concept of the death instinct and its association with aggression. He argues (particularly against Klein) that death only becomes significant some time after the infant has experienced hate.

Winnicott develops a notion of destructiveness which is not associated with anger. An essential aspect is the other's survival over time in the face of this unconscious fantasy, enabling the subject to "use" the object. By this Winnicott means that the other is, through this process, placed (temporally and spatially) outside the infant's omnipotent control and this leads to the possibility of a reciprocal relationship with the other's intrinsic difference. There is a sense of joy at the other's survival. Winnicott equates the necessity of the analyst surviving such attacks (in the form of manipulation) from the patient with the necessity of the mother surviving the infant's or child's attacks. Survival of the analyst is critical and interpretations, Winnicott claims, cannot be used by the patient at this stage. It is only when the patient has placed the other outside their realm of control that s/he can receive the otherness of an interpretation.

Winnicott's notion of "object usage" introduces, in contrast to Klein's account, the actual presence of another. However, it is rooted in the assumption (see above) that mothers and infants are initially in a state of fusion. A theory is then required to account for experiences of separateness and reciprocity. Winnicott's account also assumes the existence of a destructive drive necessary for the creation of the externality of the object. He claims that this must be inherited but that the "quantity" of aggression is also related to environmental factors. If, instead of the notions of a destructive "drive" and of an originary fusion, we emphasize the temporality in the intersubjective relation (which Winnicott does recognize), these problems are avoided. For example, Levinas theorizes the relation to the other as always temporal, located in "instants" which are a "beginning, a birth" (Levinas, 1947a, p. 74), constituted by both evanescence (fading) and expectation (see Chapter Five for more discussion of this). The "destruction" of the other described by Winnicott may be interpreted in terms of an openness to the newness of an instant in relation to the other which simultaneously involves a fading (or a "destruction") of the previous instant which becomes past. For Levinas, the relation with the other contains an absence which is time itself. The capacity for this openness to the changing experience of the other over time must be, as Winicott describes, related to an experience of the other's survival.

For Winnicott it is the fantasised death of the mother whose absence has been too prolonged which emerges as more crucial than the fear of one's own death. The fear of another's death becomes the fear of that which has already happened: the death that has occurred in fantasy in the past. The guilt associated with fantasies of destruction can make the idea of this death intolerable. Winnicott does not address the fact of our mortality as human beings and our anticipation of our death ahead in its many meanings. Certainly some of our fantasies about our own deaths are likely to be shaped by experiences that have happened to us, but for many individuals it is the knowledge that there is something absolutely unknown to us about death, the possibility of a non-being that can never be fully conceptualized, that is also terrifying.

## Lacan: time's castration

As the following discussion emphasizes, the notion of the subject's death is a recurrent strand in Lacan's theorizing. Although notable for the variable time length of his psychoanalytic sessions, his theorizing is interwoven throughout with numerous other references to the significance of time for the subject. As my critical discussion of the theme of time in his work highlights, these references contain, as O'Connor and Ryan argue in relation to his theorizing of sexuality, numerous "promises and contradictions" (O'Connor and Ryan, 1993, pp. 134–159).

Differing radically from Winnicott, Lacan is rarely concerned with the time of early parent-infant relations. He argues against psychoanalytic accounts which emphasize adaptation of the ego since, in his view, the ego is illusory and a site of alienation. The subject, for Lacan, is always the subject of the unconscious and it is a speaking subject. The significant time of the child is that of the Oedipus complex, the time at which, he theorizes, the child enters the symbolic system of verbal language. Lacan's notion of logical time underpins a number of his positions including his concept of desire, the times of the Oedipus complex and the structure of psychoanalytic practice itself.

## Logical time

Lacan distinguishes what he designates "logical time" from chrono-logical or clock time. He argues that the instigation of clock time, originating with Huyghen's 1659 invention of the first isochronic clock, inaugurated the development of the exact sciences. Although distinct from natural (cosmological or sidereal) time, clock time borrows from it, in that a unit of time must refer to "the real", that is, that which is always to be found "in the same place, whether or not one has been there" (Lacan, 1955, p. 297) and which lies outside symbolization.

His concept of logical time explicitly counters linear notions of time informing some psychoanalytic notions of "developmental stages". He claims that subjectivity involves shifts backwards and forwards, between all three temporal dimensions, through retroaction and anticipation. These shifts are, however, not between points on a continuum; they are leaps from one discrete structure (such as the imaginary or the Oedipus complex which I discuss below) to another. The "time" of these structures is conceptualized by Lacan in contradictory terms: they do not refer to clock time and Lacan claims they are "timeless", yet they have, Lacan argues, a logical time of their own. There is a further contradiction which I discuss below, namely that Lacan attributes these structures to specific ages in the child's development.

Lacan argues that logical time is not objective, it is "the inter-subjective time that structures human action" (Lacan, 1966, p. 75). However, it has a logical order, he claims, as in the irreversibility of "remembering in order to deal with the resistances of repetition" and beginning with repetition "in order to tackle remembering" (Lacan 1966, p. 40). Lacan illustrates his concept of logical time in the form of what he explicitly describes as "a sophism" (Lacan, 1955, p. 290), a story of three prisoners, of whom two can be released. They are set a test whereby they are all told that there are three white discs and two black discs, of which one will be pinned to each person's back. To gain their freedom they must calculate the colour of the disc on their own back without the use of a mirror or any communication between them. White discs are attached to every prisoner's back. Lacan argues through a number of steps (Lacan, 1955, pp. 287–289) that the colour of the prisoner's own disc is revealed through a logical tri-partite process involving an instant of seeing, a time for under-standing and, finally, a moment of concluding, which he associates with haste. Haste, he argues, is a third dimension of time, in addition to notions of being early or late, and it is particular to humans: it is "the chariot of time, which is there, close on our heels" (Lacan, 1955, p. 291).

Lacan's conclusion relies on an assumption that the prisoners take an equal time to understand, or at least will not hesitate more than a couple of times. The certainty with which this is asserted, despite its contradictions, is characteristic of his writing and illustrative of a tension throughout between his challenges to universality and his replicating of it. As Marchand (one of Lacan's students) argues, how can the prisoners all take the same amount of time to understand? Furthermore, how can the structure of any moment in time be the same for everyone? Why assume that there are just three aspects, namely seeing, understanding and haste, involved in any temporal structure? What is the value of sophistry as a form of explanation? Lacan's rebuttal of his students' arguments through various ruses, and his final patronizing dismissal of them, "it is a bit rough-going today" (Lacan, 1955, p. 293) at the end of this seminar is characteristic of his tone. He takes up the very position that he argues is illusory, namely that of the subject who is "supposed to know" (Lacan, 1964, p. 232).

## The time and timelessness of the unconscious

Lacan views Freud's claim that the unconscious is located outside time as both true and untrue and he presents a number of confusing statements, which he does not develop, to support this. He draws on Hegel's notion of the concept as "the time of the thing" (Lacan, 1954a, p. 242) and claims that, like the concept, the unconscious (as language) is "outside time" yet, simultaneously it is "in itself time" (Lacan, 1954a, p. 243). How can "the unconscious" be "like" a concept when it is a concept? If the concept *is* time, how can it be "outside" of time? What is the significance of this for the quasi-scientific "temporal pulsation" (Lacan, 1964, p. 143), the closing and opening of the unconscious to which Lacan refers? Lacan's appeal to authority (namely Hegel) offers him a sleight of hand by which he avoids clarification of his position.

In his claim that the unconscious is not located internally in the psyche but is "the sum of the effects of speech on a subject" (Lacan, 1964, p. 126), Lacan appears to promise a concept of the unconscious which allows for its uniqueness and socio-historical specificity. As "the discourse of the Other" (Lacan, 1966a, p. 16), argues Lacan, the unconscious is constituted through the symbolic order of speech which lies beyond the subject. The unconscious is thus structured like a language and its "truth" is inscribed in the body, in child-hood memories, in an individual's particular vocabulary, character and style of life, in traditions and legends, and in the "distortions" imposed by the links between the unconscious (the "adulterated chapter" of the subject's life) and other aspects of his/her life (Lacan, 1966b, p. 50). (For further discussion of Lacan's theorizing of the relation between "truth" and the "lie" see below in my section, "The time of full speech".) It is interesting to note the contrast between Jung's notion of the unconscious as "germs of new life and vital pos-sibilities for the future" (Jung, 1928, pp. 34–35) and that of Lacan's as the "adulterated chapter" of our lives.

Building on Freud's view that it is not the affect that is repressed, Lacan argues that what is repressed is the "signifier" (Lacan, 1964, p. 218). For Lacan, the "signifier" is a unit of language which derives its value from its difference from other signifiers in the symbolic system. These may be syllables, words or phrases, the effects of which form the unconscious (Lacan, 1964, p. 126) and are the focus of the analyst's attention. The drives, which are, in his view, simulta-neously sexual *and* death drives, are inseparable from their represen-tation in language; they are not "natural" (Lacan, 1964, p. 162) and (unlike the instinct), they cannot be satisfied by the object; instead, they circle around it. They are made up, like a "montage" or a Sur-realist collage, of discontinuous elements (Lacan, 1964, p. 170).

In theorizing the unconscious as structured like a language and viewing the drives as always represented in language, Lacan's theo-rizing addresses the importance of discourse in the shaping of our subjectivities. This is neglected in the work of other analysts who loosely speak of "affects", "emotions" or "instincts" without recog-nizing their specificity within language. Lacan thus points towards the possibility of a more sophisticated theorizing of the temporality of subjectivity, particularly in relation to its historical and cultural specificity. However, this possibility is undermined by his theorizing of the Oedipus complex as a universal structure of language and his emphasis on the primacy of the phallus (see below).

*Repression*

Lacan's accounts of repression contain interesting interpretations of its relation to time and the necessity of forgetting. He emphasizes the connection between the acquisition of verbal, symbolic language and repression. Disturbing events occurring in the early years of life become integrated, retroactively into language, the "human field which universalizes significations" (Lacan, 1954a, p. 191). This, he argues, parallels the role of psychoanalysis. It is at the point of their integration into language that, on the imaginary (see below) level, these events take on the status of trauma with the associated shock. The trauma is thus simultaneously repression, taking place "after the fact" (*nachträglich*). The "fact" no longer belongs to the subject as s/he is located in the symbolic structure of language which is always already in existence. It nevertheless remains there within language, "spoken" (Lacan, 1954a, p. 191).

Lacan concludes that repression and the return of the repressed are the same thing since all repression, according to Lacan, is retrospective. This means that the "return of the repressed" comes from the future and not the past (Lacan, 1954a, p. 158): the erased "signal" of something takes on its value from the future, from its integration into symbolic language and its subsequent integration into the subject's history: "Literally, it will only ever be a thing which, at the given moment of its occurrence, *will have been*" (Lacan, 1954a, p. 159). Thus, for Lacan, very subtle temporal shifts occur in repression as subsequent meanings continue to replace one another retrospectively within the context of the future. His account of the relation of the future to the past closely resembles that of Heidegger's, namely that the subject "'historicizes' out of its future on each occasion ... Its own past ... is not something which *follows along after* ... but something which already goes ahead of it" (Heidegger, 1927, p. 41), although he does not acknowledge this. See my Chapter Five for more discussion of Heidegger's theorizing of temporality.

Lacan argues that "successful symbolic integration involves a sort of normal forgetting" (Lacan, 1954a, p. 192) of what cannot be incorporated into symbolic existence, the forgetting of which is also forgotten. This is, unfortunately, not sufficiently developed by Lacan and his unreferenced and rather idiosyncratic interpretations of Heidegger's notions of forgetting and truth do not clarify his position. (See Borch-Jacobsen (1991, pp. 104–113) for an extensive discussion of this.) However, he raises an important issue in the light of the emphasis in psychoanalysis on memory. The contemporary French historian Dosse (2006), for example, argues that it is both necessary to struggle against forgetting and also necessary to forget that which prevents us from living creatively and with hope (See my Chapter Five).

Lacan's account of repression usefully highlights how subjectivity is interpenetrated by the past, present, and future dimensions. His emphasis on drives as represented in language and the role of language in relation to anticipation, memory and forgetting are an important rejection of the biologism informing traditional concepts of the drive as instinct. However, Lacan prioritizes verbal language and consequently denies the importance of the non-verbal language that is always already available to the baby or child, through gesture, facial expression, tone of voice, experiences of being held and touched, both prior to and subsequent to the acquisition of verbal language. All of these non-verbal languages are social.

## The time of desire

Lacan's account of desire frequently refers to its temporality. Arising from the unconscious, the field of the Other, desire "conveys what it maintains of an image of the past towards an ever short and limited future" (Lacan, 1964, p. 31). It is structured in logical time (see above), appearing between the moment of seeing and the "elusive moment" (Lacan, 1964, p. 32) before the unconscious closes up again in which the "absorption" of desire involves "false trails" or delusions. It arises within a dialectical relationship between one subject and another or others: the subject desires both to be the object of another's desire and to be recognized by the other. Furthermore, the subject desires what the other desires, not anything intrinsic to the object itself.

Lacan's basic assumption, namely that desire is founded on lack, contains an implicit despair. Although the naming of desire in analysis "brings forth a new presence in the world" (Lacan, 1955, pp. 228–229), implicitly pointing towards the future, desire, for Lacan,

can never be satisfied. The naming of desire confronts the subject with the lack at the heart of his being, the source of his/her existence, "the lack of being whereby the being exists" (Lacan, 1955, p. 223) and this is associated with castration and death. The notion that desire arises from lack is challenged by Grosz. She argues for a conceptualization of desire as productive, occurring between skin surfaces, rather than arising from those zones designated by Freud as specifically erotogenic. Grosz conceptualizes desire in terms of "proliferation" and "intensifications" (Grosz, 1994, p. 81) which strongly contrast with that of "lack".

The notion of desire as a universal and a logical temporal structure forecloses on the multiple possibilities of meanings (individually, culturally and socio-historically) which emerge in the uniqueness of each patient's speech. Lacan's "desire" is an abstraction which does not take into account *how the concept is used* (see Wittgenstein's 1953 theorizing of our acquisition of language through its usage, in "language-games"). Lacan's theory forecloses on the possibility of descriptions of the specificity and the variability of experienced desire. Can, for example, the notion of "lingering" be encompassed by the notions of "seeing", "understanding", "concluding" or "haste" (the structure of logical time)? His notion that we only desire what the other desires is very cynical and does not allow for any interest, conscious and unconscious, in the value of another's individual quailites to us, whether because of their perceived similarity or difference or for other reasons.

## Stages of development or not: the mirror and Oedipus

Lacan views psychoanalytic developmental theories as inherently normative, implying a natural, linear progression from one stage to another. He argues that there is a connection between the past and the future but this is not chronological. Regression is not a literal going back in time: it is a rearticulating of certain demands in the present. Furthermore, he argues that in symbolic language it is the future which has primacy: at every moment of saying 'I' there is creation (Lacan, 1955, p. 293). The past itself is a series of prior creations. We cannot know or recall exactly our early experiences in the way we experienced them then; their existence is tied to our present speech; history is therefore "the present synthesis of the past" (Lacan, 1954, p. 36) in the speech of the patient. Language and temporality are, for Lacan, intrinsic to one another.

Lacan's challenge to linear notions of development and his emphasis on how the subject is always positioned in language within a specific temporal context look promising. He appears to allow for the emergence of different perspectives in language which are not tied to any one particular truth or stage and which can shift back and fore over time. The subject is recreated through language in the context of the future. Regression must always be viewed in the context of the present. However, despite arguing against linear notions of developmental stages, he does delineate two specific stages in his theorising, namely the "mirror" (or "imaginary") stage and the Oedipus complex. Furthermore, he associates these structures with specific ages, the mirror stage occurring between the ages of six and eighteen months, and the Oedipus complex, between the ages of three and five years. While locating these historically, he claims that these are universal, timeless structures.

The "mirror stage" refers to the time when the baby, still uncoordinated, is captivated by an illusory and static or timeless image of itself in the mirror as "'whole". This contrasts with its experience of its body as, Lacan claims, fragmented. Gazing at his/her mirror reflection the baby jubilantly identifies with this imaginary wholeness and becomes alienated from him/herself. This illusory identification forms the basis of the subject's ego. According to Lacan this is not an achievement since it is based on "*méconnaissance*" (misrecognition/misunderstanding) (Lacan, 1966b, p. 307).

As Osborne (1995) argues, Lacan's account of the child's relation to his/her image denies the context of his/her relation with others, despite the necessity of another being present to hold the baby in front of the mirror. Lacan conceives of the mirror reflection as a two-person relation only, namely between the baby and itself as an object, with which it identifies. There is a temporal element to this spatial identification since it involves "an internal thrust ... precipitated from insufficiency to anticipation" (Lacan, 1966b, p. 4), that is a shift from an identification with its body-image as fragmented to an idealized body-image, that of "the master", which the baby confuses with an "image of death" (Lacan, 1954, p. 149). This fear is derived from and "psychologically subordinate to the fear of damage to one's own body" (Lacan, 1966b, p. 28). The death drive is, for Lacan, thus situated "at the juncture between the imaginary and the symbolic" (Lacan, 1954a, p. 172). The fear of damage to the body is transformed into the fear of death on the child's entry into the symbolic order (see below).

Lacan's use of Heideggerian and Hegelian "motifs" in his conceptualization of the imaginary and its relation to the death drive are critically analyzed by Osborne (1995, pp. 69–112). He raises the question as to why the child's image in the mirror is perceived as "the master" and, subsequently, confused with death, arguing that Lacan offers no clarification of this. An equally important question, in my view, is how we can "know" what the body-image of an infant is? Why should we assume that it is one of fragmentation? How can a baby know that it is uncoordinated unless it has a concept of who or what s/he might become and a concept of change and/or learning? This would require a level of thought possible only at a much later time in a child's life. It is not sufficient to claim that the imaginary is a timeless, mental structure which is projected retrospectively on to the past when Lacan is so specific about the historical time of the mirror stage, dating it between six and eighteen months. His theorizing of it as an early stage of development, prior to the Oedipus complex is in direct contradiction to his critique of the notion of developmental stages in psychoanalytic theorizing. Furthermore, Lacan's theorizing assumes that mirrors and reflections are universally accessible to everyone, regardless of their socio-historical or cultural backgrounds. How would Lacan conceptualize what happens if there is no mirror for the child?

Lacan's notion of the Oedipus complex is central to his theorising of the symbolic and he theorises it as having three "times" which are of logical, rather than chronological priority. He argues against Object Relations theorists that, implicit in the dual relation of the mother/infant, is the mother's desire for the (imaginary) "phallus", which she desires beyond the child. This signifies a lack for the child, both in the mother and in him/herself, as s/he cannot adequately satisfy the mother's desire. This is the first "time" of the Oedipus complex. The child has to face that his/her real organ is insufficient and this gives rise to anxiety. At this point (the second "time" of the complex) the imaginary father intervenes, imposing a prohibition against the mother's desires. The father is then regarded by the baby/subject as a rival. The third "time" of the Oedipus complex involves the real father who "castrates" the child by showing him that s/he cannot *be* the phallus for the mother because the father *has* it. Lacan departs from Freud in claiming that it is not identification which determines a subject's sexual position; instead it is the symbolic relation with the phallus, having it or not having it. Women do not have it, according to Lacan, and either position is precarious.

Lacan emphasises that these are not "natural" positions, they are positions within the "symbolic order" of language. His conception of this symbolic order relies on Levi-Strauss's structuralist claims that all languages are underpinned by a universal and therefore timeless grammar of thought in which women are defined as objects of exchange. Drawing on Jacobson's theory of metonymy and metaphor, Lacan claims that, in the deferral of desire (metonymy), the paternal metaphor replaces the mother's desire. The paternal metaphor, the "Name-of-the-Father" is, for Lacan, associated with the murdered father of Freud's (1913) *Totem and Taboo*, who binds himself through his death to the law, signifying the Law of prohibition against incest. The symbolic function therefore, he argues, identified the name of the father with the figure of the law "from the dawn of history" (Lacan, 1966b, p. 67). As Rose points out with regard to its implications for women, Lacan's theorizing "presupposes the subordination which it is intended to explain" and is "complicit" with it (Rose, 1982, p. 45). It is also interesting to note that, although fathers are statistically more likely to sexually abuse children, prohibition against incest is attributed by Lacan (following Freud) to the father.

Lacan's assumption of the primary of the phallus is permeated with contradictions. He claims that the phallus is a signifier which does not refer to anatomy. Yet he also attributes the origins of signifiers such as the phallus to "nature": "Nature provides ... signifiers, and these organize human relations in a creative way, providing them with structures and shaping them" (Lacan, 1964, p. 20). Derrida (1975, pp. 413–96) uses Lacan's own argument against Lacan himself in order to challenge Lacan's insistence on the phallus as primary signifier: if, as Lacan claims, every signifier is defined only by its difference from other signifiers, there cannot be a privileged signifier.

Despite the possibilities of a theorizing of language which might address cultural and historical specificity, Lacan's focus is on the negotiation of an ahistorical universal structure to which he gives primacy. He is explicit in his opposition to the feminist "culturalist" position of Karen Horney, although he does not name her (Lacan, 1966b, p. 198). He also, surprisingly, does not address Fanon's (1952) critique (published in French) of the universality attributed to the Oedipus complex. For Lacan, analysis of the Oedipus complex is pivotal in psychoanalytic work: it is the "legal, legalising coordinate", "the most uniform point of intersection" in the subject's relation to the law, it is a "ubiquitous requirement" (Lacan, 1954a, p. 198). Each of Lacan's interpretations of neurosis, psychosis, perversion, and phobia relate to specific difficulties in negotiating this universal complex. Lacan invokes hIs notion of "law" to bolster his own prejudices and to forclose on being questioned.

Lacan's theorizing of the mirror stages and the Oedipus complex are shot through with contradictions which have implications in relation to temporality. He claims that they are not developmental stages, yet he is specific about the ages at which they occur. He claims they are not "natural", yet not social phenomena, yet they are linguistic. They are "retrospective projections" yet he claims to know the ages at which they occur. Furthermore, he hides behind confused conceptualizations from philosophers while cleverly denouncing the relevance of philosophical debate to his theories of the unconscious, its structure and dynamisms, to which he claims he himself has privileged access.

*Repetition*

For Lacan "repetition" is one of the four fundamental concepts of psychoanalysis, together with the unconscious, transference and the drive. He conceptualises repetition as "the insistence of speech" (Lacan, 1956, p. 242). It occurs in the transference, as its "historicizing temporality" (Lacan, 1966b, p. 103), but it must be distinguished from the concept of transference. Central to it is the notion of missing something. An example might be the missing of a session by a patient owing to an unforeseen obstacle. It is the repetition of the discourse or circuit in which the subject is embedded and which dates back to his/her past.

Lacan stresses that repetition is not "reproduction" or a "making present" (Lacan, 1964, p. 50). The reel thrown by the child does not *represent* his mother, who is physically absent. It is *aimed at* the mother, symbolizing her departure as causing a split in the subject (a small part of a thread). In Lacan's view, if the aim is mastery, as Freud claims, endless repetition does not offer empowerment; instead, it "reveals the radical vacillation of the subject" (Lacan, 1964, p. 239) and its alienation through the split.

The problem with Lacan's (and Freud's) interpretation of the child's play is the limited knowledge we have of the child's life and relationships, and, in particular, with his mother, whose absence gives rise to his play with the reel, as well as with the observer of the game. It seems premature to speculate on and inappropriate to generalize about the meanings of this particular game for this particular child without access to such material. As I argue in Chapter One, it is crucial that, for example, a patient's actions such as cancelling a session, are interpreted within the particular context of the psychoanalytic relationship at that moment; they may or may not be instances of repetition.

### The time of treatment and death in analysis

For Lacan, analysis implicitly involves the temporal since, in line with his concept of "logical time" (see above), it allows "*time for understanding*" (Lacan 1966b, p. 48) and a "*moment of concluding*". How does Lacan allocate a time for understanding within sessions? His instigation of variable length sessions was a massive departure from the structure of fixed and mutually agreed session times to which most analysts continue to adhere, and it eventually led to his expulsion from the International Psychoanalytic Association. Sessions are terminated at any moment beyond a few seconds into the session, depending on the discourse of the patient. This intervention is one of the ways in which the Lacanian analyst "punctuates" the patient's speech in order to bestow meaning on it. A word or phrase of the patient may be repeated, met with silence, or interrupted with the abrupt termination of the session. The aim of these responses is to highlight a particular unconscious meaning or a point of resistance in the speech of the patient. The brutal termination of sessions is also intended to ensure that the patient does not manipulate the session through planning its structure or delaying the articulation of significant material until the end.

The time for termination of a session is completely in the hands of the analyst, but it is usually a shortening of, rather than the lengthening of a session. As Green (2000) argues, the decision may arise from anxiety aroused in the analyst, from their inability to make an appropriate interpretation, their desire for omnipotence, or their resistance. The possibilities are most certainly endless. Furthermore, the opportunity of being able to terminate the session at any point allows the analyst to avoid critical reflection on the conscious and unconscious reasons for their responses within the intersubjective relationship.

Termination of the session by the analyst reinforces his/her position as the "one supposed to know" (Lacan, 1964, p. 232) since it assumes that the analyst is the only one who knows what is most meaningful for the patient. It fails to acknowledge the particular importance that the patient attributes to points in the session whether articulated verbally or non-verbally, by either him/herself or the analyst, or both. These may be experienced at the time or retrospectively and may have been neither intended nor even remembered by the analyst. For Carmel, in our analytic work, her ability to begin to "see time differently", to have time and to know that she could take her own time, was extremely important. She acknowledged that time for her had always been "others' time" to which she automatically surrendered. It seems unlikely that she could have reached this point in a Lacanian analysis. The omnipotent position taken up by the analyst seems very likely to impede the patient's progress towards what Lacan argues is the end of analysis, namely the dissolution of the patient's imaginary assumption that the analyst has knowledge, is the "one supposed to know" (Lacan, 1964, p. 232) and the articulation of "full speech" (Lacan, 1954a, p. 244) in the intersubjective relationship of patient and analyst.

## The time of full speech

It is through full speech that the patient "reorder(s) past contingencies" (Lacan, 1966b, p. 48), constructing his/her history retrospectively and in the context of the future. It might be supposed that the emergence of the shifting "truths" of this (non-linear) history within a psychoanalytic relationship, in which the importance of the patient's speech is emphasized, could allow for the development of her/his individuality and imagination and for the opening out of choices in the future. Lacan's theorizing does not lead us to this but

to a postulated but, in principle, unknowable and unattainable realization of subjectivity.

Lacan's texts belie a suspicion of imagination both in his notions
of the "imaginary" and the "symbolic". The "imaginary" stretches,
as we have seen, between the supposedly fragmented body-image of
infancy and the alienating, illusory ego-identity. In psychoanalysis,
argues Lacan, demonic and monstrous images associated with the
fragmented body, reminiscent of Hieronymous Bosch's paintings,
underpin an aggressivity (ranging from poisonous to revengeful) in
the transference. The subject's relation to the analyst is narcissistic
and "specular" and their speech is "empty" (Lacan, 1954a, p. 244),
alienated from their desire. Lacan is not interested in the specificity
of the dream imagery (who is mutilating whom and exactly how,
for example) or its imaginative aspects (it is effectively reduced to a
symptom of the imaginary order) and his accounts betray an impa-
tience with its "shallow or empty speech" (Lacan, 1955, p. 216) in the
transference.

Lacan's notion of the "full speech" at which psychoanalysis, in
his view, aims, is paradoxical. As Borch-Jacobsen (1991) points out,
it may be full, but it speaks of nothing. This is because, according
to Lacan, in the naming of their desire, the subject is confronted
with the lack which constitutes their being; they are forced to accept
their castration and, ultimately, their mortality. Furthermore, Lacan
claims, the truth of desire can not only be more fully revealed in a
mistake (as Freud shows in the notion of the "slip") but also in a
lie (Lacan, 1964, pp. 139–140). The lie highlights the impossibility of
speaking the whole truth since there is always an excess of desire
which cannot be articulated. Lacan's reliance on the notion of the
lie for his argument that truth cannot be complete is disconcerting.
Truths may be sometimes partial and often contextual but this does
not give them the same status as a lie: a lie implies knowledge and
deliberate refusal. As Borch-Jacobsen concludes, whether speech is
full or empty, it seems that "everywhere, it is all one and the same
*clamor* of nothing" (Borch-Jacobsen, 1991, p. 148).

Lacan is skeptical of the normative implications of the notion
of cure in psychoanalysis. Frequently associated with the development of ego strength, cure is thus, in his view, conceived in terms of
adaptation to society. However, Lacan's pronouncements about life's
possibilities (drawn from his interpretations of Freud) in the face of

our immanent death are not encouraging, particularly with regard to his view of the understanding which one gains from an analysis, namely that *"Life is a blister, a mould, characterized ... by nothing beyond its aptitude for death ...* That is what life is — a detour, a dogged detour, in itself transitory and precarious, and deprived of any significance" (Lacan, 1955, p. 232). Furthermore, the analyst, "by pretending he is dead ... makes death present" (Lacan, 1966b, p. 140). The promises of the possibilities of language fall away leaving us only with the deadly truth of death.

# CHAPTER FIVE

# (Dis)continuous identities and the time of the other

In the previous chapters I consider the theories of time which implicitly and explicitly underpin psychoanalytic accounts of individuals' subjectivities. Although most of the psychoanalysts whose work I discuss were practising and writing at a time when modern European philosophers were questioning Enlightenment notions of subjectivity with its emphasis on science, on universality, and the priority of reason, their own theorizing is remarkably devoid of their influences. How individuals "live" time in all its dimensions is pivotal to the analyses of subjectivity of philosophers writing from phenomenological, existential, and deconstructive perspectives. Through my reflections on the theories of temporality presented by Heidegger, Merleau-Ponty, Foucault, and Levinas, I expand on some of the themes and questions raised in earlier chapters and show how their work points in the direction of possible solutions or further questions.

I particularly focus on their differing positions in relation to the question of whether the subject has a continuous identity through time (a question I introduced in my discussion of Winnicott's theorizing of temporality), and also the subject's relation to others' time. In critically presenting their very different positions one of my aims is also to highlight how very diverse assumptions and theories of time are, whether they are the reflections and arguments of philosophers or the conscious and unconscious perspectives on time which are brought into the consulting room by both the analyst and the patient. My interest is in how these theories are constructed and how particular theories might illuminate a particular patient's variable and conscious and unconscious dilemmas in relation to time. I argue against the notion that there is one universal relation to time, whether as continuity or discontinuity, which must be achieved in order for the patient's suffering to be alleviated.

## Calendar time, cosmological time and lived time

In considering the relevance of temporality to psychoanalytic practices it is necessary to distinguish "lived time" from our ordinary conceptions of time as cosmological and as dateable. As Mann's (1924) novel, *The Magic Mountain*, so poignantly exemplifies, abstract notions of time as motion, as change, as linear or circular, or as dateable, can never encapsulate the temporality of human experience. Mann explores in fictional form the effects on patients in a sanatorium of the imposition of its particular time (the time of the doctors), a time which differs radically from that which is lived beyond its walls. In the sanatorium, the smallest unit of time is the month and, in decisions regarding the length of treatments for patients, doctors treat weeks as if they are only days.

Mann's reflections on time are voiced through the musings of the central character, Hans Castorp. Castorp's time as a patient underlines for him that the time of the calendar, the units of minutes, hours, days, weeks, months and years are "purely arbitrary, sheer conventions" (Mann, 1924, p. 66): the second hand on a watch may complete the same circuit each time to indicate the passing of a minute, but our *experience* of the time it takes is variable. For Castorp, most often, days in the sanatorium are exceedingly long yet, retrospectively, in their emptiness, they seem to "scurry by like dead leaves" (Mann, 1924, p. 105), indistinguishable from today, blending into "the always" (Mann, 1924, p. 546). Since the sanatorium is up in the mountains even the calendar cycle of the seasons is non-existent: there are spring and autumn *days*, burning hot summer days in winter, and snowfall in the summer, all incongruent with the seasons designated arbitrarily by the calendar. Mann's novel conveys vividly the operations of institutionalization in temporal terms and its alienating effects on the patients' subjectivity: time is organized such that "one should get used to things, even if the getting used consisted in getting used to not getting used" (p. 349).

The questions which Mann raises through his character, Castorp, regarding the relation between cosmological time, dateable time and "lived time" extend far beyond the particular context of the institution that he describes in the novel. The impossibility of an exact correlation between, for example, the times of sunrise, sunset, and planetary movements, and any system of calendar time indicate that time and dates are relative, not absolute. In his Special Theory and his later General Theory of Relativity (1911) Einstein argues that time is affected by mass and also by relative speed. (See Ellis, 1973, for an accessible overview of theories of scientific and cosmological theories of time.)

Osborne argues that calendars themselves are "socially specific versions of cosmological time" (Osborne, 1995, p. 67). He traces the connection between the development of capitalism and the establishment of world standard-time: time synchronization in the organization of transport and communications became crucial to the success of capitalism. However, as Osborne points out, world standard-time is no more than one abstract measure alongside the myriad of other diverse time measurements existent in local social practices.

The question of how individuals "live" time, as highlighted in Mann's *The Magic Mountain,* is a major theme in modern European philosophical thought. Time is neither objective, nor observable as something "outside" the subject. We are always "in time" or as Merleau-Ponty (1945) claims, we *are ourselves* time (see below). The variability of our lived experiences of time is, as this book argues, of particular relevance to practising analysts. I begin with a discussion of Heidegger's theorizing of our ordinary conception of time. His work has been of particular influence on the theorizing and practices of existential analysts such as Binswanger and Boss.

### Heidegger's Future-time

Heidegger (1927) emphasizes that clock-time, as public time, is necessary and that temporality is the condition for its discoverability and its necessity. He argues against common-sense views of time as a sequence of "nows" (originating with Aristotle) and claims that these obscure the dateability and significance of time. Heidegger challenges dichotomies between the self and the world and theorizes Dasein (the "Being" of persons) as always already in the world through its "thrownness" (Heidegger, 1927, p. 174). Dasein is grounded in temporality, constituted by the phenomena of the future, the past and the present. He designates these dimensions the "ecstases" (Heidegger, 1927, p. 416) of temporality. In designating them as "ecstaces", Heidegger means that they "stand out". Dasein is carried beyond itself, transcending the world, through the unity of the ecstases. However, the beyond to which it is carried is not limitless; each of the ecstases have a different "horizontal schema" (Heidegger, 1927, p. 416). Dasein's relation to its future is disclosed in the horizontal schema of "*for-the-sake-of-itself*", its relation to the past is defined by the horizontal schema of "thrownness", and the horizontal schema for the present is framed by the "*in-order-to*" (Heidegger, 1927, p. 416). Each of these dimensions temporalize themselves in relation to the other dimensions.

In contrast to much psychoanalytic theorizing which, as I have shown, prioritizes the past as most formative of the subject, Heidegger prioritizes the future. In his analysis of "care" which he defines as "concern and solicitude" he distinguishes between "willing" and "wishing" which both signify a particular relation to the future. In "willing", one's "potentiality-for-Being" is unavoidably modified by the limitations posed by the social context, i.e. "everydayness" (Heidegger, 1927, p. 239 and pp. 421–422). "Wishing" is constituted by"being-ahead-of-oneself" such that whatever is available is "never enough" (Heidegger, 1927, p. 239) and he associates this with the notion of "hankering" and "addiction" (Heidegger, 1927, p. 240). In addiction, all other possibilities of being are subsumed in the craving for intoxication.

Heidegger argues that authentic temporality depends on our recognition of the finiteness of our individual "Being-towards-death". Our awareness of our own mortality structures our relation to the present and the past. In the face of death, Dasein "stands before itself in its ownmost potentiality-for-being" (Heidegger, 1927, p. 294). Concepts of time as a series of "now" points imply an infinite continuity in which there is no death. If Dasein immerses itself in this everyday view of time, in flight from an acknowledgement of its own death, it loses itself: it is closed off from its authenticity and its potentiality. Dasein "is a "not-yet" which any Dasein, as the entity which it is, has to be" (Heidegger, 1927, p. 288). According to Heidegger, anxiety is rooted in Dasein's fear about its potential individuality (see my Chapter Seven for more discussion of this). For further clarification of Heidegger's arguments I recommend Rée's (1998) publication, *Heidegger, History and Truth In Being and Time* to the reader.

Heidegger's interpretation of the relationship between "authentic" living and our awareness of our own mortality resonates with the thoughts of a patient who had recently been diagnosed with an illness from which she might eventually die. She described how she had always lived in the future and that "now, as I don't know if I will have a future, I have to live in each moment". For her the future had been, in her words, "like a false self, an ideal self" and she felt that her focus on this had stopped her paying enough attention to her health in the present (or her recent past). Although she had been focusing on the future, this was a future conceptualized as being without death (without imperfection). Now death had revealed itself as a possibility in the future she could consider living in the present (which included taking up her past).

The problem with Heidegger's analysis of death is its individualism (Levinas 1947, Osborne 1995). He claims that death "By its very essence ... is in every case mine" (Heidegger, 1927, p. 284). Furthermore, others' interpretations of death deny its "ownmost possibility which is non-relational and not to be outstripped" (Heidegger, 1927, p. 307). Heidegger implies that an authentic relation to our own death and to our own existence is only possible if we repudiate the meanings derived from our experiences of others' dying and also the dominant social and religious discourses on death. As Osborne (1995) points out, there is a tension between the individualism within Heidegger's analysis of death and his emphasis on our "Being-with" others, even when we are alone, as an essential characteristic of Dasein (Heidegger, 1927, p. 156). However, despite this tension, Heidegger's acknowledgement that the knowledge of our own death ahead profoundly affects how we live our lives is, in my view, extremely important in psychoanalytic work with patients at any stage of their lives.

Osborne incisively discusses the relation between Heidegger's support of National Socialism in Germany and his philosophical theories, an issue which has been widely debated amongst modern European philosophers. He argues that Heidegger's position was not based on anti-semitism but rooted in his opposition to technology and mass industrialization. Osborne's analysis of the relation between National Socialism's stance as a "reactionary avant-garde" and Heidegger's theorizing of Being points to a problem in Heidegger's theorizing of time. In Osborne's view, these converge in their shared commitment to a " 'return to a new beginning' " through a revival of the importance of tradition (Osborne, 1995, p. 172). He argues that this gives rise to a paradox in Heidegger's thought since it implies an originary sense of Being which is located beyond or before time and is, itself, the source of historicity. It is, of course, vitally important to be attentive to the reactionary aspects of Heidegger's thought and its political implications. Not withstanding this, there are many aspects of his work which can contribute to a consideration of the subject's experiences of temporality which are of value to practicing analysts.

## The times of world-designs

The existential psychoanalyst Binswanger, a close friend and colleague of Freud's, was strongly influenced by Heidegger in his theorizing of subjectivity. He emphasizes the temporal modes of individuals' "Existential A Prioris" or "world-designs". According to Binswanger, a "world-design" is a mode through which Dasein is structured. Dasein's existence may be structured through one mode or through several, one or some of which are more dominant than others. Binswanger designates the term "Geworfenheit" ("thrownness") for a state of being constricted by a particular world-design. In psychosis the individual is completely overpowered by a single world design. Binswanger emphasizes that a world-design is revealed in the specificity of an individual's language. Furthermore, it is neither conscious nor unconscious: it lies beyond these dualisms. A world-design neither precedes subjectivity nor imposes on an already existing subjectivity; a world-design is, rather, a relation to the world.

Binswanger draws on Von Gebsattel's notion of "lived time", differentiating it from the *experience of* time, and extends this in his concept of the "self-temporalizing of the existence" (Binswanger, 1946, pp. 301–302). By this he means that Dasein transcends itself in the ecstases of the future (the *"toward which"* or "being-ahead-of oneself"), the past (the *"upon which"* or "having-been"), and the present (the *"with which"* or "being-with") (Binswanger, 1946, p. 302). Existence is determined by both its future and its past, its "thrownness", such that "All futurity of the existence is therefore 'has-been' and all having-been is of the future" (Binswanger, 1946, p. 303). With Heidegger, Binswanger claims that the future dimension, however, is primary for Dasein since existence concerns being-able-to-be, which he equates with understanding. The present is given meaning through decisive action.

Throughout his clinical illustrations Binswanger analyzes the individual's relation to the different temporal dimensions. He emphasizes, however, that the analyst's attunement to her/his patients' temporalities does not rely on their conscious or explicit articulation of how they live time. Binswanger's case-example concerning the suffering of a young woman whose world-design is structured by the temporal mode of continuity, is of particular relevance since the question of the continuity of subjectivity continues to preoccupy many psychoanalytic theorists (see below). Binswanger describes how, as a five year old girl, the young woman had experienced a panic attack and fainted after an incident when her heel separated from her shoe and got caught in her skate. From then on she had become overwhelmed with anxiety at any loosening of her heel, any talk of heels, or if anyone touched her heel.

In Binswanger's view, the young woman's world had shrunk to the one category of significance, namely *"continuity,* of continuous connection and containment" (Binswanger, 1946, p. 203). Any disruption to her world in the form of the new and unexpected was experienced as a suddenness that "explodes continuity, hacks it and chops it to pieces ... exposes it to the naked horror" (Binswanger, 1946, p. 204). Her phobia of heels was a way of safeguarding herself from this horror, the anxiety of existence itself, and the movement of time towards the future. Behind her fears of loose heels were birth phantasies which revealed her fears of separation from her mother. The young woman fixed herself in past time, the "already having-been-in" (Binswanger, 1946, p. 205). However, paradoxically, the more she constricted her world to preserve it from her anxiety, the more anxiety she felt in the face of a possible threat to this.

Binswanger vividly describes the structure of the young woman's experience of her world and her specific and troubling relation to time and change. He argues against a Freudian reduction of her phobia to her "predisposition" and proposes a more "anthropological angle" (Binswanger, 1946, p. 203). He contends that the birth phantasies were not phylogenetic but arose out of this young woman's particular "world-design". He challenges the notion that an overly intense pre-Oedipal tie to the mother might be the source of the young woman's world-design of continuity and her fear of suddenness. In his view such a causal explanation is inadequate. Instead he interprets the strength of this tie as arising from her world-design: her attachment to her mother was her way of having a "hold on the world" (Binswanger, 1946, p. 203).

As Needleman (1967) emphasizes, a world-design of continuity is not in itself necessarily problematic to an individual. What is problematic is the extent to which this temporal mode restricts an individual's freedom to risk exploring other possibilities of living. I focus on the question of the importance of a sense of continuity through time in the light of current debates within psychoanalysis below. Firstly I want to consider the value and limitations of the notion of a "world-design". Laing (1961), for example, indicates that this concept does not sufficiently take into account the actual influence of others on an individual, whether in the present or the past. Certainly, the effects of, for example, living in a patriarchal society, are not addressed in Binswanger's case studies of women. Binswanger was unavoidably affected by his own "thrownness" into a time at which such analyses of gender were undeveloped. However, his theorizing and his case illustrations do not exclude a recognition of the effects of others; throughout they allow for an attentiveness to the particular and unique lived experience of an individual in all its intersubjective manifestations as revealed through their language.

Binswanger takes into account the extensiveness of an individual's world which cannot be completely circumscribed by notions of the drives, the intra-psychic, early development or immediate family relationships. It is important to stress, however, that in practice, it is equally essential, to be attentive to the significance of the moments at which an individual departs from his/her world-design. Although his emphasis on the specificity of an individual's language does allow for this, this aspect is not sufficiently developed by Binswanger.

## Merleau-ponty's lived present

Merleau-Ponty, the phemenologist, emphasizes the present temporal dimension over the future in his theorizing. Against Heidegger he argues that we can only perceive time from the point of view of the present: "it is always in the present that we are centred, and our decision starts from there" (Merleau-Ponty, 1945, p. 427). Merleau-Ponty rarely mentions the subject's mortality. He regards temporality as integral to the motility of the lived body: a bodily movement in the present always dovetails with a previous instant of movement and anticipates a future movement. Each movement contains within it the succession of the previous positions and the outline of those to come. We actively assume time non-reflectively: the human body belongs to or "includes" time. Furthermore, he emphasizes, our relation to time is intersubjective; we are alive to and share in the temporalities of others with their histories and future aspirations.

For Merleau-Ponty, time arises "from my relation to things" (Merleau-Ponty, 1945, p. 412). With Heidegger, he argues strongly against Aristotle's linear conception of time as a series of instances of "now". He also critically reflects on the common metaphor of time as a river flowing from past to future. He draws our attention to how, if an observer is introduced into this picture, those time dimensions are reversed. For example, a perception of a volume of water flowing forward with the current quickly becomes a past perception to the standing observer. Merleau-Ponty's view is interesting in the light of recent research (Nunez, 2006) on the Aymara people who live in the Andes, in Chile. For the Aymara, the past is in front of them and the future is behind them. Nunez speculates that the reason for this might be that their language emphasizes the visual. The past that they have "seen" (experienced) is therefore in front of their eyes. The future is behind as it is, as yet, hidden from view. It appears that such metaphors are culturally and/or historically specific.

Phenomenology is a method of describing experience, not an empirical, deductive, or inductive theory of the "reality" of our existence. As a phenomenologist Merleau-Ponty (1945) argues that time is perspectival: for the subject "the past is a former future and a recent present, the present an impending past and a recent future, the future a present and even a past to come" (Merleau-Ponty, 1945, p. 422). Time is a dimension of our existence, a "network of intentionalities" (Merleau-Ponty, 1945, p. 417) and we are carried forward by lines of "intentionality" which trace out the style of our futures. These lines do not originate in us; we are situated within a perceptual field which is run through with "retentions" and "protentions". "Retention" refers to the transition of a present moment into the past, whilst remaining present, and "protention" refers to the overlap between the present and the impending future moment. Although past, present, and future are distinguishable, they are nevertheless embraced within a single flux which is present. Furthermore, Merleau-Ponty argues that we must conceive of the subject as temporality itself, both thrusting and being thrust towards the future: "We must understand time as the subject and the subject as time" (Merleau-Ponty, 1945, p. 422).

Merleau-Ponty specifically addresses how the meanings of certain "symptoms" can be illuminated through a consideration of them as a reflection of the subject's conflictual relation to time (in any of its dimensions). This is vividly illustrated in his interpretations of a woman's loss of speech and appetite (a case of Binswanger's). The woman is no longer able to eat or to speak when her mother prohibits her from seeing a young man with whom she is in love. The young woman had previously lost her speech twice in her childhood, following firstly an earthquake and then another frightening experience. Merleau-Ponty argues against a Freudian interpretation which would interpret her later loss of speech as a young woman in terms of a fixation at the oral stage of sexual development. He claims that, on the contrary, what has become fixated for her is not only her sexual existence but her spoken relations with others. Her mother's action threatens to cut her off from the possibility of a future, just as her earlier frightening experiences also carried the threat of death and the loss of co-existence. Her loss of speech is a means of escape from the conflict; it is a refusal of co-existence and of life itself. Moreover, by not eating she is refusing to assimilate events that are part of the flow of existence; she is refusing to "swallow" her mother's prohibition from seeing the man whom she loves.

Merleau-Ponty's account imaginatively captures the specificity of this woman's relation to time and to language. An interpretation which reductively locates the source of her loss of speech and her appetite in a fixation at an early infantile stage of development does not adequately address the present conflict, namely between her own and her mother's desires, its connection to those past experiences where she feared losing her life, its threat to her future, and the shifting of her past perceptions in the light of her current experiences.

Merleau-Ponty (like Binswanger) does, however, fail to address the "time" of gender. From a Foucauldian perspective (see my Chapter Six), the woman's inability to speak might be interpreted both as a powerful point of resistance and an (almost satirical) embodying of the silencing of her sexuality. This "silence" is required of her by her mother within the context of a time and a culture whose dominant discourses convey women's sexuality as threatening. She refuses to swallow the prohibition of these, as transmitted within her relationship with her mother. Although, from Merleau-Ponty's presentation of the case, we do not know enough about the young woman's relation to food and to her body-image, we might speculate on this in the light of the power of social discourses regarding historical and cultural expectations of women's body size. It is important to stress, however, the socio-historical context of Merleau-Ponty's writing, namely that of the mid twentieth century, before the emergence of European and American feminist psychoanalytic perspectives on women's development, not withstanding the groundbreaking work of Simone de Beauvoir in *The Second Sex* (1949). (See Chapter Six for more discussion of socio-historical time).

Merleau-Ponty's view of temporality as synonymous with subjectivity and his theorizing of the subject's shifting relations to all three dimensions, each with their own temporal horizons, offers a valuable contribution to psychoanalytic practices. The stories of patients' experiences told in the present in the consulting room shift from present to past to future. Contained within each of these dimensions are other presents, pasts and futures, extending back and forwards through time. Merleau-Ponty's theorizing alerts us to the limitations of the naturalism of Freud's developmental theories and the constraints of Klein's prioritizing of the time of the baby.

### Identities continuous in time?

In my critical presentation of Heidegger's, Binswanger's and Merleau-Ponty's theorizing of temporality my intention is to raise questions for psychoanalytic theorizing and practices. What conception of time with its transitions between the past, present, and future does the analyst bring to the psychoanalytic relationship? What normative assumptions about a "healthy" relation to time might be at play in the clinical work? Does the analyst take the view that, for example, an acceptance of temporal gaps and discontinuities is more psychically mature or, the converse, that the experience of a continuous sense of self through time is an aim of psychoanalytic work, as Winnicott argues?

According to Merleau-Ponty, drawing from Heidegger, "I" am "one single 'living cohesion', one single temporality, which is engaged from birth in making itself progressively explict, and in confirming itself in each successive present present" (Merleau-Ponty, 1945, p. 407). There is no "I" external to this, an agent which synthesizes perceptions taken in from a number of different perspectives. Nor is there an "I" which is consciously experienced in each act of perception. Rather, he argues, the unity of the "I" is "invoked" (Merleau-Ponty, 1945, p. 406) in the present and through this the unity of all my thoughts is achieved. Merleau-Ponty stresses that this unity does not depend on the retention of memory, since we do not in any physiological sense possess a store of memories which we have to consciously recall in order to affirm the existence of our past. We feel and assume the presence of our past.

Although the subject is a single "living cohesion", Merleau-Ponty does not deny that the subject is contextual; he argues that "Inside and outside are inseparable. The world is wholly inside and I am wholly outside myself" (Merleau-Ponty, 1945, p. 407). This means that we extend towards, are open to, and affected by the temporalities of others with their histories and future aspirations and we acquire backgrounds of shared meanings (see my Chapter Six for further discussion of this). There is therefore some fluidity implicit in Merleau-Ponty's concept of subjectivity: it is contextual and relational.. However, it does not go far enough in allowing for the very radical breaks in self-continuity that are experienced by many individuals.

Hoffman's autobiography, *Lost In Translation* (1989), spans the years of Hoffman's childhood, firstly in post-war Poland and then, from the age of thirteen, in Canada, through to her adult life in New York. Her account is movingly punctuated by her reflections on the significance to her of her frequent experiences of gaps and discontinuities. Her departure from Poland in a ship bound for Canada for her marked for her the end of the "narrative of her childhood" (Hoffman, 1989, p. 95). Much later, as a student at Harvard she unexpectedly encounters a childhood friend from Poland. Looking together at an old photograph of themselves as children, they realize the impossibility of crossing "such a large time canyon" (Hoffman, 1989, p. 222). In her relationship with her mother, Hoffman is thrown back and fore across so many generational divides, she is conscious of how emigration has "bollixed up the time distances between us" (Hoffman, 1989, p. 250). For her, memory "emits an intermittent glow" (Hoffman, 1989, p. 242) and, in revisiting Crakow, the town of her childhood, her past is revealed to her, reassuringly, as "only a story" (Hoffman, 1989, p. 242). Perceptions of the past are thus narratives which emerge in different ways at different times. For further discussion of this see my Chapter Eight.

Hoffman warns of the dangers of nostalgia ("an ineffectual relationship to the past" in which time is static) and of alienation ("an ineffectual relationship to the present") as defences against discontinuities. (Hoffman, 1989, p. 242). In her personal psychoanalysis she realizes that these gaps, although at times a source of suffering, are also a source of her aliveness. Healing her suffering does not mean the development of a sense of herself as continuous. It also does not mean denying discontinuity. She discovers how to shift between Polish and English without sealing over their differences, and also without being split by them. The gaps are what sharpen her sensitivity to diversity. Many of Hoffman's references to experiences of time resonate with Merleau-Ponty's accounts (see also my Chapter Six) but her attention to the inevitability and the value of the discontinuous is more congruent with Foucault's theorizing.

Foucault, who had been a student of Merleau-Ponty's, argues that any notion of continuous history erases occurrences such as sudden accidents and discoveries which unavoidably cut across the continuous. His concern is with the relation between discourses and practices in relation to subjectivity. His methods are "archeological" and "genealogical". The "archeological" method is concerned not with whether discourses express the truth or make sense but with the rules that govern them. From this Foucault developed the "genealogical" method in order to thematize the relation between truth, values and practices. Genealogy is an approach to history which seeks out discontinuities as against continuity and rejects notions of fixed essences,

underlying laws or metaphysical finalities. Counter to those historical narratives in which events have often been "rearranged, reduced,
effaced in order to reveal (their) continuity" (Foucault, 1969, p. 8),
Foucault argues for an attentiveness to the small shifts, gaps and
crises in history.

According to Foucault, the notion of history as continuous is problematic. It relies on an assumption that the subject can be certain of
restoring everything that has been lost, that everything will eventually be reconstituted in the unity of time, and that s/he will be able to
absorb everything s/he perceives to be different. Foucault's critique
is an implicit challenge to Merleau-Ponty's theorizing. As we have
seen, Merleau-Ponty claims that, for the subject, the totality of his/
her experience including the past and anticipation of the future is
operative within every present thought and action. For Foucault, this
would be to place the subject as the source or origins of historical
development. Against Merleau-Ponty's view that a person whom
we know in the present is the same person as we met in the past,
Foucault (1969) poses the example of Nieztsche. He argues that there
cannot be the same relation between the name Nieztsche and his
philosophical writings, his letters, notebooks, sketches and laundry
lists.

An interesting conceptualization of the relation between continuity and discontinuity of identities through time emerged in a professional development workshop I ran for art therapists entitled
"Image and Embodiment", focusing particularly on the work of
Merleau-Ponty. In response to my reflections on Foucault's challenge
to Merleau-Ponty, one of the participants used the time allocated
for personal artwork to explore this question. She cut a spiral into
a square piece of black paper. Flat, with the spiral cut into it, the
paper had one identity. When she pulled at the centre of the paper,
the spiral extended outwards in a three-dimensional spiral, revealing a radically different identity. Both these, and also the shapes in
between, depending on how far the participant pulled the spiral
were equally possible from the same piece of paper. The participant's
work offered a creative solution for a conceptualization of identity as
simultaneously continuous and discontinuous.

The different positions taken up by Merleau-Ponty, Hoffman and
Foucault alert us to the importance for analysts of both acknowledging and questioning the assumptions that they make about the

relation between time and subjectivity and the implicit value judge-
ments they attach to these. How do these influence their aims for the
patient? If a patient feels that their sense of continuity between past,
present, and future offers them security, is this to be interpreted as a
defence or a sign of psychic health? If the patient's experience is predominantly one of gaps and discontinuities, does this indicate that s/
he is "dissociated"? What are the implications of these different perspectives in relation to how the psychoanalyst views the possibilities
and the experience of change?

A consideration of the notion of "forgetting" highlights some of
the problems and paradoxes involved in the question of the subject's
continuity. In his presentation of the analysis of Regular Zürcher,
the existential psychoanalyst, Boss, includes an extract of a letter in
which she appreciatively describes how, towards the end of the psychoanalytic work, she had begun to think of herself "more and more
outright as a *woman without a past* or earlier life" (Boss, 1979, p. 17). In
Boss's account he conveys how, at the beginning, Zürcher's memories
had been exceedingly intense and overwhelming, and he stresses
that the analyst's "steadiness" through this time, during which her
extensive psychosomatic symptoms disappeared, was crucial. Boss
does not comment on the connection between Zürcher's recollec-
tions of her past and the amelioration of her symptoms. I suspect
that Zürcher's memories or stories about her past were important in
enabling this particular shift (see Chapter Eight for more discussion
of this) but I think that her pleasure at now being a "*woman without a
past*" deserves reflection.

Although more dramatically conceptualized, Zürcher's words
resonate with those of my patient, Laura, who said to me after many
years in analysis that she sometimes tried to remember the times
when she had been treated abusively by men "but the memories are
fading. I feel more distant from them". The relief she felt from this
was very evident, but she was also wondering whether this meant
that they were once again repressed. It felt to me that it was appropriate that these memories were receding. Our earlier work had
been important in enabling Laura to remember and/or construct (see
my Chapter Eight) these memories or experiences in order for their
power over her to diminish.

Freud's theorizing emphasizes the importance of a *complete* remembering of that which is repressed, resisted, and defended against,

denied or disocciated from (an unrealistic expectation against which I argue in Chapter One). Lacan claims, but does not expand on the idea (see my Chapter Four), that in analysis there is an aim integral to this remembering: the patient is encouraged to remember in order to be able to forget. As Ricoeur reminds us, "the specter of a memory that would never forget anything … we … consider … to be monstrous" (Ricoeur, 2004, p. 413). However, as the examples above indicate, it is important to consider what this "forgetting" entails. Dosse, the contemporary French historian, argues against a notion of continuous history but he is also concerned with the "duty of memory" which, he argues, must be preceded by the "work of memory" (Dosse, 2006, p. 79). For example, if the extreme and extensive suffering experienced by the Jews at the time of the holocaust is forgotten, we cannot, as Ricoeur emphasizes, protect the future from the errors of the past. This duty of memory extends beyond oneself to others. However, a certain "forgetting" is necessary in order not to be "held captive by unhappiness" (Dosse 2006, p. 82), which is what Bosse's and my own patient are referring to (see above). In response to this problem Ricoeur theorizes an "oubli" (a "forgotten"), which is a "memory-as-care" (Ricoeur 2004, p. 505) available for recall as "what has been". Ricoeur conceptualizes this as "Carefree memory on the horizon of concerned memory, the soul common to memory that forgets and does not forget" (Ricoeur, 2004, p. 505).

The work of psychoanalysis is, in part, a project of remembering in order to release the individual from the compulsive hold of unconscious memories. When these memories recede, finding their place in the individual's past, they are nevertheless accessible to a re-remembering which allows them to be, consciously and unconsciously, creatively learnt from and reshaped, according to different contexts, opening out a different relation to the future. This neither relies on a concept of time as linear nor of a unified subject containing an internal store of memories; it is a dynamic process.

The importance of resisting notions of analysis which claim to enable the patient to discover or construct a solid unified self is argued for by Flax. Such an aim is bound to be disappointed since, according to Flax, in line with much post-modernist thought from Lyotard (1979) on, the subject is "a shifting and always changing intersection of complex, contradictory, and unfinished processes" (Flax, 1993, p. 108). The temporality of subjectivity is implied in her account of the subject as always changing. She argues that the illusion of a unified self relies on "relations of domination", namely dissociation from, or repression or control of, other aspects of one's own and other individuals' subjectivities. Resistance to domination, politically and personally, requires instead "multiple and fluid subjects" (Flax, 1993, p. 110) and the recognition of these as contextual.

Laing, by contrast, describes the precariousness of individuals in schizoid states who do not feel embodied (which he views as the foundation for a sense of continuity) and live with the constant threat of "attack, mutilation, disease, decay, and death" (Laing, 1961, p. 67). A person in a psychotic state may be so unable to assume a continuity of being in time to the extent that, for example, s/he loses any sense of her/himself as the agent of her/his own perceptions, believing that someone else is using her/his eyes and ears. However, Laing also acknowledges that subjects exist "between being and non-being" (Laing, 1961, p. 51), and that non-being does not necessarily carry the threat of disintegration. The ability to be absorbed in listening to music or other creative activities requires an ability to tolerate a state of non-being which, he argues, is integral to human subjects as finite. Although Hoffman's (1989) position appears closer to Flax's, her subtle differentiation between being "split" by the differences between Polish and English and moving between them resonates with Laing's distinctions.

Ryan, a relational psychoanalyst, poses the possibility of a " 'fine balance' between the experience of an 'illusory', constant, continuous self and the experience of a less conscious, discontinuous, changeable self" (Ryan, 2000, p. 154). He compares the relational worlds of two women living in a therapeutic community (these could be described as "world-designs" in Binswanger's terms). One of the women relies on maintaining a rigid and unchanging perception of herself as needy and deprived (sometimes through various somatic complaints) to ward off her fears of disintegration. The other woman's relationships are characterised by (con)fusion, indecision, and lack of separateness. Ryan alerts us to the dangers of either a too rigid or a too fragmented self identity which, although he does not say it explicitly, both cut the individuals off from their future.

The subtle differentiations between different states of being and non-being, of continuity and discontinuity in time, some of which productively opened out future possibilities and some of which were limiting were vividly conveyed to me by my patient Owen. In one session he said to me that he frequently felt he was "somewhere else". He struggled to articulate how this felt, saying to me, "you may have experienced this in reading". He described shifting imperceptibly from an awareness of the act of reading into being absorbed by a reality which is very different and extremely far away from one's own (usual) reality. Owen then went on to clarify that what really concerned him were states in which it was "more like gazing at landscapes through a train window". Emerging from them, he was unable to recall any of them" knowing only that he had been "elsewhere", completely absent in someone else's presence. These states seemed to him to be "timeless". He thought this happened when there were tensions or conflicts in his relationship with another person.

For Owen, it seemed that these breaks in the continuity of his (usual) being served different functions. Complete absorption in reading enabled him to imaginatively live in and be affected by the world offered by the book; the state he was specifically concerned about occurred at times other than reading. In our discussion it emerged that this particular "not being there" was an unconscious movement away from others into a time which was unreachable by others. He realized that he had developed this early in his childhood, while growing up without any private space of his own and so rarely any time on his own. When the time of others threatened to consume him he drifted away into another time, the events of which he did not remember on his "return". This posed a particular problem for him as an adult as it prevented him from acting in the world he shared with others, from changing or challenging what felt difficult or frustrating for him.

My work with Owen raises the question as to the problem of normative or universalizing assumptions regarding the time of the subject. The discontinuity in his sense of identity was, at times, useful and at other times restrictive. Sometimes it opened out possibilities for the future, sometimes it fixed him in the present. His disappearance into a different time provided an important means of survival for him in his childhood. It had now, however, become problematic to him, hindering his ability to make life changes that he later came to see as necessary for him. His ability to absorb himself in reading was important to him: he loved language and he soon began, in his analysis, to experiment with writing (an interest he had had as a very young man). This became a way to reflect on his relationships with other people and on future directions in his own life. His absorption in the activity of writing opened out the possibility of his taking action in relation to the future. It was my attentiveness to his descriptions in language of the precise differences in these states of non-being which was critical to my understanding of them.

### Timeless absorption

The absorption required for creative activities deserves greater attention in psychoanalytic practices, particularly since, for many individuals, the inability to "concentrate" (as it is often described) can be a particularly debilitating aspect of their suffering. The importance of absorption is recognized in Jung's and Winnicott's theorizing of creativity and also in Freud's concept of "evenly-suspended attention" (Freud, 1912e, p. 111). Freud develops this with his warning to the analyst not to take notes during or after sessions as this may interfere with the spontaneous emergence of the analyst's unconscious associations in the state of suspended attention. Bion (1970) takes this further in strongly advocating that the analyst approaches sessions without memory in order to be more fully attuned to what arises in the present between the analyst and the patient.

Classical descriptions of absorption as a state of "eternity" or "transcendence", with their religious or English Romantic associations have resulted in the assumption that this state is of another era or another realm and not relevant contemporaneously or compatible with the speed and immediacy of our technological culture. However, it is precisely because of its neglect in Western contemporary culture that we need to open out conceptualizations of it.

As Owen described in relation to his reading and, later, his writing, many individuals experience creative absorption as "timeless". In this state we are not conscious of time passing in any quantifiable, chronological or linear way. We are, as Rickman describes, "lost in what we are doing, caught up completely in the 'now'. '... you are the music while the music lasts'" (Rickman, 1964, p. 192). This absorption does not necessarily require solitude; it can be experienced in intimacy with another or others. The ability to experience this depends on being able to relinquish attention to everything other than what is being focused on in the present. In the case of writing or producing work which we want others to see or hear, we simultaneously include in our absorbed attention a relation to an other or an imaginary other.

Absorption, if it is to be productive, requires a relaxing of self-protectiveness ("defences") and an openness to the "otherness" of what might emerge, particularly the "otherness" of unconscious thoughts and feelings (one's own and others' if they are present with us). These thoughts are often the source of originality and, as Jung and Winnicott indicate, point towards the future and they do not always appear to us in any linear sequence. Assumptions that the "timelessness" of absorption is necessarily reminiscent of the early undifferentiated mother infant relationship, such as Sabbadini (1989) implies, do not allow for the way in which absorption can involve an opening out to the otherness of the other. Freud's (1912) notion of "evenly-suspended attention" (Freud, 1912e, p. 111), which he regards as essential to effective listening on the part of the analyst does, in contrast, crucially constitute such an openness. (For a critique of the view of the mother and infant as merged, see Chapter Four).

For some individuals such profound immersion in one activity may be associated with loss of control and with vulnerability. For others, the interruption in their sense of identity as continuous in time, or the possibility of being "at one" with an activity, or with another, can feel too threatening. If the analyst is sufficiently able to be absorbed by the experiences as conveyed through the patient's language, whether verbal or non-verbal, the specific meanings of, and associations to, these states of timelessness and their significance for the individual's creativity will emerge.

### Time and the other

The phenomenological method of attending to the descriptions of a person's lived experiences enables us to expand traditional psychoanalytic analyses of lived time. Owen's descriptions of states of disappearing into another time and my subsequent reflections on creative forms of absorption raise the question as to how far we ever share the same time as others. According to Merleau-Ponty, individuals' temporalities are not entirely separate "because each one knows itself only by projecting itself into the present where they can interweave" (Merleau-Ponty, 1945, p. 433). Our present opens back into our past, forward into our future, and towards the temporalities of others of which we become a part and take forward in our lives. In contrast, Levinas, who was a phenomenologist working contemporaneously with Merleau-Ponty in Paris, argues in his theorizing of temporality that the subject and the Other never share the same time. Levinas uses the term "the Other" for the other person whom one encounters in the "face-to-face" relationship. In contrast to Heidegger's theorizing of the "mineness" of death (see above), Levinas argues that what is crucial about our relation to our death is that it allows us to be *in relation to* that which is absolutely Other; in recognizing the unknowability of death, we realize the otherness of the Other. The Other is, like death, ungraspable and ultimately mysterious to us: "the Other is what I myself am not" (Levinas, 1947b, p. 83). Furthermore our awareness of the mortality of the face of the Other demands of us a responsibility to them, requiring us to be neither an accomplice to, nor indifferent to, their death. This responsibility does not rely on reciprocity. For Levinas, writing within his Talmudic interpretation of his Jewish tradition, it is "for-the-other-person" (Levinas, 1947, p. 137) and it is an openness to beyond being, to God and to infinity.

The Other's time disrupts my own and, as the Other as "future" reveals to me my relationship with the future. Our temporality is therefore intrinsically intersubjective. This is emphasized in Levinas's analysis of the caress as not knowing what it seeks in touching, as opening out what is ungraspable: "The caress is the anticipation of this pure future [*avenir*] without content" (Levinas, 1947, p. 89). He connects avenir (French for "the future") and à venir (French for "about to come"). He contrasts this notion of the erotic with Freud's theorizing of the libido as searching for a definite "content" or "fact", namely pleasure. For Levinas what is intrinsic to sexual intimacy is the search for the mysterious. His notion of the relation with the Other as being a relation with the future also contrasts strongly with Lacan's notion of the third term (the law of the Father) as necessarily disrupting the fusion of the early mother-infant relationship. For Levinas, the relation with the other contains an absence which is time itself and he argues against such a notion of an "intermediary" (Levinas, 1947b, p. 94) or of alterity as spatially differentiated (Levinas, 1947b, p. 84).

Levinas's challenge to the idea that the erotic relation is one of fusion is original. However, surprisingly, he argues that it is in the feminine that the dimension of alterity appears. This does assume a heterosexual intimacy and, in order to understand this, it is important to take into account the particular socio-historical context in which Levinas was writing. Although (as he acknowledges), feminists at this time were already voicing their demands for equality with men, within the field of philosophy his recognition of gender difference (in contrast to notions of the generic "man" or the sexually neutral Dasein) was a radical move. Furthermore, despite the stereotype implied in his equation of the feminine with the mysterious, Levinas's view of the feminine as Other does not designate her as subordinate to the masculine as De Beauvoir (1949) wrongly assumes. He prioritizes her as the Other that is not possessable and cannot be encompassed by the Same. O'Connor's feminist reading of Levinas emphasizes that "The otherness of the feminine cuts through the self's egoistic self-inherence ... (allowing us to) begin 'to think' the possibility of voluptuosity which does not exclude the social, the practice of differences" (O'Connor, 1988, p. 67).

Levinas's view of the instant as an original moment which disrupts continuity contrasts with Merleau-Ponty's notion of identity as continuous through time, identified with time. Like Merleau-Ponty, Levinas challenges the classical Greek (Aristotelian) abstract representational view of time as linear, spreading from past to future, with separate instants, as inert measurements of time, placed between. However, he retains the notion of instants as separate. They are, for Levinas, insubordinate to time as a whole and interrupt its duration. They are a "beginning, a birth" (Levinas, 1947a, p. 76) and they are constituted by both evanescence (fading) and expectation. They therefore do not in themselves have duration. In each instant what is absolute is the materiality of the relationship between the subject's mastery of existence and the weight of concrete existence bearing down on the subject. This materiality is derived from the present. Each instant is "like a breathlessness, a panting, an effort to be" (Levinas, 1947a, p. 79). This resonates with Hoffman's conclusion in her very last sentence in Lost in Translation: "Time pulses through my blood like a river. The language of this is sufficient. I am here now" (Hoffman, 1989, p. 280). According to Levinas, engagement with the world depends on the evanescence of the instant and the presence of the present bestows an appearance of being to the past and "defies" the future which cannot eradicate it. It is nevertheless free of the past; as "'the occurrence of an origin", the present "turns into a being" (Levinas, 1947a, p. 79). What is crucial about the instant, moreover, is its "stance" (Levinas, 1947a, p. 77). By this Levinas means that the instant enables the subject to "take position" (Levinas, 1947a, p. 81) towards the world, thereby coming into existence.

For psychoanalytic practices which are concerned with a sensitivity to the uniqueness of the patient's experience Levinas's view of the Other as absolutely other is an important contribution. Otherness, as theorized by Levinas, exceeds rational understanding, a gathering into the "same" and requires an originality of response to the patient which allows for those individual possibilities that escape overarching theories. The universalism claimed for many psychoanalytic theories does not allow for the irreducible otherness of individuals. It contributes to the possibility of this being feared, ignored or denied by the psychoanalyst who is in flight from both their own and the patient's anxiety and confusion regarding the limits of knowledge and understanding. The critical importance of this is highlighted in working with people from cultural and religious backgrounds, ages, and sexualities which may differ considerably from the analyst's own. Levinas's theorizing reminds the analyst of the importance of their responsibility in relation to the specificity of the patient's experience as always beyond their own. This does not mean it cannot be responded to, but it requires us to be attentive to the limits of empathy, with its implicit assumption that the psychoanalyst feels exactly the *same* as the patient.

Individuals' relation to time varies considerably between cultures and is shaped by cultural and religious traditions (for example, specific perspectives on death and immortality, understandings of history, the role of memory and narrative), work patterns, the climate, and the length of daylight time as well as many other factors. In psychoanalytic work with couples the differences in individuals' relation to time is particularly highlighted. For one couple it was a relief when they identified how one of them always lived in anticipation of the future, planning for every eventuality, including the possibility (or likelihood) of death. The other was unafraid of death and lived more in the immediacy of the present, often feeling at risk of being consumed by others' demands which she felt she had to respond to immediately.

Levinas's notion that the Other is always in a different time is very relevant to the relation between patient and analyst. Although they both agree on the frequency and duration of the session in clock time (except in Lacanian psychoanalysis, see my Chapter Four), the lived time of the session is not however shared (Green 2002). In their speaking and their gestures, in the rhythms, gaps, unconscious slips and silences, both the analyst and the patient weave in and out of different times, between their pasts, presents and possible futures. Moreover, the difference between the times of the participants is itself critical to the psychoanalytic work. When, for the patient, the future closes down under the shadow of despair, the analyst must both remain alive to its possibilities, and also responsive to the drudgery of endless suffering. In listening to the dread of what may happen in the future, the analyst may turn her/his attention to the patient's past. Incidents in previous sessions, memories recalled and reforgotten by the patient, each with their own horizons, seize the analyst's attention together with the personal associations which may elucidate or obscure the otherness of the patient's experiences.

In the patient's transferences past experiences may be lived as present with their "pastness" torn from them and their difference from the present precluded from consciousness. Or, as I discussed in Chapter One, the transference may be a form of experimenting with new possibilities of relationships, pointing towards the future. The newness of the instant as theorized by Levinas is the promise of the opportunity for change in psychoanalysis. The appearance of an instant in which the past cannot be present and where the future does not yet exist offers the possibility of the taking up of a new position, of breaking the compulsion to attempt to repeat that which, in fact, can never be repeated. This taking up of a new position occurs in the relationship between the analyst and the patient, in the difference between them, in the time that points towards the future. It is an original unrepeatable instant in which both individuals are changed, consciously and/or unconsciously. The new position is a creation that is born between them and, in its freedom, it carries, paradoxically, the weight of responsibility to oneself and to others.

## Conclusion

The work of Heidegger, Merleau-Ponty, Foucault and Levinas en-
hance the possibilities for psychoanalytic practices which are more
sensitive to individuals' experiences of time. As I indicate at the
beginning of the chapter, I do not claim that any one of these positions is more relevant than another and, moreover, there is not one,
"mature" perspective on time for which psychoanalytic practices
must aim. Through an appreciation of their diverse positions, the
analyst is alerted to the importance of an attentiveness to the dominance of particular time dimensions in individuals' speech, their
relation to these dimensions and to others' time, and to whether and
how these temporal experiences are sources of conflict and suffering
and/or of hope. Similarly, the specificity of *how* individuals experience their identities, whether as punctuated with gaps or as continuous through time, must not be assumed to be *in itself* productive or
problematic for the individual in psychoanalysis. This differs for
different individuals at different times.

# CHAPTER SIX

# Places lived in time

In previous chapters I have argued that the theories of Freud, Klein, Jung, Lacan and Winnicott do not adequately address the question of the socio-historicity of the subject. Developing this theme further in this chapter I argue that a theorizing which prioritizes the temporality of the subject (as opposed to the interpretations of classical psychoanalytic writing which draw primarily on the spatial metaphors of internal/external) allows for more inclusive interpretations of individualities as lived in their socio-historical and cultural specificity.

It might be anticipated that Andre Green (2002), as a contemporary French psychoanalyst, would in his book, *The Psychoanalysis of Time*, consider this aspect of temporality. However, Green asserts that it is unimportant whether fantasies are transmitted genetically or culturally from generation to generation. His theorizing of time emphasizes the value of Freud's notion of the unconscious as "timeless" and of resurrecting Freud's drive theory. Green's lack of interest in the socio-historical is particularly surprising given the accessibility of modern European philosophical thinking in France. The concept of "historicity" in the hermeneutic and phenomenological traditions in philosophy, introduced in Chapter One, is very relevant to psychoanalytic practices. "Historicity" denotes an individual's lived experience of their past and present in anticipation of their future possibilities. Furthermore, the individual's historicity is contextual; the subject is intrinsically social and linguistic, embedded in a network of human relationships at a particular moment in historical time; we are always already in the world and this is a world of others. This is highlighted in the historian Bourke's book *Fear*. Assumed to be timeless and universal, the emotion of fear instead "acquires meaning through cultural language and rites" (Bourke, 2005, p. 7).

I begin this chapter with a consideration of the contributions of some psychoanalysts who explicitly struggle with the question of the relation between the individual and the socio-historical and cultural contexts. They offer radical and courageous challenges to the emphasis on the intra-psychic in mainstream psychoanalytic theorizing. However, their work founders on contradictions arising from arguments reliant on spatial metaphors, with the exception of Samuels (1993). O'Connor and Ryan (1993) point to this problematic in their innovative analysis of psychoanalytic theorizing of lesbian sexualities. In this chapter I argue that it is through our attentiveness to the temporality of the subject and through relinquishing discrete notions of "external" and "internal" that we can allow for a notion of subjectivity in which the psychic and the social are integral to one another. I return again (see Chapter Five) to the work of the French philosopher, the phenomenologist, Merleau-Ponty and also to that of Hoffman, the contemporary writer and novelist, to explore the possibilities of this for psychoanalytic practices. Hoffman's work illustrates clearly the limitations of any theorizing which perceives the individual primarily in terms of alinguistic drives, mechanisms or universal complexes.

Why is an attentiveness to the socio-historical in individuals' narratives important in psychoanalytic practices? In this chapter I highlight how important this is to an understanding of the richness and complexity of patients' experiences (experiences which could not have occurred at any other historical moment) in their multifarious aspects. An acknowledgement of socio-historical specificity also allows for a notion of change: each of our experiences arises from a specific moment in time; they are not fixed and unchanging. This does not mean that it is always appropriate to interpret the socio-historical specificity of an individual's experience directly; rather the orientation of the therapist to this aspect of the material can in itself convey an openness to subjectivity as fluid and changing.

*Gender in time*

The late 1970s, 1980s and early 1990s saw the emergence of a range of critiques of traditional psychoanalytic theorizing regarding its failure to sufficiently attend to the relation between gender and the wider socio-historical context. A range of differing and challenging perspectives were developed by psychoanalysts in Britain and the United States, such as Mitchell (1974) who draws on Lacanian theory, Dinnerstein (1976) who is influenced by Klein, Chodorow (1978), Eichenbaum and Orbach (1983) whose work is rooted in a critical appreciation of Winnicottian theory, and Benjamin (1988) whose theorizing draws on the work of the Frankfurt School. In France, psychoanalysts such as Irigaray (1977) and Kristeva (1979) were exploring the question of gender against the background of contemporary French philosophy and the rise in popularity of Lacanian psychoanalysis, with its emphasis on the phallus as primary signifier (see my Chapter Four). All of these writers in their radical critiques take the socio-historical and socio-cultural into account. Focusing specifically on the conceptions of temporality which explicitly and/ or implicitly underpin their theorizing with regard to socio-historical specificity, I discuss two examples here, one from the Anglo-American feminist discourse (Eichenbaum and Orbach) and one from the French (Kristeva).

Eichenbaum and Orbach's project arose from questions raised by the Women's Liberation movement in Britain and the US in the 1970s regarding the relation between the personal and the political and posed a strong challenge to Freud's lack of attention to the socio-historical context in configurations of gender. Developing Chodorow's (1978) argument against his theorizing of the Oedipal stage as determining gender they argue that, from the very beginning of life, the child's relationship with his/her mother arises from a social context in which women are expected to be the main carers (of children and others). This expectation is transmitted to the girl baby through the ways in which the mother touches, holds, feeds, and communicates with her. In theorizing women's ego development Orbach and Eichenbaum claim that the ego boundaries between mothers and daughters, since they are of the same gender, are more blurred. This arises from their identification with one another and also from the social expectations of mothers to produce daughters whose priority will also be the care of others (as mothers or carers). In their relationships girls consequently experience themselves, consciously and unconsciously, as merged with and continuous with others. Furthermore, girls develop an unconscious internal boundary, splitting off those qualities which are regarded as unacceptable in women, such as strength, anger and independence in thinking and in action.

Eichenbaum and Orbach's conceptualization of the unconscious is a radical one, theorized as continuous with the wider social context, reflecting its social structure and its organization of gender. This stands in strong contrast to notions of the unconscious as containing raw and primitive forces which are assumed to be ahistorical and asocial in their origins. They are sensitive to the particular social pressures on girls and women at different stages of their lives, from infancy, through childhood, adolescence and adulthood, and they include in their analysis the role of the media and cultural attitudes which shape girls' and young women's identities, consciously and unconsciously.

Eichenbaum's and Orbach's theorizing is, however, constrained by their over-valorization, in line with other Object Relations theorists, of the spatial metaphors of "inner" and "outer". In so doing they assume a split between the subject and the world, the very split which their theorizing challenges. Self-understandings in terms of an "inner world" arise from a desire (particuarly in the psychoanalytic relationship) for recognition of what is individual, personal and private in a person's experience. As Scarfone argues, in relation to the notion of phantasies arising from within or from a "prehistoric past" (Scarfone, 2005, p. 37) it is problematic if the status of a psychoanalytic theory is uncritically assigned to a particular self-description. If an individual experiences what is individual to them as "inner", this does not mean that this dichotomy exists, or should exist, for everyone universally. As I discuss below, an analysis which, by contrast, emphasizes the temporality of the subject, allows for more specific interpretations of the shifting conscious and unconscious relationships that subjects "live" in the world.

Eichenbaum and Orbach conclude that, for a shift to occur in the binarism of gender roles, men and women must equally be involved in childcare, but they rely on a biologistic position (see Parker 1995) which repeats the binarism. Their claim is that because mothers and daughters share the same biological sex, particular patterns of relating are reproduced. This does not sufficiently take into account the individual circumstances of mothers in very diverse socio-historical contexts, class, and cultural backgrounds. It raises the question as to whether, if the father is necessary for a developing girl's sense of autonomy, all daughters of lesbian parents are therefore destined for particularly merged relations with others. It is clear that Eichenbaum and Orbach do not hold this view, given their openness to interpretations of lesbian identities as non-pathological and their critiques of how women's sexualities have been subjected to control in patriarchal cultures. (See also Stacey and Biblarz's 2001 study of the effects of the sexual orientation of parents on children which concluded that there were no differences between children raised by heterosexual parents and those raised by lesbian or gay couples.) Orbach and Eichenbaum's theorizing of the presence of the father as a necessary condition for changes in the organization of gender to occur throws their critiques open to question in their own terms.

It has been very evident to me in my own practice that Orbach and Eichenbaum's theorizing is acutely relevant to the experiences of many white middle-class women born in the late 1940s and 1950s in Britain and the U.S. This was at a time when women were being stridently encouraged through institutional and discursive practices such as education, medicine, and psychoanalysis to relinquish the work and activities they had enjoyed in war-time and to become full-time wives and mothers. As Cunningham(1999) in his novel *The Hours* describes through his character Laura's reflections:

> Because the war is over, the world has survived, and we are here, all of us, making homes, having and raising children, creating … a world of order and harmony where children are safe (if not happy), where men who have seen horrors beyond imagining, who have acted bravely and well, come home to lighted windows, to perfume, to plates and napkins. [p. 42]

The daughters of Laura's generation of women suffered greatly from the notion that to become a woman was to become a mother or a carer like their own mothers. Furthermore, the mothering promoted as beneficial to families in post-war Britain and the U.S. emphasized, as Cunningham conveys, detailed attention to physical care and comfort in the home, often at the expense of children's happiness and the development of their individuality. At the end of this chapter I discuss a dream reported by a woman patient born in the mid-1950s which illustrates the effects of this style of mothering on her sense of subjectivity.

Orbach and Eichenbaum's theorizing developed within a specific socio-historical context, namely the early 1980s, and they reflect on the lives of women whose childhoods extended back some decades before. It is heartening that since the time at which they were writing, and in part, owing to the influence of their work, there have been many historical shifts which have profoundly affected women's lives. For example, adolescent girls' shame and embarrassment about their bodies and sexualities are less widespread and women are feeling more confident in defining their own sexualities. Men are feeling more able to develop closer emotional ties with their children and to accept their own emotional vulnerabilities as well as their sexualities. The availability of artificial insemination by donor and changes in adoption law have had a significant effect on how lesbians experience their sexualities, both consciously and unconsciously. This, of course, has different meanings for every lesbian, depending on, for example, their age and their attitudes to parenting. Historical and cultural shifts such as these have radical effects on women's subjectivities, whether they constrain or open out different possibilities of existence.

Across the channel from the London Women's Therapy Centre founded by Eichenbaum and Orbach and other women, Kristeva, a Bulgarian born psychoanalyst living in Paris, explicitly addresses the question of time in relation to women's subjectivity. Kristeva's theorizing of language is influenced by Lacan's theories. However, she extends his concepts of the imaginary and symbolic to include her notion of the "semiotic", a modality which is neither temporal nor spatial. Its origins are in the pre-Oedipal, and, according to Kristeva, it is indicated in Freud's concept of the primary process. The "semiotic" refers to an articulation of the pulsions or drives, predominantly oral and anal, and it is discernible in the ruptures in the grammatical rules of language, and through metonymy and metaphor. The drives are gathered in the "chora", "a non-expressive totality" (Kristeva, 1974a, p. 25) which is both "mobile and extremely provisional" (Kristeva, 1974a, p. 25). The "chora" is organized through its orientation to the mother's body, and through familial and social constraints, not via the "law" which relies on symbolic language. Kristeva emphasizes that the "chora" is neither a sign nor a signifier; she equates it with vocal or kinetic rhythm (music, according to her, is a non-verbal signifying system produced through the semiotic).

Kristeva's emphasis is on "abjection" and the separation from the pre-Oedipal mother, rather than castration. She describes abjection as the "violent, clumsy breaking away, with the constant risk of falling back under the sway of a power as securing as it is stifling" (Kristeva, 1980, p. 13); it is also timeless, a time of "oblivion" (Kristeva, 1980, p. 9). "Abjection" precedes the intervention of the father and the introduction of the child into symbolic language, through which the chora and the infant's connection to the maternal is repressed, albeit precariously. However "abjection" returns in the interruptions, gaps and rhythms within symbolic language.

Kristeva maintains Lacan's notion that it is the father who introduces the growing child into the symbolic order: the tie with the mother is severed and the child is forced to accept its castration. In "Women's time" she argues for an extension of the notion of castration (beyond the penis as main referent) to signify, for men and women, all that limits totality, namely "the break indispensable to the advent of the symbolic" (Kristeva, 1979, p. 198). However, this does not lead Kristeva to substantially question her equation between the father, the symbolic order, and time itself: "There is no time without speech. Therefore there is no time without the father". The father is "sign and time" (Kristeva, 1974b, p. 35). The time of the father is linear time.

In "Women's time" Kristeva seeks to redress the emphasis accorded to space in the theorizing of psychoanalytic theory, anti-psychiatry, matriarchal religions, and in Plato's philosophy. She differentiates between "monumental time" (Kristeva, 1979, p. 189), which is "all-encompassing and infinite like imaginary space" (Kristeva, 1979, p. 191) and associated with the maternal, and linear historical time. She argues that traditionally, female subjectivity has been connected with the former and also with the "cyclical time" of nature and biological rhythms (Kristeva, 1979, p. 192). She equates linear time with obsessionality and the "hysteric" (male or female) in flight from memory with cyclical and monumental time.

Kristeva claims that the struggles of suffragists and existential feminists for equal rights with men signified the desire for a place in linear time. Consequently, she argues, they rejected qualities such as the maternal which might jeopardize their inclusion in that time. She describes the next generation of feminists (from 1968 on), by contrast, as repudiating linear time in favour of fluidity and plurality and, furthermore, a valorization of mythical memory and cyclical and monumental time. Through their writing and artistic productions (about which Kristeva is scathing) these feminists were attempting to articulate bodily and intrasubjective experiences which had been previously silenced.

Kristeva regards the lesbian's or "homosexual" woman's position as characterizing a problematic within both linear and monumental temporalities. In *About Chinese Women* she presents the lesbian as one of the "supermen" (Kristeva, 1974b, p. 37), identifying with masculine values and, in "Women's time", as destructively rejecting the "paternal function" (Kristeva, 1979, p. 205) along with terrorists and single mothers, if she becomes a mother. Kristeva concludes with the offer of an alternative to those she characterizes as belonging to the first two generations of feminists. She argues for a position which, she claims, allows for the "*singularity* of each person" and "the multiplicity of each person's possible identifications" (Kristeva, 1979, p. 210). As an ethics, it involves drawing on the "cutting edge" of the symbolic to deconstruct the power-positions inherent within it and to open out possibilities for *jouissance*, responsibility, challenges, and differences.

Kristeva's explicit engagement with the themes of time, language, and gender appears to offer a promising analysis of the socio-historicity of the subject which might allow for differences (as opposed to universals). She is particularly original in her consideration of how different genders may be inserted into different times. Her account is, however, permeated with contradictions. Although Kristeva emphasizes the early relation with the maternal body her perspective relies on the Oedipus complex as pivotal. She unquestioningly equates femininity with the maternal, and the symbolic with the father's intervention, while implying the possibility of a deconstruction of this. She assumes that women can insert themselves into a different time without questioning how the very equations she makes (between femininity and maternity, fatherhood and the symbolic) paradoxically have the effect of maintaining that which she criticizes. Women who do take up particularly radical challenges to these positions (such as lesbian mothers or professional women who choose not to have children) are denigrated by Kristeva. This stands in strong contradiction to her argument, in the same paper, for the possibility of a time which can allow for individual differences and a plurality of identifications which are free of the constraints of both male and female sexism.

## The time of the political psyche

Introducing the notion of "the father of whatever sex" Jungian psychoanalyst Samuels (1993) goes further than Kristeva in opening out possibilities for multiple identifications in relation to gender and sexuality. His concern is less with the question of language but, rather, with addressing notions of "inner" and "outer" in the Anglo-American psychoanalytic literature. Challenging the rigidity of such distinctions in *The Political Psyche* (1993) he argues that "Subjectivity and intersubjectivity have political roots; they are not as 'internal' as they seem" and that "the demarcation between the inner world of psychology and the outer world of politics has no permanent existence" (Samuels, 1993, p. 4). Although Samuels does not explicitly acknowledge it, it is striking that his analysis relies on a recognition of human temporality: his work contains many references to time and to the socio-historical contexts of particular theories, including his own. The influence of Jung's recognition of the significance of the present and future, as well as the past temporal dimensions is evident in his work and allows him to develop a more complex theorizing of the subject's socio-historical and political specificity. He particularly challenges object relations theory with its causal and sequential explanations in relation to origins, emphasizing the importance of the dimension of the future and potential for political change. Instead, he argues, the question for the psychotherapist should be "Where's it going? What does it mean? Not, what are its roots?" (Samuels, 1993, p. 74). The notion of "development" is not natural; it is a fantasy and is contingent. He argues that the father-infant relationship is not universal but subject to mutability within specific socio-historical contexts.

Samuels does, however, find it difficult to sustain his critique of the assumed division between inner and outer realities. On the last page of *The Political Psyche* he refers to his struggle to "negotiate a tension between respect for historical specificity and context on the one hand and the limitless, playful vitality of imagination and fantasy on the other" (Samuels, 1993, p. 339). He is explicit that psychic and political realities are different and implies, therefore, that freedom in imagination relies on its being ahistorical, acultural and alinguistic. Samuels's conclusion risks replicating the very split that he challenges at many other points in the book.

Samuels's work raises challenging questions as to how and whether human imagination can exist outside or beyond history, language and culture and, also, whether a recognition of its historical and cultural specificity is necessarily restrictive? In my discussion below of the work of the philosopher Merleau-Ponty and the autobiographical writing of the writer and novelist, Eva Hoffman, I argue for the possibility of a conceptualization of subjectivity as located in and moving between constantly shifting matrices of complex webs of connections in which there are numerous possibilities of play, of creating and breaking connections, of originality produced from the extraordinary criss-crossings of the fibres and intricacies of all of our relationships. Integral to such a conception is the recognition of the subject as temporal.

## Desires, identities, and historicity

It is predominantly in relation to the significance of the emergence of lesbian and gay identities that the most radical theorizing of the historical specificity of subjectivities has emerged. For example, the contemporary philosopher, Butler, argues that many philosophical accounts search for an "internal feature" of the subject which guarantees the continuity of their identity across time. She contends that the stability of the term "person" is severely challenged by the "cultural emergence of those "incoherent" or "discontinuous" gendered beings who appear to be persons but who fail to conform to the gendered norms of cultural intelligibility by which persons are defined" (Butler, 1990, pp.16–17). "Identity" is thus a normative concept which is itself socially and historically specific. Of particular relevance here is the theorizing of analysts O'Connor (also a contemporary philosopher) and Ryan in *Wild Desires and Mistaken Identities, Lesbianism and Psychoanalysis*. Influenced by Merleau-Ponty and Foucault, O'Connor and Ryan challenge psychoanalytic notions of same-sex sexualities as necessarily pathological arguing that such an interpretation arises from a reliance on "over-arching and universal metapsychological concepts" (O'Connor and Ryan, 1993, p. 15) which do not acknowledge socio-historical or socio-cultural specificity.

O'Connor and Ryan present a thorough and wide-ranging critical analysis of how lesbianism is positioned within psychoanalytic theorizing and practices. Acknowledging the particular socio-historical contexts which have produced this theorizing, their work vividly demonstrates how the issue of homosexuality within psychoanalysis has been "largely split off, inadequately discussed and understood, subject to rigid and sometimes attacking theorizing, and to excluding practices" (O'Connor and Ryan, 1993, p. 9). Central to their critique is a challenge to the notion of the Oedipus complex as universal. Drawing on Fanon (see below) they argue that it does not allow for the diversity of patterns of child-rearing, historically and culturally, and also assumes a split between desire and identification: to be a (mature) man, one has to desire a woman.

O'Connor and Ryan are innovative in drawing on contemporary European philosophy with its emphasis on historicity and on the importance of language; in their view there is no "true" sexuality that lies outside language. They argue that the meanings of both homosexuality and heterosexuality are not "exhausted by reference just to intra- or interpsychic events; they both denote significant aspects of the 'deployment of sexuality'—to use Foucault's term—within the social order" (O'Connor and Ryan, 1993, p. 21). For Foucault, there is no body prior to history or to discourse; it is "produced" by and saturated with historical forces. Designations of the body and of sexuality as, for example, "natural" or "unnatural" are not factual distinctions given at the level of the body. These are interpretations which arise from the dominant discourses of the time, whether religious, medical, pedagogic, psychoanalytic etc. As O'Connor and Ryan argue in relation to psychoanalytic theories of sexuality, theories are never value-free. They arise from within particular socio-historical contexts and are saturated with the values of particular people at different times.

O'Connor and Ryan emphasize the multiplicity of sexualities and sexual identities and how these are produced from within particular socio-historical contexts. They argue that there are no essential features of lesbian desire which are necessarily shared by lesbians but acknowledge that homophobia may "constitute or contribute to (its) forms of expression" (O'Connor and Ryan, 1993, p. 234). An example of this, as I suggest elsewhere (Ellis, 1997), is the difference between the same-sex sexuality of an upper middle-class white women in the 1920s, such as Virginia Woolf and Vita Sackville-West, and that of a black working-class young woman who defines herself as "queer" and enjoys "gender bending" contemporaneously.

### Race in time

Fanon's critique of the universality of the Oedipus complex in his book *Black Skin, White Masks*, is supported by his evidence that in the French Antilles at that time "97 per cent of the families cannot produce one Oedipal neurosis" (Fanon, 1952, p. 152) and that every neurosis there has its source in the cultural context. Fanon is explicit from the beginning of the book that his analysis of black identities and the sources of racism includes both the socio-cultural (the context of place), and simultaneously, the socio-historical. In his warning to the reader, "I do not come with timeless truths" (Fanon, 1952, p. 9) he acknowledges the historical specificity of his own work.

Fanon's theorizing is influenced by French existential and phenomenological thought; he studied and worked in France as a psychiatrist before being assigned to a hospital in Algeria during the war of independence from the French. References to time in all its dimensions run throughout Fanon's conceptualization of subjectivity: the time of previous generations, the time of childhood, present time, and future time. His emphasis on temporality challenges the notion of a reductionistic "black psychology", one which he keenly repudiates. He also argues against the temptation to revive or attempt to romanticize the richness of previous, forgotten civilizations. According to Dalal, the fact that Fanon implies in his work the existence of a "pure "race" of Negroes before the Diaspora" (Dalal, 2002, p. 95) signifies a weakness in his position. However, not withstanding this critique, it is important to emphasize Fanon's refusal to make himself "the man of any past … I do not want to exalt the past at the expense of my present and my future" (Fanon, 1952, p. 226). The past has only relevance as a support for solidarity in the struggle against future subjugations of any group and he warns against being determined by the present. He emphasizes the future dimension of subjectivity: "In the world through which I travel, I am endlessly creating myself" and "I am part of Being to the degree that I go beyond it" (Fanon, 1952, p. 229).

Fanon analyzes the various culturally and historically specific influences on the development of black people's subjectivities, particularly in colonized cultures such as the Antilles where he grew up. He traces the role of magazines, comics, and stories in the development of black children's identities. Produced mainly by white people (the colonizers), they depict the characters of savages, evil spirits, and the devil as black people or Indians. Fanon argues that the black (boy) child invests his own aggression in the white hero of the story and identifies with him. Since he does not see himself as black ("black people live in Africa"), but as an Antillean, it is only when he moves to Europe and faces overt racism that he realizes, in Fanon's words, "he is a Negro" (Fanon, 1952, p. 148). Although Fanon is writing in the 1950s and addresses the particular issues of black identification for young black men, many aspects of Fanon's analysis continue to be relevant in Europe and the U.S. Contemporary children's literature contains fewer stereotypes but there continues to be a dearth of black people in positions of power, including in the media. Education services are failing to address the needs of young black men and success is equated with being white. However, owing to the increasing strength of demands from black people for equality, together with an acknowledgement of differences, there is a much greater diversity of black identities, including those with high social status, available to black people in Europe and America contemporaneously.

Fanon analyses the unconscious anxieties on which anti-black racism hinges. Black people are associated with the biological, the instincts and genitality: "… one is no longer aware of the Negro but only of a penis; the Negro is eclipsed. He is turned into a penis" (Fanon, 1952, p. 170). White men attribute their ideal of sexual potency to black men and seek revenge for their supposed possession of this genital superiority. It is in his theorizing of white women's fear of black men's sexuality, however, that contradictions arise. His interpretation of it as primarily an expression of early developmental anxieties contrasts strongly with his emphasis on the socio-historical and socio-cultural in his theorizing of black subjectivities. Drawing on the work of Helene Deutsch and Marie Bonaparte he claims that the little white girl (aged five to nine) observes her father beating a sibling rival. When he does not take up her unconscious aggression (previously directed clitorally towards her mother) she invests this in black men, in accordance with the prevailing discourses of the culture. However, its original source is the infantile need to "disembowel the mother" (Fanon, 1952, p. 179) which Fanon conveys as implicitly ahistorical and acultural. He concludes that the unconscious wish is that the black man "rip me open as I would have ripped a woman open" (Fanon, 1952, p. 179). The fear of being raped thus arises from the wish to be raped.

Fanon does not offer any argument to support his retention of the Oedipus complex as central to his theorizing of white European women's sexual development, despite his fervent critique of its supposed universality. He uncritically accepts Freud's account of female development (expanded on by Deutsch and Bonaparte) through negotiation of her "double Oedipus complex" (Fanon, 1952, p. 178) and the attainment of "mature" vaginal sexuality. In relation to black women's "psychosexuality" he admits, "I know nothing about her" (Fanon, 1952, p. 180), except that her fears are of the "all-but-whites" such as Senegalese men, whom she regards as inferior.

The contradiction between Fanon's interpretation of white women's racism as arising from early infantile drives and his emphasis on the socio-historical and socio-cultural in his accounts of the shaping of black identities is striking. His position is particularly surprising given his critique of the psychoanalyst Manoni's assumption that a "dependency complex" (Fanon, 1952, p. 85) exists in colonized people which predates, and makes them susceptible to, colonization. However, his detailed analysis of the role of power and discourses in the production of socio-historical and culturally specific black identities was extremely radical for his time, anticipating Foucault's later analysis of the production of sexualities.

Fanon's analysis extends back to previous generations of black people including their experiences of slavery. Fletchman-Smith (2002) draws on her clinical experience with black men and women in analysis to support her argument that some of the dynamics of their intimate relationships contemporaneously can be traced back to the time of slavery and echo those which occurred between slaves and also between slaves and slave-owners. Fletchman-Smith does not claim that the transmission of these occurs in any biological or archetypal way. Rather, she implies, particular notions of intimacy are generated within and through parent-child relationships consciously and unconsciously from one generation to the next. She is also not claiming that there is one "black psychology". This would be to deny the diversity of the cultural backgrounds of people who define themselves as black and to assume that their conscious and unconscious experiences of their identities are fixed in time. Aaron (1994), a Welsh literary theorist, shares Fletchman-Smith's interest in the cross-generational transmission of patterns of behaviour. She describes how restrictions on Welsh women's sexuality inculcated by the colonizing culture (England) outlived the retention of these in English culture. She refers to a Welsh language text (Rowlands 1966), which describes how a woman's guilt at unknowingly having had an affair with a married man was nearly as acute in 1966 as if it had occurred in the late nineteenth century. During this latter period Welsh Non-conformity had introduced a strict policing of women's sexuality in order to prove to the English colonizers that Welsh women were not, as they believed, promiscuous and wild in their sexuality. This self-policing had continued to be passed down over generations and to have profound effects on women's sexual lives.

## Ambiguity, language and embodiment

I shall now focus on some of the resonances between the texts of two writers from the fields of philosophy and literature, Merleau-Ponty, the modern European philosopher, and Eva Hoffman, the contemporary literary theorist and novelist. As I have discussed in Chapter Five, the themes of time and language are central in the work of both of them. Their particularly extensive analysis of the socio-historical specificity of subjectivity is highly relevant to psychoanalytic practices.

Merleau-Ponty, in *Phenomenology of Perception*, theorizes how we are embodied through and by the passage of time, including our anticipation of the future. He argues that subjectivity is always contextual and his theorizing is rooted in his challenge to Cartesian mind-body dualisms, including distinctions between "inner" and "outer", "internal" and "external". He criticizes the claims for universality in psychoanalytic theories with their failure to take into account socio-cultural and socio-historical contexts. Hoffman's (1989) autobiographical work, *Lost in Translation*, is a highly personal account of her reflections, questions, and struggles as Polish and Jewish, as a girl and a young woman, through her shifts between different cultures across decades of radical political changes.The individuality and originality of her writing emerges from the intricate interweaving of the specific temporal and cultural contexts through which she moves. Some of Hoffman's reflections reveal her engagement with psychoanalysis (as both an academic and also, later, as a patient) but her work goes further than much psychoanalytic theorizing in addressing questions of time and subjectivity. Although there are significant differences in Merleau-Ponty's and Hoffman's views on the question of the continuity of the subject's identity through time, which I address in Chapter Five, they both share an understanding of the subject as socio-historical.

*Lost in Translation* ends with the words "Time pulses through my blood like a river. The language of this is sufficient. I am here now" (Hoffman, 1989, p. 280). As well as resonating with Levinas's notion of time (see Chapter 5) these words also echo Merleau-Ponty's conception of subjectivity as temporality itself: "we must understand time as the subject and the subject as time" (Merleau-Ponty, 1945, p. 25). "Catapulted across so many generational divides, backward and forward at the same time" (Hoffman, 1989, p. 250), Hoffman is acutely sensitive to the temporal shifts in her experience between past and present time, and her ambitions for her future. Folded into her experience are the stories of the times of her parents' lives, their experiences as Jews before and after the first world war, their suffering, the enormity of their losses, their struggles to survive.

Throughout her autobiography it is evident that Hoffman's most private reflections are deeply rooted within, and shaped by the various socio-historical and, therefore, political contexts in which she lives and in which her parents lived. Writing of her childhood in post-war Poland she recalls falling asleep as a small child amidst conversations which "weave in and out", such that she has the "sense that I am immersed in a stream, and that when I wake up there will be more stuff, more talk, more life" (Hoffman, 1945, p. 56). For Hoffman, this context is not "added on" to personal experience or viewed by her simply as the "external" world. It forms the texture of her experience: "politics infiltrates daily lives in the most porous ways ... we kids pick up reverberations of half-finished political phrases like bat signals" (Hoffman, 1989, p. 57). These "reverberations" include the times of the stories of her parents' lives before her birth and, most recently, the political atmosphere of terror, killing, and flight from the holocaust. As a small child Hoffman is intent on searching the world for her mother's younger sister, who was killed in a gas chamber, in the hope of healing her mother's grief. She believes it is a "matter of honour" (Hoffman, 1989, p. 24) to remember, yet she is too young to understand what she remembers. Moreover, to relive it all with her mother is a way for her to "atone for what happened" (Hoffman, 1989, p. 24). Hoffman's father's stories eventually emerge out of the silence on which he has relied for so long for his sense of dignity. By then, his experiences, with more distance, have become "fables" (Hoffman, 1989, p. 23); it is a friend of his who reveals to Hoffman (when she is an adult) the profundity of his suffering as he carried her mother, who had had a miscarriage, on his back, trudging several kilometers through snow. This friend's account weighs on her, forcing her to acknowledge "that this—the pain of this—is where I come from, and that it's useless to get away" (Hoffman, 1989, p. 25).

Hoffman's account of how she absorbed the shifting political climate together with the stories of her parents' past (which were specific to the particular socio-historical context in which they had lived), resonates with Merleau-Ponty's theorizing of "sedimentation" (Merleau-Ponty, 1945, p. 130). He argues that, in our relations with others, we accumulate a background of shared meanings which inform our conversations without our needing to reassemble them on every occasion: they constitute a "sediment left by our mental processes, which enables us to rely on our concepts ... without there being any need for us to resynthesize them" (Merleau-Ponty, 1945, p. 130). This sediment is not, however, an inanimate layer within us, but a dynamic process, whereby every acquired meaning is revivified by a present thought.

This notion of "sedimentation" allows for the acquisition and retention of historical and cultural meanings which inform our ways of being in the world. As we have seen in Chapter Three, such meanings are, according to Jung, inherited in the form of the collective unconscious. For Merleau-Ponty these meanings are, instead, acquired through our intersubjective relationships through the languages of bodily gesture and verbal language (which may be transmitted from one generation to another through language). He argues that in listening we do not listen to a succession of words or facts, but rather follow the flow of a particular account. The story has a "style" (Merleau-Ponty, 1945, p. 133) that is accessible to the subject because h/she is able to extend him/herself beyond his immediate experience to the events recounted. This account of listening emphasises that listening is itself a form of embodiment through which "… my world is expanded to the dimensions of that collective history which my private existence takes up and carries forward" (Merleau-Ponty, 1945, p. 433). Merleau-Ponty argues that, furthermore, it is impossible to delineate "where historical forces end and ours begin … since there is history only for a subject who lives through it, and a subject only in so far as he is historically situated" (Merleau-Ponty, 1945, p. 173). In writing about class he stresses that economic systems and societies are not "impersonal forces" and that the identity of, for example, being a proletarian, arises from how we carry these institutions within ourselves and experience living within their framework (Merleau-Ponty, 1945, p. 443).

Hoffman vividly describes how she becomes embodied through her experiences of alienation as a young immigrant in Vancouver struggling to find a place in a radically different culture whose collective history she does not share. Out of time with this new culture and severed from her childhood in post-war Poland she swirls in a world where her previous "grid of mental imagery", the historical and cultural structuring of her perception which informed her previous existence, no longer has relevance. Now, in this strange country, her vision is literally blurred (Hoffman, 1989, p. 134). Her alienation is "inscribed in my flesh and face" and her shoulders are "bent with the strain of resentment and ingratiation" (Hoffman, 1989, p. 110). An older Polish woman initiates her into the exacting requirements of early 1960s' femininity in Canada: shaved underarms, plucked eyebrows, a bouffant, high-heels, lipstick and incessant smiles. Underneath this "elaborate packaging" her body is "stuff, sulky, wary" (Hoffman, 1989, p. 110). When she meets up with a Polish woman friend, after living some time in America as a young woman, her embodiment as an American is accentuated for her. Her stride is more assertive than Danuta's but her face is more controlled. Hoffman mourns the loss of its lively expressiveness which characterizes femininity in Poland. Her features and her friend's have been shaped by "different ideologies of femininity, different loci of restraint and expression (Hoffman, 1989, p. 236).

Hoffman rages at the impossibility of inhabiting Canadian English with the deftness and spontaneity she enjoys in her native Polish. The enormous cultural shift is simultaneously a temporal one: for Hoffman time stops as she desperately tries to freeze the past and resist the future: "I want to stop the flow. As a punishment, I exist in the stasis of a perpetual present, that other side of 'living in the present', which is not eternity but a prison. I can't throw a bridge between the present and the past, and therefore I can't make time move" (Hoffman, 1989, p. 117). Later on, as a young woman in New York, Kennedy's assassination highlights how, for her, not knowing the historical background makes the "foreground" harder to grasp (Hoffman, 1989, p. 190). At college she finds that aspects of her history and her present, now that she is older, do seem to converge with those of other young Americans, including her sense of "dislocation". But the historical sources of their dislocation differ from hers and her American peers consequently refuse assimilation, while her own "uprootedness" (Hoffman, 1989, p. 197) is underpinned by a longing for a sense of home.

Hoffman recognizes that she has "been written in a variety of languages" (Hoffman, 1989, p. 275) and it is an important moment when she dreams in English, discovering that words can be "a transparent medium in which I live and which lives in me" (Hoffman, 1989, p. 243). Her realization echoes Merleau-Ponty's view that, in our listening, words become "the transparent envelope of a meaning *within* which (we) might live" (Merleau-Ponty, 1945, p. 133) and not signs to be deciphered. Her descriptions challenge the dichotomies of "inner" and "outer" that permeate much of psychoanalytic theorizing. Subjectivity is, for her, intrinsically socio-cultural and socio-historical. Later on in her book she muses that it is if as though she has two unconsciouses, an American one and a Polish one. These both carry their own histories and the histories of others with whom she has been connected. This is a radical departure from notions of the unconscious as containing alinguistic or ahistorical impulses; for Hoffman the unconscious is historically and culturally constructed and this is evident throughout her descriptions of her life.

Hoffman's concept of the unconscious converges somewhat with Merleau-Ponty's. He (1960) strongly criticizes naturalistic notions of the unconscious prevalent in psychoanalysis and, drawing on Freud's later work, presents a new formulation in which "conscious" and "unconscious" are not conceptualized as such discrete realms. He questions how the unconscious can be made up of instinctual impulses if it selects what it admits to consciousness and makes us avoid thoughts or situations that we are resisting. (For Freud, the super-ego is located in both the conscious and the unconscious). Merleau-Ponty concludes that the unconscious is "*not un-knowing* but rather an un-recognized and unformulated knowing that we do not want to assume" (Merleau-Ponty, 1964, p. 229). It is this, Merleau-Ponty claims, that Freud leans towards in his later work, and he suggests that it may be better formulated as "*ambiguous perception*" (Merleau-Ponty, 1964, p. 229). A closer analysis of this concept reveals how it allows for more inclusive interpretations of the complexities of subjectivities in their conscious and unconscious aspects within particular socio-historical contexts.

Merleau-Ponty associates ambiguity with dialectic such that dualisms between, for example, inner and outer, mind and body, conscious and unconscious, are in an interdependent, rather than a contradictory or superceding relationship to one another. They may deny one another but they rely on one another for their existence. Perception, for Merleau-Ponty, is an act which gives meaning to data. As acts of ambiguous perception, dreams, humour, and mistakes are meaningful or condensed groupings of what he describes as "symbolic matrices, a language of self to self, systems of equivalences built up by the past" (Merleau-Ponty, 1960, p. 69). They are embodied, linguistic and social, and are therefore shaped by specific socio-historical and cultural contexts. Their meanings are sometimes conscious and sometimes unconscious. As Merleau-Ponty argues, we know about them to the extent we do not know about them and we do not know about them to the extent that we know about them.

Merleau-Ponty's critique of the notion of biologistic conceptions of the unconscious and his notion of ambiguous perception opens out further possibilities. If there is a dialectical shifting between conscious and unconscious experiences, this must as occur in time. The associative chains revealed through discussion of, for example, a dream may be more usefully viewed as connected horizontally back and forth across time, rather than vertically downwards into the so-called "depths" of "the unconscious" with its repressed impulses. Rather than *possessing* "an unconscious", in the form of a discreet chamber of instincts, it is our actions which possess conscious and unconscious meanings. "Conscious" and "unconscious" may thus be better used adjectively or as adverbs.

Hoffman's and Merleau-Ponty's accounts lead us in the direction of a new solution to the question posed by analysts concerned with the socio-historical and the socio-cultural, namely, how we can theorize the relation between an individual's "internal" and "external" worlds. If, instead, we focus on the individual's temporality, on *how* they live, consciously and unconsciously, amongst the temporalities of others and how they carry forward the temporalities of those that have lived before them, the socio-historical specificity of their experiences is revealed as neither "inner" nor "outer".

It is important to emphasize that if, as I argue, subjectivity is socio-historically specific, this does not mean that subjectivity is unalterably shaped, as if layer upon layer, by its socio-historically specific experiences. This fear is expressed by Hoffman when she furiously rails against the constraints of her socio-historical and cultural identities:

> How trite and tedious ... to see oneself as a creature formed by historic events and defined by sociological categories. I am a Jew, an immigrant, half-Pole, half-American ... I suffer from certain syndromes because I was fed on stories of the war ... I haven't escaped my past or my circumstances; they constrain me like a corset ... [Hoffman, 1989, p. 198]

This perspective on herself arises, in part, from what she assumes is the perception of some rich Bostonians she encounters as a student. Reading Nabokov's fiction she longs for the freedom of Nabokov's pure, aesthetic and individualistic world, "untrampled by history, or horrid intrusions of social circumstance" (Hoffman, 1989, p. 197). However, in her question as to whether it is aristocratic privilege which provides access to this world, she paradoxically acknowledges the socio-historical and cultural specificity of the possibility of such access and also assumes that it can be transcended. Hoffman concludes that "perhaps it's not possible to transcend our circumstances entirely after all" (Hoffman, 1989, p. 198).

From Hoffman's dilemma as to whether we remain defined by our histories and our cultures or whether we can transcend them, a third possibility emerges. This is not articulated explicitly by her, yet it is lived by her, from moment to moment, in its joys and its discomforts: through and between the shifts and contradictions in her identities new possibilities and new configurations arise from complex matrices of identifications which stretch back and fore in time as well as across places. In the vulnerability of being an "outsider" she fights fiercely against the possibility of subjection to the dominant (American) culture. She moves between the voices of her Polish past, including her parents' creativity in their deter-mination to escape from the Holocaust, her adolescence in Canada, and her new life, beginning as a student, in America. It is the inter-weaving of these different and sometimes conflictual voices across time, as well as place, which produces a critical questioning and is the source of Hoffman's individuality, and originality, not impedi-ments to it.

Said recognizes the creativity that can emerge from exile: "Exiles cross borders, break barriers of thought and experience" (Said, 2000, p. 185). Movement from one culture to another does not involve only a spatial shift; it is also temporal. He emphasizes, as Hoffman's work so vividly conveys, that every experience in the new culture "occur(s) against" the memories of those in the previous culture (Said, 2003, p. 8). What is recalled of the past and how it is remem-bered also shape the individual's perception of the future. This is not, as Said and Foucault (1969) emphasize, to assume that identities are continuous through time. Hoffman is, for example, explicit as to how the journey from Poland to Canada marks the end of "the narrative" of her childhood (Hoffman, 1989, p. 95). Foucault, Said, and Hoffman all highlight the importance of gaps, discontinuities, and contradictions in allowing potential for new thoughts and the emergence of resistances to a dominant order. Their theorizing offers a solution to the question posed by Samuels (see above), namley how to "negotiate a tension between respect for historical specificity and context on the one hand and the limitless, playful vitality of imagi-nation and fantasy on the other" (Samuels, 1993, p. 339). Hoffman's autobiographical work implicitly cuts through this split, revealing it as being, itself, a cultural-historical construct.

In the analyst's awareness of the socio-historical as intrinsic to our conscious and unconscious experience there is, implicit in this, an orientation to the possibility of change: every moment produces a new context for a different possibility of experience. This is vividly illustrated through a comparison between two possible interpretations of a dream reported by Elsa, aged fifty and born in the mid-1950s:

> My mother is serving food that I have prepared, substituting a particularly important dish of mine with one she has cooked. I become enraged and lose my temper, screaming at her that her breasts are hoovering up everything in sight.

For Elsa her dream encapsulated in an almost surreal way her experience of 1950s mothering. The cost to her individuality was enormous, she felt; her mother's "care" could not nurture; it imposed on her, and as the dream indicated, denied her own creativity and seemed to suck her very existence out of her. Elsa recalled the power of her mother's large and heavy vacuum cleaner which generated so much noise that, as a child, she felt she could not be heard. Although I did not comment explicitly on the historical period, I think that my orientation to the atmosphere and values of that particular time increased my sensitivity to Elsa's particular experience.

I was also attuned to the dream as containing a reminder for Elsa of the importance of her own creativity, symbolized by the various dishes she herself has cooked. In her fury she fights for this creativity which, unconsciously, she *is* able to value. These interpretations, arising from a phenomenological psychoanalytic perspective, encompass both the socio-historically specific restraints on Elsa's individuality which dated back to her childhood and also her capacity for creativity within her present life. They contrast radically from interpretations which assume the existence of an unconscious containing timeless instincts.

A Kleinian interpretation would, for example, tend to view Elsa's dream primarily as an expression of the patient's aggressive instincts; for example, her envy is projected on to the breast, producing schizoid anxiety and infantile rage in the face of the fantasized potential annihilation. Such an interpretation denies the temporal (envy is universal and ahistorical, according to Klein) and, furthermore, fails to address the specificity and complexity of this particular patient's experience of her own mother at a particular historical time. It also does not recognize the possibility of future developments of her creativity.

## Conclusion

The interpretations which arose in the discussion about the dream, between the patient and her analyst, exemplify clearly how an acknowledgement of the socio-historical aspects of temporality can contribute to a richer and more complex understanding of an individual's experiences. This should not be reduced to a "collapse into sociology" (an accusation leveled at one therapist by her supervisor when she wanted to discuss a black patient's experiences of racism), or assumed to be merely generalizing. As Hoffman's autobiography so vividly conveys, a recognition of socio-historicity, in contrast, individualizes the experiences that are brought to the psychoanalytic relationship.

I have highlighted how the familial constellations in which individuals grow up are shaped by specific socio-historical contexts and cannot be adequately theorized in terms of Oedipal (or pre-Oedipal) dynamics. Reductive interpretations of this type which are generalizing and do not address the uniqueness of the positions within which individuals recurrently discover themselves, amongst matrices of criss-crossing identifications stretching back to the past and forward into the future.

Psychoanalytic attunement to the socio-historical requires an acknowledgement of difference and of change. This orientation in the analyst's relationship with the patient is vital for the emergence of new possibilities of being in the individual's life. In contrast to notions of "instincts" as raw, alinguistic impulses or of the universality of the "archetypes", it allows for multiple meanings of experience which shift as they are perceived from within different temporal contexts.

# CHAPTER SEVEN

# States of time

> *"Time travels in divers paces with divers persons. I'll tell you
> who Time ambles withal, who Time trots withal, who Time gallops
> withal and who it stands still withal"* (Shakespeare, *As You Like
> It*, Act 111, Scene 2).

This chapter aims to explore a diversity of individuals' ways
of living time and their articulations of these. I highlight
the importance of an attentiveness to these in psychoanalytic practices. In line with my challenge to the universalizing positions in some psychoanalytic theorizing, I do not claim that specific
temporal states *always* coincide with particular forms of distress.
My case illustrations demonstrate that attempts at such a correlation would be inadequate and unuseful. Through reflecting on
individuals' experiences from a phenomenological perspective, I
emphasize instead the uniqueness and complexities of individuals'
lived experiences of time. I aim to raise questions as to what *might*
be revealed if we consider the temporal aspects of any particular
experience and how an attention to these might usefully extend
psychoanalytic perspectives in theorizing and practice. It is important to emphasize that when I indicate that there are shifts in an
individual's experience of time in their analysis I am not implying

that my relationships with them are underpinned by any linear notions of change and progress.

Throughout the book I have referred to phenomenological theorizing in relation to time and historicity, language, embodiment, and the unconscious (see, in particular, Chapters Five and Six). As has been evident, my psychoanalytic perspective is strongly influenced by my reading of phenomenological texts (see also Ellis, 2000 and 2005), in particular those of Merleau-Ponty. It is important at this point to briefly reiterate and highlight those aspects which are particularly relevant to psychoanalytic practices and which, together with psychoanalytic theorizing, informed many of my responses to the patients whose struggles I describe below.

As a philosophical method, phenomenology was founded by the German philosopher, Husserl (1859–1938), a student of Franz Brentano's in Vienna, who also taught Freud. It aims to investigate phenomena as they appear in human consciousness. Its primary emphasis is on attending to the specificity of our *descriptions* of states of being rather than explanations of experience in terms of causes. Phenomenologists are concerned with the everyday world of human existence, with descriptions of states of being in relation to oneself and to others, such as anxiety, the anticipation of death, love, desire and sexuality. These are, of course, themes that arise throughout psychoanalytic work with individuals.

Phenomenologists challenge the Cartesian dualisms of mind and body, subject and object which permeate Western culture. As Merleau-Ponty elucidates, we *are* our bodies and they are neither simply subjects nor objects, they are "our general medium for having a world" (Merleau-Ponty, 1945, p. 146). Phenomenologists view the meanings of experiences as crucial. They argue against the idea that we can possess a complete understanding of our own origins since, from birth, we are thrown into an already constituted world of language, of family constellations, and our culture. This contrasts with Freud's emphasis on the analyst acquiring a "complete" picture of everything the patient has repressed (check Freud, 1937d, p. 258). A phenomenological perspective holds that such understanding is always only partial and disclosure of existence always depends on the context. This context is always intersubjective and linguistic (verbally and non-verbally). We are always already in a world of others, whether in the presence or absence of them. Attention to the specificity of individuals' conscious and unconscious languages in their descriptions of their worlds is crucial to a phenomenological approach.

As I have emphasized (see Chapters Five and Six), phenomenologists emphasize the temporality of the human subject. For example, Needleman stresses that "it is just as significant that the patient experiences time-sequence in the manner he does as it is significant that he hates his father" (Needleman, 1967, p. 30). Merleau-Ponty's (1945) interpretation of a child's jealousy of his younger sibling emphasizes that a particular temporal structure might be integral to an emotion itself. The child, in his jealousy, suffers from a fixed notion of himself as the only child. According to Merleau-Ponty, overcoming such jealousy involves an acquiescence to the temporal schema of past-present-future, namely that the child has *been* the youngest, but *is* no longer the youngest and that s/he *will become* the biggest. Minkowski (1923), in his phenomenological analysis of a patient who had been diagnosed as schizophrenic goes further by prioritizing the subject's relation to time; it is *fundamental* to the structuring of her/his world. He claims that his patient's delusional fears of execution had arisen *because of* his having a distorted attitude to the future (see further discussion of this below).

Through the case studies in this chapter I emphasize the variability of an individual's conscious and unconscious temporal experiences: they shift in importance and are articulated in a multiplicity of ways, verbally and non-verbally. Such experiences may be the source of, or arise from, a particular delusional structure. Sometimes it may be helpful for the analyst to address the patient's experienced temporality directly, at other times it is sufficient for them to be sensitive to its significance as a context for, or within a context of, other experiences. Temporality may appear to be more or less important than other aspects of what is being communicated to the analyst, but it is, nevertheless, intrinsic to all of our actions and modes of being in the world.

### Time's urgency

#### Colin

Colin began his analysis complaining that his body was breaking down; he was undergoing medical tests for neurological diseases, he was terrified, exhausted, and was on extended sick leave from his work as a part-time community worker in a very deprived urban area. Colin's wife had a demanding full-time job in management and he was primarily responsible for the care of their two sons, now aged three and five. His anxiety was palpable from the moment he arrived at his first session. He believed he was going to die and was terrified of the possible consequences for his family if this was to happen.

In Binswanger's terms Colin was overwhelmed by a world-design of urgency. His whole being, including his speech, conveyed this urgency in relation to time. There was barely time for him to breathe; he spoke fast without ever fully drawing his breath. He spoke particularly about his anxieties about his children, his fears of not doing enough for them and what that might mean for their futures, psychologically and educationally. It was as if their survival was under threat and time might "run out" if he did not respond instantly to their every demand.

A crucial association between Colin's lived experience of time as urgent and the death of his mother when he was aged twelve (and an only child) emerged. She had died falling over a cliff-edge in mist. Colin and his father had been running after her as she walked ahead of them, calling her to slow down and to watch out for the edge. They had been too late; time had "run out" and she had not heard their warnings. For Colin, his "lived experience of time" was of a present consumed by his terror of the death of another in the future, a death for which he would be primarily responsible. He was working himself to death to avoid the death of others and, more difficult to admit to consciousness, his own death. Later, he admitted that his own death might also signify the possibility of relief from his frantic drivenness.

Colin remembered his mother (who was a full-time mother) as lively and affectionate, although sometimes irritable. An atmosphere of loss and confinement surrounded his father. He was from a working class background and financial problems in his family had meant that he was unable to go on to study music for which he had had a passion. Instead, he opted to become an electrician. He had been previously married but his wife had died of cancer early in the marriage. His hopes for the future were thus constantly disappointed and this was confirmed for him by the loss of his second wife, Colin's mother. As his therapy continued Colin connected his inability to develop more professionally with his identification with his father's losses and the closures on his future.

For Colin, his world was one of relentless, and anxious effort against a background of extreme urgency. However much energy and commitment he put into anything, he felt he was achieving nothing. The future as possibility was screened from him by the immediacy of his endless activity and however much he did, there was no guarantee that he could ensure his children's survival. Instead it (the future) threatened to take everything from him in a way that he could never fully anticipate. The speed of his breathless speech and the contortions in his body spoke his anxiety more than any of his words. It was as if even taking a breath for himself might take the time he owed primarily to others. In the transference I was a further demand and he often missed sessions. When he came it was because I seemed to want him to, but he resented seeing me as it took him away from his responsibilities to others.

My attunement to the language of Colin's embodiment was crucial. It was a surprise and a relief to him when I pointed out that he seemed unable to take the time to draw breath in our sessions. He had not been aware of it. I also reflected on whether the constraints of his breathing may have been producing physiological effects: all of his medical tests were presenting negative results, yet his pains were continuing. As Colin gradually allowed himself to take time and to receive my attention and my interpretations, his breathing slowed and his body began to unfold from its pain and contortion. A lessening of his driven urgency was revealed in his feeling, several days after taking his youngest son for a medical test and now awaiting the results, "it can wait". He was beginning to develop the capacity to wait and for things to take their own time.

In my work with Colin, my attentiveness to his experience of time as conveyed in the specificity of his language, verbal and non-verbal, was crucial in my response to his interpretations. Merleau-Ponty's view of the subject as embodied and of temporality as being integral to this (see Chapters Five and Six) was particularly valuable in enabling me to attend to the language of Colin's embodiment and its articulation of urgency in relation to time and, especially, to the future. Minkowski's position (see above) raises the question as to whether Colin's anxiety in relation to responsibility and the death of others had arisen because of a distorted relation to the future or whether his concerns had created a problematic relation to the future. My experience of working with Colin, however, suggests that this may be a false dichotomy; for Colin, certainly, these were integral to one another. I think it is more useful to think of Colin as being placed/placing himself within a relational matrix or network of linguistic connections stretching forwards and backwards through the times of his life, and horizontally towards the times of others in the present, in which a notion of the future is produced as an atmosphere, that of promised, yet uncertain death, and the guilt associated with it. This is not to underemphasize the importance of gaps and ruptures within this network of meanings, but to emphasize that, notwithstanding his loss, Colin was in a "speaking present".

Heidegger (1927) differentiates fear from anxiety arguing that fear is the fear of something definite and known about and that anxiety involves the threat of what is indefinite and unknown. Our anxiety is anxiety about our "Being-in-the-World" (See Chapter Five for more discussion of his analysis of time and being). Anxiety is grounded in our "having-been", taking Dasein back from its worldly possibilities to a realization of one's authentic and individual "Being-towards-death" (Heidegger, 1927, p. 310). Through this the present and the future are temporalized. For Heidegger anxiety is thus fundamental to the possibility of authentic being; death is certain but we cannot be definite about when. In my view, Heidegger (Heidegger, 1927, p. 233) is addressing one particular form of anxiety and his account of it as a sense of the "uncanny" or "unheimlich" does not address the intensity of Colin's particular anxiety which was filled with urgency. However, his description nevertheless opens out the possibility that a strong aspect of Colin's anxiety concerned his flight from his own individuality of which he felt utterly undeserving. This was certainly connected to the death of his mother (to which we often returned) and to his father's losses, although not, I would argue "caused" by them. It was vital that in my work with him I was sensitive to any glimpses of possibilities of pleasure or creativity that emerged, often unconsciously, in our conversations and attentive to how dangerous he perceived these to be.

*Endless time*

States designated as obsessional in psychoanalytic theorizing have tended to be interpreted as having their source in, for example, fixation at the anal stage (Freud), the effacing of pleasure so as to avoid the anger of the "master" (Lacan), and intolerable guilt (Winnicott). These accounts do not sufficiently recognize the range of forms of obsessional ways of being and their specific meanings for each individual. They also do not include a sufficient analysis of the temporal intricacies of these states. Binswanger draws on the psychoanalytic notion of anality to exemplify his existential critique of the causal and biologistic interpretations of Freud's account, arguing that "no world can be constructed from sensations and urges" (Binswanger, 1945, p. 319). Anality may be one form of filling emptiness; however, it is neither the reason for, nor the cause of, an experience such as his patient's (Ellen West) of the world as a hole or a grave. In the vignettes below I reflect on a diversity of states referred to as "obsessional" or "compulsive" by the individuals themselves or which would be interpreted as such in classical psychoanalytic theorizing. As I emphasize above, I am not claiming that the temporal aspects are necessarily as or more significant than other aspects but, rather, that to disregard them limits our understanding of the possible meanings of the experiences.

*Jack*

Jack had come for analysis initially because of his concerns about his drug and alcohol consumption. He would describe evenings out with friends, having a drink or taking drugs, and wanting to prolong the effects endlessly, meticulously calculating how to make sure he would reach off-licences on the way home to his house after his night out. Gaps were unbearable: "I hate waiting for anything", Jack said. He would plan his holiday in endless detail, "totally obsessed with it" (in his words). As soon as he was away, he would be planning for what he would do the minute it was over. "I am not like everyone else who feels that they *have* time, I don't know what that means". The existential psychoanalyst, Boss, drawing on Husserl and Merleau-Ponty, offers an interpretation of "having time" which is relevant here. He stresses that no-one ever "has" time in the sense of being able to possess "it" as an object, rather, *"Any time I "have", I have in such a way that I am expectant of that which is to come, aware of what is present, and retentive of what has been"* (Boss, 1979, p. 99). In wanting to ensure that time was endless and developing compulsive strategies of preserving it for the future, Jack cut himself off from both his present and his past and deprived himself of the sense of extended time through which his activities might become meaningful in more creative ways.

*Elaine*

The struggle for the possibility of having time in the way Boss describes was a crucial aspect of Elaine's analysts work (Ellis, 2000). Her relation to time and mortality was articulated both through relentless work and through the pain of her embodiment. Elaine was a mixed-race woman, the only child of a black Afro-Caribbean father and a white mother. She had been persuaded to seek psychotherapy by her gynecologist who had been unable, for two years, to diagnose or cure a soreness in her vaginal area. Elaine spoke of never being able to set limits, of feeling a "huge hole" inside her, of working endlessly, and feeling interminably responsible for the deprivation of her clients (she was a social worker). She felt drained and desperate, believing that her soreness was her fault (for not looking after herself) and that everything was her fault. Elaine also described herself as being "the sort of person who wants everything yesterday" and this became explicit in the transference in the enormity of her demand on me. In her sexual relationship with her partner, which she described as addictive, she craved completion.

It seemed as if, in its "furious" redness, Elaine's soreness stood for that which makes perfection impossible, namely the limitations of humanness, particularly mortality, against which she unconsciously raged. In her relationships with her partner she insisted that she washed her hands before touching her, that the kitchen surfaces were spotless. She began to realize that her desire for perfection in part mirrored her father's with his rigid belief in his own rightness and in absolutes. Her father had been desperately anxious for her to succeed where he had not as a black immigrant in the racist atmosphere of 1950s Britain. Her father's control, while frustrating, promised the possibility of certainty, contrasting with Elaine's experience of her mother as anxious and fragile. Elaine's experiences of racism had also contributed strongly to her belief that everything was her "fault". It was crucial to Elaine that I acknowledge the significance of both her own, and her father's, experiences of racism in her life. Her distress was specific to the socio-historical context in which she was raised.

For Elaine her analysis felt endless. In one session she spoke of two dreams in which she was told she had cancer and then wondered aloud how I could have the patience to listen to this for so long but "perhaps it reflects that I can't, it seems endless". I reflected on how perhaps it was exaclty endlessness that she was caught up with and how much she feared loss if anything was to end. It seemed that the dreams were calling on her to attend to her unbearable mortality.

In an important dream Elaine dreamt of having a watchstrap of silver birch bark which, she then noticed, was actually made of evergreen leaves. Delighted, she reached out to hide her actual watch under her pillow (which she discovered in the morning). Elaine associated the silver birch with a childhood song about a busy beaver, which I connected with her compulsive absorption in her work. Elaine linked placing the watch under her pillow to the visits of the tooth fairy who always left her a coin, in her childhood. For her, losing her childhood teeth signified getting older, gaining maturity. Elaine then went on to reflect on the question of how losses are necessary for change. In giving up her desire for immortality (the evergreen leaves) to the tooth fairy, she was given something in exchange, the coin which she could spend in any way she wanted. The tooth fairy appeared to symbolize the possibility of encouragement for and acknowledgement of maturity and change and the development of her individuality, countering the severity of her father's control and also her own experiences of racism. She (the tooth fairy) was also, I reflected, connected to myself in the transference.

Gradually, through our work, Elaine risked more spontaneity with me and this coincided with her attending a Latin-American dance class with her lover. At first she had felt awkward and "out of time" but suddenly she had felt an enormous shift, feeling herself carried "in time" to the music with her partner. She was amazed at the individuality of all of the dancers despite dancing to the same music. Elaine had been finding a way to be "in time" in which she felt comfortable in her own separateness and difference. Furthermore, this being in time allowed for endings and mortality. When our work ended she gave me a gift of flowers *because* they do not last, saying from our work, she could now allow for and enjoy what was temporary.

## The times of depressions

In my experience, conscious and explicit references to experiences of time appear most often in individuals' descriptions of their depression. This may be specific to the socio-historical context of the West in which time, contemporaneously, is equated with pressure to achieve. The differences in the lived times of different cultures, historically and geographically, is considered by Hoffman. She describes the slow time of her childhood in post-war Poland and the possibility of having free time without guilt. She contrasts this with the "compressed, speeded up" (Hoffman, 2004, p. 60) time of nineteen-seventies America in which people were compelled to produce and to fulfill ambitions, a mode which is still operative in the West. The guilt at having time which cannot be used productively may therefore be highlighted in depression, particularly where themes of guilt and responsibility are accentuated. However, although time may be a common theme in the narratives of people who are feeling depressed, it nevertheless appears in individuals' language in multifarious ways and through a range of metaphors. These vignettes highlight how diverse these experiences are.

*Sarah*

In one session Sarah, who had sought analysis at a time of intense depression, described how the time of her childhood had felt "awfully long". She felt she had always been waiting and that time had never been her own. Her mother, she said, had been "ruled by time" so that lunch, for example, would appear at one o'clock "whether you were hungry or not". Most poignant was her waiting from the age of nine onwards for her mother's return. Her mother had left the family suddenly and had been unable to contact Sarah or her sister until many years later. Sarah described the huge frustration she feels now if she ever has to wait for anything, saying that "time feels awfully long if you are an adult in pain". She often ate at home in her flat to fill this time and to distract herself from her depression and would then feel disgusted with herself. Through our conversation it emerged that these feelings of self-disgust echoed her disgust at her own vulnerability, particularly in relation to the loss of her mother. It had, she said, felt evident to her that her father was experiencing a much greater sense of loss when her mother left (he became very depressed) and needed her, as the older daughter, to be strong. Time that was unstructured had become for Sarah the time of waiting, rather than time that could be used for herself productively. It is significant that in her next session she said she had begun to give

herself time to think about what she might want to do. She had gone
out on her own to have a coffee and a cake, and was surprised at not
having felt lonely doing this.

Sarah's waiting is the opposite of the "awaiting" of anticipation
and expectancy described by Heidegger (1927, p. 386). It is characterized by passivity and the impossibility of agency through which
something can be altered (her mother's absence, for example).
Mann's account of waiting is particularly relevant here: in waiting,
time and the present moment are regarded "not as a boon, but an
obstruction" (Mann, 1924, p. 239). He equates waiting with a greed
in which "the digestive apparatus works through quantities of food
without converting it into anything of vaue or nourishment to (the)
system" (Mann, 1924, p. 239). Waiting is both long and short since it
"consumes whole spaces of time without our living them or making
any use of them" (Mann, 1924, p. 239). The "awfully long" time spent
waiting had also, paradoxically disappeared for Sarah.

*Karen*

Karen's depression took the form of wishing her life away and this
included her analysis. She felt that she never lived in the present:
she was constantly regretting decisions that she had made in the
past and often worried about the future. She was anxious about
what would happen after her course of study ended, whether she
or her parents might die and she might be left alone. It seemed that
her fantasizing about death served as a way to avoid the present as
possibility, opening out the newness of the future. She described the
present as "nothing", and said that she "circled around its edges, the
past and the future, in order to 'have control' ". In response to my
comment that it sounded as if the present was like a hole she might
fall into, Karen talked about the unpredictability of the present; she
felt impinged on by its demands and she could not take it up for
herself. It emerged that her fear of the present was, in part, related to
her difficulty in managing the negative aspects of her feelings which
threatened to be explosive and destructive to others. Circling around
the edges of the present she sought to contain them.

Karen's relation to the future was not one of waiting as Sarah's
was, but they both share a passivity in their relation to it. Sarah passively hopes the future itself will bring change and feels frustrated at
the impossibility of this occurring in the way she that she longs for.

Karen feels passive in relation to her creative resources for changing the present. She lacks belief in the sustainability of her volition which she experiences as threatened by "unpredictability" and her ambivalence.

### Margaret

Margaret's present, with its overwhelming depressions interspersed with terrifying panic attacks and claustrophobic and agoraphobic feelings, was lived in the shadow of death: "all the time I am alive, I am thinking about death". She did not just fear death ahead sometime in the future; death was certain and very imminent, and she was terrified. Margaret was surprised and appreciative when I commented on how often she referred to death since she said this had not been acknowledged in her previous years of therapy with someone else. She spoke of a fantasy of a body which was her own that was "clinically dead, yet alive inside", wanting to live. Sometimes the image seemed to symbolize her wish to break out of her immersion in death, at other times it symbolized her hope of immortality. This was reminiscent of Laing's notion of "death-in-life" in order that "one cannot die, and one cannot kill" (Laing, 1959, p. 176).

Margaret was from a working-class Catholic background and, in the early part of her therapy, she spoke often of God. Rarely appearing in the form of goodness, God was to be feared as he watched the devil take grip of her in his long claws, laughing. Various images of her parents appeared as she spoke. Identifying with each of them—an agoraphobic mother and an asthmatic father—Margaret was furious at their inability to parent her as a child. In drunken rages her father threatened to kill her; in the next moment he would be gasping asthmatically and Margaret had to run to find a doctor for him. Her mother was absent to her, locked in her phobias and depression. Margaret felt abandoned to a confusing world, a "house of horror" in her words. In the early years of her therapy with me my holiday breaks were intolerable to Margaret. She was explicit about her anger at my neglect of her, abandoning her to the "blackest depression" or the worst anxiety she had ever experienced.

When I directly addressed the fury involved in these panic attacks and her relentless search for a mothering which kept proving to be an impossibility, Margaret said that she had been thinking about this; it was not what she really wanted, it was the idea of it. Some weeks later she began to talk of finding her "own resources", of beginning to do some voluntary work (she had been unemployed for many years). However, she complained of feeling thrown by me into the huge task of getting on with her life: it was like, she conveyed through a dream, being faced with a man with a gun, the devil. To live was to kill or be killed. Thoughts of evil and murder surfaced. In a taxi she had almost told the driver that she had seen a murder (which she had not); putting her coat on to come to therapy she had thought "I'll kill Mary"; her miscarriage many years back confirmed for her that she was a killer, as did her fantasies of strangling her daughter when she was small. She felt she really wanted to kill her parents. Margaret's fantasies of killing did not evoke anxiety in me; instead I was greatly moved by the extent of her terror and the despair in her depression.

In fantasy Margaret wanted to kill whoever disappointed her and prevented her from finding totality. To be out of control, subject to anyone's authority (such as a manager or a teacher), threatened her with her life. Everything that was unknown or unexpected was equated with death; in her search for an absolute mothering she sought refuge from its threat. It was an important moment when she knew, in response to a woman friend's wish to look after her, that this woman would fail. She felt very sad about this and experienced a sense of loss, as she was gradually relinquishing her belief that there was someone who could protect her from everything. Moreover, she realized that if this fantasy could have been realized, she would have felt "powerless and confined".

This realization marked a shift in Margaret's life which was to lead her, several years later, to taking up a very powerful pastoral role in a voluntary organization and to performjng in an amateur dramatic company. As Margaret herself acknowledged at the beginning of our work, it was important that I directly addressed her relation to her mortality in its different meanings. She lived time as either already dead or on the point of death. Her terror of the unknownness of the future deprived her of a present in which she could experiment with the expression of her many unlived intellectual and creative abilities.

## The threat of the other's time

In his forty-six years Kevin had never worn a watch and he was stubborn in his refusal to submit to others' time. Railing against his age he dressed impeccably in the style of a challenging twenty year old: every garment was "up-to-the-minute", as he put it. Kevin was from a Northern working-class family and was the second youngest of seven children. There were nine years between himself and the youngest child, a sister, whom, he said, he had always hated (and had now lost touch with), and for whom he was expected to be responsible ("I had no parents and I was supposed to parent her", he would say). His mother had been extremely depressed after his, and also his sister's birth. She had tried several times to leave Kevin's father, sometimes with, and sometimes without the children. Kevin's father had had a "breakdown" when Kevin was two; he remembered his "dark depressions" and also admiring his father's physical strength. He often criticized his mother for her "selfishness" and her rules and he felt that he could never trust her.

The possibility of my "inconsistency" was terrifying to Kevin and he tried to ward this off in every possible way. At times he was menacing and, in the counter-transference, I felt transfixed and as if any "wrong step" would take me into a landmine. At these times interpretations in relation to his transferences to me were intolerable (and unhelpful); the effect on Kevin was that he had to fight for his life. It was too dangerous for him to admit that he had a relationship with me as this, he said, gave me power over him. Furthermore, it seemed to me that it represented my imposition of my temporality over his; the link between his past and the present were humiliating to him. He demanded that I give him my holiday dates months in advance so as to ensure he could go away too. This was not only to save paying fees if he was away when I was working, but also as a way of asserting his independence, and often he would miss sessions before breaks. Kevin was always meticulously on time for sessions however, despite not having a watch. This seemed to ensure that he could not be criticized for breaking an agreement. My holiday breaks were, by contrast, interpreted by him as a breach of our contract; my temporality was intruding on his.

From the beginning of our work together any small changes in my consulting room were experienced by him as an imposition and his anxiety was voiced in furious rage. Despite Kevin's fear of change, the unbearability of the present could also drive him to the verge of violence and he fantasised about stabbing anyone who might get in the way of whatever he needed to distract him from his terrifying anxiety (he had been involved with some serious fights in pubs when he was younger). At times I felt fearful of my own physical safety. When I said to him it seemed as if he was trapped in the present, he experienced this acknowledgement of his "state" as a relief. Later on in his analysis he was increasingly able to recognize that an experience would pass. However, this often took the form of "getting (something) over with" or "getting rid of" someone, such as a dentist, as soon as his treatment was over. Kevin had to be the agent of change; others' temporalities threatened him profoundly. He was explicit about his anger with his mother, conveying how from his birth she could never be relied on. Kevin had been trapped in the vicissitudes of her temporality and never put first.

Kevin would say "I want everything and I want it immediately". He particularly wanted money and status and resented that he had to work for this. Most of all, he wanted to be loved. He hated having to think of the consequences of his actions in the future, but he did care about the consequences of not getting what he wanted and calculated carefully as to how he could get what he needed, without risking loss of the others' love. Kevin was contemptuous of others' passivity: it reminded him of the unavoidable passivity that is integral to humanness: being mortal and being vulnerable to suffering. Kevin was eternally vigilant; he could never allow himself the passivity of sleep. When he felt vulnerable to me he would drift into a repetitive fantasy of running round and round a sports field, perhaps in an identification with his father which reassured him of his strength. Kevin was triumphant each time he felt he had won a battle: his idealization of his aggression protected from his unconscious experience of extreme vulnerablity to others' rules, their time. His search for a diagnosis was also rooted in his thirst for omnipotence and, from time to time he, would make an appointment with a psychiatrist in order to determine what his problem was. It seemed that if he could have undisputable scientific knowledge about himself, he would be more in control. He could research it and predict its course, which he could not do with our psychoanalytic relationship.

As I have highlighted, a crucial aspect of Kevin's analysis was the question as to whether two subjects with their own different temporalities could exist without one consuming the other. Winnicott's (see Chapter Four) theorizing of the importance of "holding" in the spatial sense (as "containing") and in a temporal sense (enabling the continuity of the infant's self through time) is relevant to Kevin's experience. His parents' inconsistency had been, and continued to be, a source of endless anxiety for him. In response he tried, as some theories of "narcissistic" states describe, to omnipotently "freeze" time (Boschan, 1990, p. 343). Levinas's accounts of the Other's time as necessarily disrupting one's own (see Chapter Five) contributes further to a more extensive understanding of the intersubjectivity of Kevin's temporality and my own. The Other (the analyst) in his/her difference opens out the future and intrinsically exposes the subject to uncertainty. For Kevin every movement of mine that was unexpected threatened to throw him violently into the unknown of the future. The moments when he could enjoy the surprise of my difference, however, were profoundly moving, as was his ability to express gratitude to me for these.

### Time and psychosis

The specificity of a psychotic person's spatial relationships, and their experience of a body that is disintegrating or fragmented, and confused with the bodies of others, has been documented and discussed extensively (see, for example, Laing 1959, Sass 1992 and 1994, Roustang 1976). Sass's (1992) analysis specifically includes an exploration of the relation between spatial and temporal experiences in psychosis, highlighting how spatial experiences subsume temporal ones: the use of spatial adverbs such as "where" replace chronological adverbs such as "when". Sass (1992) extends his analysis of psychosis in individuals to an exploration of the socio-historical relation between schizophrenia and Western modernism. He argues that traits attributed to schizophrenia (emotional detachment, extreme introversion, lack of spontaneity, extreme abstraction, deliberation and fragile self-esteem) appear to correspond with an increasing socio-historical and socio-cultural emphasis on individualism, self-reflection, and detachment. Hesitant to attribute a direct etiological link to this, Sass suggests that the latter provide "prerequisites" (Sass, 1992, p. 369) for schizoid and schizophrenic tendencies and that a schizophrenic individual exists in a dialectical relation to modernity "not just as a product of but also as a reaction against the prevailing social order" (Sass, 1992, p. 372).

In this section I focus specifically on one individual's lived experience of psychosis in its temporal aspects. I consider both the limitations of MInkowski's account and also the more extensive contribution of Roustang (1976) with his emphasis on the time of the parents as the foreclosed "other" in psychotic experience.

Minkowski's clinical work with an individual patient suffering from a depressive psychosis leads him to conclude a distorted relation to temporality leads to the development of psychotic delusions; they arise as logical explanations for the individual's more fundamental relation to the future as "blocked" and of "time and living disintegrating" (Minkowski, 1923, p. 134). Minkowski describes how his patient lived every day with the certainty, communicated to him everywhere, whether in the form of small pieces of rubbish on the street or crumbs left on a table, of being tortured and killed that night as a punishment for his crimes. Minkowski focuses on the question of why, despite the expected punishment never being meted, the patient continued to believe day after day, that it would arrive. It was if neither his present nor his past experiences bore any relation to his future. Each day was an isolate, and the same as every other, and his future was blocked. Minkowski contasts this perception of the future with our more usual one which is open to its possibilities, allowing for desires and actions, despite our awareness of our mortality.

The problem with Minkowski's position is that he does not explain sufficiently how or why the patient's fundamental relation to the future may have arisen. He (Minkowski, 1923, p. 137) describes it in terms of the modification of the "natural phenomenon" of the orientation of our desires towards the future. His account does not adequately address the specificity of the patient's fears of being punished and executed which, interestingly, he believes everyone, *except his family*, knew about. Furthermore, Minkowski's account assumes a subjectivity in the individual who is psychotic which more recent theorizing (Roustang, 1976, see below) questions. This is underlined in his description of his patient's attempt to express the problem of his relation to the future "by *borrowing* thoughts from his former life and, thus, ends by expressing delusional material" (Minkowski, 1923, p. 137, my italics). In the discussion which follows I show how an individual's psychosis may occur as a response to his fears of the future but it is also interconnected with his experience of living an "expropriation" (Roustang, 1976) of his subjectivity.

## John

John had consulted me for an initial session a few days before his psychosis began. This was shortly after abruptly ending a very extensive period of analysis during which he had had a number of psychotic crises. John told me that he had been taken with a statement, which he attributed to R. D. Laing, that "you can show people the door of their cage and all they want to do is wonder how they got in there". He no longer wanted to continue reflecting on the past experiences which made him feel so "stuck". I suggested that perhaps what might be more relevant to him was the question of what he feared about leaving the cage. In this session John described his fears of being judged by several people he knew. A few days after this initial session, John was admitted to hospital in an acute psychosis. I spoke to him on a weekly basis during his stay, either on the phone, or visiting him.

A strong aspect of John's psychosis involved his fears of being the devil and of being killed for his evil. This killing was both a punishment and a "sacrifice"; if he was killed, the world would then be "alright". He felt, however, "too much of a coward" for this but, whatever plan he tried to make, others were always a step ahead of him. He was particularly frightened that his older sister would kill him. John thought too that if he killed himself it would be better for everyone else: "If I get better I will make things worse for everyone else". He said that the devil liked "devilry, sexual practices, and smoking"; the smoking "murdered people". On another occasion he said to me that he was afraid of caring about people: if he did not care he was "protected from punishment, remembering, hurting". John said that he only cared about himself, his sadism and his sexual thrills and then pleaded with me to help him not to forget the damage he had done to people. At many times during his psychosis he asked me to remember for him that he had hurt people and said that he feared getting better because he would once again forget his problems. On John's recovery from his psychosis he told me that he had very much appreciated my introducing the question of what might prevent a person from leaving a cage. He could not remember whether I had said that to him before he had been in hospital or while he was there. The other important thing John he told me that I had said during his psychosis was that even if he was evil, why could we nevertheless not have a conversation. He had felt met "head-on".

John's shifting modes of temporality are interesting to reflect on in the light of Minkowski's claim. My comment in the first session, regarding the risks of leaving the cage, resonated with John's own hesitation and fears about the future. Minkowski would have interpreted John's subsequent delusional thoughts regarding punishment and death as explanations for his perception of the future as cut across. This does not, however, sufficiently address the origins of John's perception or the specific content of his delusions (regarded by Minkowski as thoughts borrowed from the patient's earlier life).

Freud's (1937d) theorizing of psychotic delusions has some similarity with Minkowski's. He claims that they are constructions which replace a fragment of reality which has been repudiated in the present with a fragment that has already been repudiated in the remote past. However, it conveys more strongly the passivity and lack of subjectivity which is integral to psychotic experiences. It seems that the intolerable fragment of reality for John was the reality of the future as signifying change and possibility. His belief that he would be punished for his crimes, which he now felt acutely in the present, could be seen as a "fragment of the past" which acts as a kind of patch, covering over his present reality.

The French psychoanalyst Roustang's interpretation of psychosis, however, allows for a more extensive understanding of John's subjectivity. He argues that the psychotic person is inhabited by the thoughts, words, and acts of his/her parent or parents. The parental figures (the "other") are foreclosed upon (rather than repressed); they are empty of thoughts because their thoughts inhabit the psychotic person's consciousness. Reciprocity is closed to the psychotic person since there is only room for one; to live as a subject oneself means that the other dies. The parents themselves are foreclosed upon as one, not two. Living as if s/he does not have a body, the psychotic person lives instead in ideas as a "him": "If something happens to him, he is the theatre in which it happens, but he is not the actor" (Roustang, 1976, p. 133).

In the light of Roustang's account, how can we theorize John's psychosis in temporal terms? It is likely that John's wish to orient himself to the future, instead of being "stuck in the past" was a precipitant of his psychosis. This desire had emerged tentatively from a precarious sense of himself as a subject, threatening the foreclosed parental figure (s) who sought appropriation of his subjectivity. Their

ideas, which had been (unconsciously) inserted into John's "uncon-
scious-consciousness" (Roustang, 1976, p. 146) in the past, equated
desires, including sexuality, with evil. These ideas contained the past
of one or both parents but were not in any way experienced by John
as "past" or as in any way belonging to others, since "he does not
know if he is the other or himself" (Roustang 1976, p. 149).

Sass refers to the many descriptions of people diagnosed as schizophrenic of their experience of time, its "immobility … the loss of
past and future … the difficulty of arranging remembered events in
the correct order" (Sass, 1992, p. 156). This is not to imply that John
was conscious of the present as present. Instead, in his psychosis, he
lived in an immediacy in relation to others which precluded a subjectivity which could not differentiate between "now" and "then",
or what had gone before; it was a state of timelessness. This allows
us to understand how John's speech could contain completely contradictory statements within one sentence. For example, he told the
therapist that he only cared about himself and also pleaded with him
not to forget the harm he had done to others.

Roustang's reflections on the psychotic person's relation to death
are not without contradiction. He describes how the idea of killing
oneself, as in John's fantasy of self-sacrifice in order to cure the
world, may also contain the hope of being "the 'absolute master'
that the *him* will identify himself" (Roustang, 1976, p. 139). This
hope is rooted in an extreme sense of powerlessness. Roustang interprets the "delirium" of uncontrolled and uncontrollable ideas as
being also an attempt of the "him" to defeat the other: it "contains
within itself both the accusation and the judgement" (Roustang,
1976, p. 139). However, he argues that there cannot be a notion of
wishing to kill another in psychosis as this presupposes a notion of
subjectivity. Roustang claims that, if a psychotic person does kill,
this will be experienced as suicide. Although he uses the pronoun
"him" in the first two examples, he does convey that the individual
has some sense of agency, even if located in the "him" and not conscious. In his theorizing of the position that the psychoanalyst must
take up, he emphasizes the analyst being attentive to the cry of the
"him" and the crucial necessity of avoiding imposing a discourse on
the patient. This allows for the possibility of "resubjectiviz(ing) or
subjectiviz(ing)" (Roustang, 1976, p. 155) the psychotic person's discourse (see Chapter Eight in my discussion of the relation between

time and narrative in the psychoanalytic relationship). The significance for John of my reassurance, that even if he *is* bad, a conversation might still be possible, can be understood in the light of Roustaing's remarks.

## Death on the horizon

In acknowledging that death has many different meanings to individuals, it is important, as I have indicated in earlier chapters not to deny the importance of the fact of our death which is always already inescapably present for us on the horizon of our lives. Many psychoanalytic accounts are limited in their interpretations of fears of death in purely metaphorical terms and neglect the way in which the presence of death in the future shapes every subject's life.

Death presented itself to many of the patients whom I have described above in a multiplicity of ways and was intertwined with their current and past thoughts and fears, as well as those pertaining to the future. Working with an individual who is facing death in the form of terminal illness presents other challenges for the therapist. Schaverien (2002) movingly describes her experience of an analytical relationship with a young man, "James", who in the course of his analysis was diagnosed with an incurable lung cancer. From the point of his diagnosis her relationship with him was bounded by a new temporal structure: James's future was shortened although the extent of time he had left was unclear. Instead of moving towards the opening of possibilities extending beyond the end of analysis, in his analysis he was moving towards the finiteness of death.

The heightening of the immediacy and intimacy of the relationship between her and James in the context of his death ahead required Schaverien to reflect on and reassess the anaytic boundaries. This demanded a particular attentiveness to her counter-transference. Withstanding James's wishes that she become his friend, rather than his analyst, given the short time he had left, Schaverien retained her commitment to the importance to him of the uniqueness of their relationship as analyst and analysand with its special value in enabling him to live with his imminent death. Shifts in the usual analytic boundaries of time and space were necessary to include, for example, phone calls and hospital visits, in order for the analytic work to accommodate the deterioration in James's health. Schaverien's account is impressive in its honesty in relation to the challenges to analytic practices posed by the imminence of her patient's death.

Schaverien's patient was facing premature death. In psychoanalytic work with elderly people facing death, whether through the experience of illness or a more general or gradual lessening of their abilities, there are both similar and different issues. For example, Jung's (1959) emphasis on the importance, in old age, of living as if there are centuries ahead, while not denying the fact of death, is appropriate to elderly people in good health, but not necessarily to people in the last stages of terminal illness.

According to Freud, people over the age of fifty cannot benefit from psychotherapy owing to the loss of the "elasticity of the mental processes" (Freud, 1905 [1904]), p. 214). It is ironic that Freud was himself nearly fifty when he wrote this (Pollock 2006). He was moving into an extensive period of production through which he clearly sustained his ability to learn and to critically question his own conclusions. This view is challenged by Reggiori (2004) who argues that, while aging unavoidably and variously brings about a deterioration in some capacities, it may also enable increased playfulness and creativity. It may also bring about the recovery of interests and activities previously enjoyed at a younger age. Reggiori (2004) strongly argues for the crucial importance of recognizing the creative possibilities in an elderly person. As I indicated in Chapter Two, in my discussion of Jung's theories, these may be partly subsumed by the strength of historically and culturally specific stereotypes of old age which have been embodied by the older individual. It is crucially important to be sensitive to the effects of such stereotypes on an elderly person's perception of their aging.

Jung (1959) warns against the dangers of looking back to the past in old age, while recognizing (Jung, 1960) that this is also inevitable and argues that unconscious fantasies about the past may also contain the seeds of new possibilities for the future. This raises the question as to how an elderly person might position him/herself in relation to the different temporal dimensions and the analyst's response to this. My experience of working with Jonathan confirmed to me the value of analytic work for elderly people. In his late seventies, he came to analysis engulfed by his grief at having recently lost several close friends and relatives. In addition to the massiveness of these bereavements, deep feelings of failure weighed on him.

Jonathan frequently berated himself for not being as active or as productive in his work with me as he felt he should. Over time, the unconscious connection between this and his experience of the exacting and intrusive demands of his father in his childhood emerged. These demands had been particularly focused on physical achievement, an aspect of his life that was now, unavoidably, decreasing. His reflections on this gradually opened up the question of other possibilities of expression and he began to consider taking up painting again (he had enjoyed doing watercolours in his twenties, but this interest had been consumed by the demands of his career). Jonathan also felt ashamed at having to decrease his workload (he was self-employed) and this was also connected to the stringency of his father's demands. However, it also evoked a later experience, when his career had been threatened by an envious colleague. He was surprised to realize how this had become, once again, so significant.

At times Jonathan felt extremely isolated. He had left his partner twenty years previously and lived alone. His two sons lived some way away. Although he did not discount the possibility of another sexual relationship, it was difficult for him to imagine that he could be attractive enough at this stage of his life to anyone else with his "flabby body and thinning hair". Stereotypes of elderly people as asexual or unattractive (which are particularly pervasive in relation to women), together with his own self-critical feelings, contributed to this.

Jonathan's feelings of dependency on me were, at times, very difficult for him. His dependency was associated with inadequacy in relation to his father but it also re-evoked anxieties as to the availability of his mother whom he described as often being "distracted". Jonathan was appreciative of my making connections with his past as he realized that he needed to mourn aspects of it that were not as resolved as he had thought. In particular, his own aging revived memories of his parents, their own aging and deaths and also his earlier relationships with them. He did wonder occasionally, when he was in the midst of a particular struggle, whether he was too old for analytic work and whether the pain was worth it. However, the emergence new perspectives which opened out possibilities for his future reassured him. It also highlighted for me, that age is not necessarily a factor in an individual's ability to change.

Jonathan had no idea when he was going to die as he was in good health. He was tentative about his wish to talk about his death, feeling it would be offensive to me as a younger person. However, it was clear that he was also desperate to discuss this, together with questions about his will. This became the focus of questions about his self-value, what he had achieved in his life, and how this would be reflected in what he was leaving to his two sons. His fears about death were not concerned with what might happen to him after death; the question which obsessed him at times instead was whether it would be "messy" for those who might find his dead body. He agreed with my interpretation that perhaps this particular fear was connected to his father's early objectification of his body. His focus on death also seemed, at times, to protect him from the question of how he could feel worthy enough to develop his own creativity in the present.

Throughout my work with Jonathan I was acutely aware of the differences in our lived temporalities; I was only a few years older than his older son. It was crucial that I was attentive to counter-transference aspects arising from my relation to my own parents and to my own aging and death. Junckers (2006) additionally warns of the dangers of the younger analyst wishing to please their older patients (drawing on Hinze, 1987) or to avoid causing them pain (Plotkin, 2000), and of an older person's use of their age as a defence against facing their destructive feelings. These admonitions focus on possible negative identifications; there may be others (derived from an analyst's relation to their grandparents, for example) which may positively contribute to a sensitivity to an elderly person's experience.

The relevance of Levinas's view of the Other's time as disrupting one's own temporal inherence and his emphasis on the intersubjectivity of time (see Chapter Five) are particularly relevant. He argues that the Otherness of the Other, always exceeds rational understanding, a gathering into the "same". It is through our awareness of death that we recognize the absolute Other and come face-to-face with mystery. A respect for this mystery is crucial to our ability to be original in our responses and to a recognition of individual possibilities which cannot be contained within over-arching theories.

## Conclusion

In this chapter I emphasize the crucial importance of individuals' descriptions of time as they emerge consciously and unconsciously in the psychoanalytic sessions. This is not to claim that the theme of time is always as, or more, important than any other aspects of patients' material. Time is however, integral to all their experiences in their shifts between between past, present, and future dimensions.

My examples highlight the multiplicity of ways that individuals articulate their embodied relationships with others in time. In my discussion of how one individual struggles with living with old age I emphasize the importance of a recognition of the significance for individuals of different stages of their lives, depending on their particular socio-historical and cultural contexts. In exploring the theme of death, both of oneself and of others, I emphasize the importance of acknowledging meanings of death in relation to our past, present and future in psychoanalytic practices. I challenge the notion that it is ever too late for psychoanalytic work and the opening of possibilities for change.

# CHAPTER EIGHT

# Finally... speaking of time

T hroughout the book I argue for the importance of sensitivity to individuals' lived temporalities in the context of the
psychoanalytic relationship. I challenge the pervasiveness
of spatial metaphors in much psychoanalytic theorizing because of
their reification of individual experience. Interpretations of early
infantile relationships as being determinative of an individual's
relation to their present and their future do not adequately address
the variability and complexity of individuals' temporal experiences.
This reductive tendency is reinforced furthermore in a theorizing
which is rooted in ahistorical notions such as inherited, phylogenetic
phantasies and archetypes. I argue that interpretations of subjectivities which address their historicity and their temporality allow for an
attentiveness to fluidity and to monotonous fixity, to gaps and to dis-
ruptions, and to the opening and closing of imaginative and creative
possibilities, lived by individuals consciously and unconsciously.

Through my critical analyses of Merleau-Ponty's and Levinas's
theorizing of temporality and subjectivity, I emphasize the "intertemporality" of subjectivities. Individuals live their lives within
intersubjective networks in which their own past, present, and
future temporalities are interwoven and are in constant flux. The
fabric I describe is not one of continuous threads since, as Foucault's

genealogical analysis emphasizes, this would be to deny the breaks, separations and deaths integral to every relationship with another.

In this final chapter I draw together some of the main themes in the book and focus further on the temporality of the relationship between analyst and patient. I begin with the question of the time frame of analysis, which is located in shared chronological time. In addressing the differing temporalities of patient and analyst I particularly focus on the much debated question of change in psychoanalysis. I discuss how psychoanalysis can open out possibilities for change which are not underpinned by normative notions of "health" or of change as linear and progressive. Developing Schafer's (1983) reflections on the role of "narrative" in the psychoanalytic relationship in the light of Ricoeur's theorizing of the relation between time and narrative, I discuss the importance of language in opening out possibilities of ways of being. I emphasize the role of imagination in allowing for new ways of existing in the world.

### Frames of time

The time frame of an psychoanalytic relationship such as the mutually agreed times, frequency, and length of the sessions is structured by chronological time. This structure has been a source of considerable debate, which has heightened over the last decade in Britain, Europe and the U.S. Some groups of psychoanalytic practitioners are allied in their claim that the efficacy of an analysis requires a minimum of three sessions (preferably four or five) weekly for a number of years and must reach a definite end (in that the patient can never return again to the analyst). Other groups argue, instead, for the value of once weekly and above, and are often more flexible as to what constitutes the "end" of an analysis.

The argument for three to five times a week analysis is founded on a quantitative view of time ("more is better"). Aside from the economic implications of this in relation to the question of accessibility of psychoanalysis, this position is based on a confusion between a chronological notion of time and how individuals live time. Many analysts, particularly in the Object Relations tradition, are attentive to the particularity of the unconscious significance to the patient of the time frame, including the endings of sessions and the analyst's breaks (See Chapter Two on Melanie Klein). However, the quantitative argument for five times a week analysis denies the extent to which individuals live time in multifarious ways. Individuals' abilities to continue the psychoanalytic work between sessions varies considerably; for some individuals in weekly analysis, the psychoanalytic relationship is as intense and as productive as it is for those in five times a week analysis.

The extent to which patients can "hold in mind" the psychoanalytic relationship cannot be universally predicted or measured in terms of chronological time. The argument for more frequent sessions is often based the notion that "more" offers the safety necessary for "deeper" and for "earlier" exploration, which is claimed to be "better". However, even within the model of the analyst/patient as mother/infant, this assumption is questionable. The patient may not necessarily feel more "held" by seeing the analyst more frequently. Anxieties aroused by too frequent contact may prove too difficult to work with: less frequency may provide more security, allowing for a more gentle encounter with these over time. These considerations are also relevant to interpretations of individuals' experiences of breaks in their analysis. For some patients breaks may raise profound anxieties which have their roots in their histories, for others the breaks may offer a valuable opportunity for exploring possibilities of independence. This is specific to each patient at different times in their analysis. It is crucial that the analyst is attentive to the individual meanings patients attribute to the breaks in the time of their analysis.

How long is a session? In Chapter Four I argue strongly against Lacan's variable length sessions and his view that the patient is manipulative and that his/her resistance must be cut through by the analyst's unpredictable termination of the session. My argument for a mutually agreed session length does not arise from a developmental position (the patient/analyst as mother/infant relationship). It is an acknowledgement of the vulnerability of any individual who is engaged in the exploration of unconscious aspects of his/her experience (whether pertaining to the past, present, or the future) and of the necessity for a sufficiently secure time frame within which to do so. My position is also rooted in a respect for the individual temporality of the patient and in an openness to the specificity of their conscious and unconscious experience of the session. The analyst who ends the session whenever they consider it appropriate imposes his/her own time and defines what is significant and what is to be taken away. This cuts across the various significances attributed by the patient to the session, or to elements of it, many of which the analyst will not be conscious.

How long should an analysis last? As I discuss in Chapter One, Freud bases his conviction about the necessity of an analysis being open-ended on his theorizing of the unconscious as "timeless". Although, as I argue, this latter premise is problematic, Freud's commitment to open-ended work does recognize that the timing of the emergence of unconscious aspects of subjectivity is unpredictable. The conscious setting of a specific length of a contract from the outset can place constraints on the patient's exploration; there is an implication that something definite has to be achieved within the time, even if conscious goals are not explicitly set. Most analysts agree that several years of analysis is necessary for its efficacy, even if there is little agreement as to what it might achieve (see below) and this is my preference. However, the value of short-term, time-limited psychodynamic work should not be dismissed; it can produce significant shifts for some individuals if it is offered at the right time in an individual's life (whether it is the "right time" may, of course, be only recognized as such retrospectively).

How complete is an analysis? For many analysts, the timing of the ending is a crucial constituent of the preceding ongoing analysis and its end is final. There is an underlying assumption, often made explicit, that an analysis must aim at completion. This is addressed by Freud who, while not offering a definitive answer, questions the "optimism" of this position and its implication that it really is possible to "inoculate (the patient) against any other instinctual conflicts in the future" (Freud, 1937c, p. 203). Whether or not the conflicts Freud alludes to are interpreted as "instinctual" (see my critique of this concept in Chapter One), Freud's hesitancy about the notion of a completed analysis is important. Such a notion assumes that an analysis can enable an individual to become consistently conscious of that which s/he is unconscious, which would be both unrealistic and also undesirable. It also begs the question as to how far we can be aware of the possible conscious and unconscious impact of experiences and events on individuals' lives which are beyond their control and may create unforeseen disruption after the analysis has ended.

The notion of a "complete" analysis is thus based on a decontextu-alization of an individual's life, historically and culturally. It assumes that, in the end, analysis is a linear and self-enclosed process with its own internal continuity and does not sufficiently recognize that different times in an individual's life give rise to different challenges and struggles. The finality of an end to an analysis is also based on a simplistic notion of separation: it is claimed that if the possibility of any further periods of analysis in the future is left open by the analyst, this signifies a collusion with the patient's fear of separation or with their denial of mortality. However, if the end of an analysis is treated as having the same finality as death, the definiteness implied by this is likely instead to cut across the complexities of important questions for the patient pertaining to the future: those of independ-ence, dependence, desire, gaps, continuity, separation (including the possibility of the mortality of the patient or the analyst), and uncer-tainty, in relation to a living individual (the absent, as opposed to the dead analyst). The desire to return to analysis (if the relationship appears likely to continue to offer productive psychoanalytic work) therefore does not necessarily signify a failure of a previous period of analysis. The patient has recognized that separation does not have to signify death; it is a part of the continuity of relationships. It also signifies that they have been able to be attentive to their own knowl-edge that they would benefit from further exploration of previous or of newly emergent themes. An assumption that the work has been done risks constituting a denial of these.

### The time between: time and narrative

Throughout the book I have questioned the over-emphasis on the past dimension of time in psychoanalytic theorizing. This is not to deny its critical importance in people's lives. Individuals' percep-tions of their past are often voiced in analysis in the expectation that this will increase their understanding of present experiences, break the repetitiveness of their suffering, bring longed-for recognition or, alternatively, preserve the past and protect them from the feared future. As Irving Hoffman (1983) argues, an individual's realization of how their past has contributed to their particular experience of the psychoanalytic relationship can enable them to recognize the possibility of different ways of relating in the future. It is important, however, to critically reflect on how this notion of the "past" is constituted. As Freud describes through his concept of deferred action ("Nachträglichkeit"), memories of the past are interpretations of previous memories from new perspectives. These are also, as a phenomenological approach emphasizes, interpreted by us in the light of our anticipation of the future. If an individual's attitude to the future is, for example, one of despair, this will shape their conscious and unconscious interpretations of their past experiences.

Freud (1937d) also emphasizes that it is the construction between analyst and patient of those many aspects of our histories which cannot be directly recalled which is crucial (see my Chapter One). Psychoanalytic theorizing over recent decades has developed the notion of the mutual co-construction of the patient's past through the notion of "narrative" (Schafer 1983, Cavell 2000). Schafer (1983) emphasizes the inseparability of experiences and of narrative accounts. These are not linear and they are replete with gaps and contradictions to which the analyst attends. Schafer argues that every description is an interpretation and that the possibilities of interpretations are "interminable" (p.186). Moreover, reconstructions are "coauthored" between analyst and patient. Schafer also extends the notion of "narrative" to transference and resistance. He distinguishes his position from the traditional view of regression within the transference in which the life-history is conceived as "static, archival, linear, reversible, and literally retrievable" and emphasizes instead "new experiencing and new remembering of the past that unconsciously has never become the past" (p. 220) such that "regression is necessarily a progression" (p. 220). Surprisingly he regards this as a "timeless version of past and present" (p. 197) despite the notion of "new" implying a sense of time. He also describes psychoanalytic work as "temporally circular" in that the past and the present are interdependent, which does not adequately encompass his own recognition of the way in which reconstructions are also forms of orientation towards the future.

The philosopher Ricoeur's theorizing of the relation between historical and fictional narratives is particularly relevant to psychoanalysis. He argues that temporality and narrative are integral to one another: "… time becomes human time to the extent that it is organized after the manner of a narrative; narrative, in turn is meaningful to the extent that it portrays the features of temporal experience"

(Ricoeur, 1983a, p. 3). Ricoeur explores how the relation between historical and fictional narratives illuminates human temporal experience. He argues that history is an interpretation of the past: the past can never be known directly. Fiction is an imaginative process which "collides" with, and accordingly recreates the real world (Ricoeur, 1983b, p. 142). Ricoeur concludes that human temporality involves an interrelationship between history's "indirect reference to the past and the productive reference of fiction" (Ricoeur, 1983b, p. 143). Although Ricoeur's theorizing resonates somewhat with Schafer's, Ricoeur goes further in emphasizing the imaginative aspects of narrative. It is these imaginative possibilities within the relationship between analyst and patient that I wish to emphasize, particularly in relation to the question of change in psychoanalysis (see below).

In considering the relation between time and narrative, it is important to briefly address the question as to whether our auditory experience is unavoidably that of a succession of words in (linear) time. This is the claim of Lessing (1766) who distinguishes between painting as a spatial art and poetry and music as temporal arts (see Rée 1999). Lessing argues that vision is the only sense which can grasp a plurality of realities instantanously. This view is challenged by Rée who argues that if we were to experience words only as separate sounds in succession, we would be unable to "recognize words ... grasp their meaning and syntactical relations, or appreciate their tunes and rhythmic patterns" (Rée, 1999, p. 352). Listening to speech and to music involves "memory and anticipation" (Rée, 1999, p. 352), memory not only of the previous word or note, but also of words and notes prior to those, all of which may be repeated and returned to. Just as our auditory experience is not limited to the sequential, our visual experience is not only spatial. As art therapists are very aware, the imagery of art reflects temporal dimensions, or rather as Merleau-Ponty says of the subject, the imagery *is* time itself (see my Chapter Five).

*Changing times*

In my discussion of Jung's theorizing I stressed the importance of his attunement to the patient's relation to the future. For example, his interpretation of the notion of regression addresses its creative role in the subject's orientation to a new future. He also views the transference as not only a repetition of significant relationships in the past but also as enabling the individual to move beyond his/her immediate family, a task s/he has not yet sufficiently achieved. Merleau-Ponty's (1945) reflections on the question of how change occurs in psychoanalysis resonate somewhat with Jung's. He emphasizes that within the unique context of the psychoanalytic relationship aspects of the past are relived and given significance. Change does not occur through insight into the past, but rather through the way in which psychoanalysis "bind(s) the subject to his doctor through *new* existential relationships" (Merleau-Ponty, 1945, p. 455, my italics). As I argued in Chapter One, Freud's notion of the transference as a "playground" which functions as "a motive for remembering" requires extension: it is crucial that the notion of the "playground" includes its possibilities for experimentation in the psychoanalytic relationship with new ways of relating.

Through the case studies that I have presented I have illustrated how this occurs. I emphasize that it is the analyst's attentiveness to the subtle emergence of these new possibilities which is crucial. These tentative steps can be easily stymied through a reductive interpretation which is focused solely on their connection to, and sometimes causation by, early relationships. Levinas's notion of the originality of the instant (see Chapter Five), which is constituted by both evanescence (fading) and expectation, illustrates how a new position can be taken up, in which the compulsion to attempt to repeat is broken, in the relationship between the analyst and the patient. It is in the difference between them, in the time that points towards the future, that both individuals are changed, consciously and unconsciously. This instant is unrepeatable and brings with it, in its openness to the future, the weight of responsibility to oneself and to others.

The limits and the possibilities which are realized in the psychoanalytic relationship depend on the different times which are "lived" by the analyst and the patient. As I have emphasized throughout the book this relationship, particularly within Object Relations theory, is conceptualized in the spatial metaphors of "inner" and "outer", "internal" and "external", "projection" and "introjection". Notions of transference and counter-transference hinge on these. For example, the analyst experiences the patient as defensively projecting or pushing feelings into her/him. A recognition of the shifting temporalities of the analyst and the patient allows for a more complex understanding of the interweaving of their subjectivities, including their own and each others' different conscious and unconscious perspectives of their historicities. It throws into question the assumption that there can be an absolute clarity as to whether what is experienced by the analyst in the "counter-transference" belongs to her/his past or to the patient's. It also more readily allows for the more complex interpretations of "truth" in psychoanalysis which do not assume that there is an objective reality which is available to the subject once the "distortions" of unconscious projections have been peeled away. It allows for the dynamic interplay of "co-created" and contingent "truths" which arise from the specific and shifting temporalities lived from moment to moment between the analyst and the patient within the frame of the psychoanalytic "hour".

It is through the interplay of these co-creations in the psychoanalytic relationship that change occurs. Individuals usually seek an analytical relationship in the hope of alleviating a suffering which may appear to be endless and of discovering more satisfying relationships. For some people there may be a hope or a belief that analysis will enable them to find permanent happiness. Intrinsic to these hopes may be a wish or a fear (or both simultaneously) of emerging from analysis as a completely "changed person", with a new identity. There may also be the expectation that change will be linear, in the form of progress, and that "curing the symptoms" will not take very long.

As I discuss in Chapter Four, Lacan is sceptical about such conscious hopes and about the risks of analyses which aim for adaptation to "reality". In his view, the end of an analysis involves a confrontation with death and a recognition of life as a "dogged detour, in itself transitory and precarious, and deprived of any significance" (Lacan, 1955, p. 232). It is ironic that Lacan, while challenging the concept of goal-orientated work, is very explicit about what he regards as the goal of a successful (and thus complete) analysis. His position contains an uncompromising despair which resonates with the view of a senior Kleinian psychoanalyst involved in training at the Tavistock Clinic, whom I interviewed in 1991, who assured me that the criterion for a successful analysis was the realization of "how jolly sick" we are.

These positions avoid the question as to whether and how our lives can be satisfying and creative enough within the restrictions of specific socio-historical and socio-cultural contexts (see the next section "Change in contexts"). In my experience, the psychoanalytic relationship can open out possibilities for hitherto unimagined experiences and ways of being which may be pleasurable, discomforting, exciting, or even intolerable. It may end because of the evocation of such feelings. If the ending is mutually planned and worked towards it is likely be accompanied by feelings of deep appreciation of the work on the part of the patient and of the analyst, even if these are not articulated verbally. Even if the ending occurs too quickly, my hope is that at least some of an individual's suffering has been alleviated and that more and new possibilities of being and relating to others have emerged through the work. This does not at all mean that I argue either for the value of a predictable outcome (as the setting of goals implies) or for normative notions of "psychic health" or maturity. Rather, as Levinas describes in relation to our awareness of our own death (see Chapter Seven) analysis brings us face-to-face with the creative possibilities of the Other, of mystery.

*Change in contexts*

As Levinas argues (see Chapter Five), intrinsic to our relationships with others is a responsibility to them. This both curtails our freedom and enables intimacy. Merleau-Ponty in his reflections on freedom claims that freedom arises paradoxically precisely from that which simultaneously limits us, namely our "psychological and historical structure" (Merleau-Ponty, 1945, p. 455) through which we embody a style of existing and which gives us access to the world. Infinite freedom is impossible since we are "a network of relationships" (A. de Saint-Exupery, quoted by Merleau-Ponty, 1945, p. 456) and our "commitment" to the world necessarily involves contradictions. We can transform our pasts only through making other commitments elsewhere (to a psychoanalytic relationship, for example) and this brings other constraints on our aspirations for freedom.

As a Marxist, Merleau-Ponty stresses the relation between one's own freedom and the freedom of others: "*your* freedom cannot be willed ... without willing freedom *for all*" (p. 456). This raises the question of the relation between the possibility of our individuality and the wider socio-historical and cultural contexts within which we live. For Fanon (see Chapter Six) the solution to this question was engagement with political struggle. Leaving his post as a psychiatrist Fanon joined the war for Algerian independence from France. His decision explicitly signified that, for him, individual change was impossible without wider social change. Merleau-Ponty does not prescribe how an individual should respond to their concern regarding others' freedom, characterized by such questions as "Shall I make this promise? Shall I risk my life for so little? Shall I give up my liberty in order to save liberty?" However, he emphasizes that these are questions that must be faced; they are irrefutably intrinsic to our relationships with one another.

### Opening futures

Psychoanalysis offers the creative possibility for individuals of opening out a time, as well as a space for themselves. In the psychoanalytic relationship an individual can explore possibilities of hitherto not glimpsed decisions and actions in relation to present dilemmas. It is important to emphasize that the future is not something that we can represent to ourselves in advance with any certainty.

Wood reflects on how we can conceptualize our relation to the future without recourse to a metaphysics. He questions whether Derrida's argument for the notion of a plurality of histories, "different in their type, rhythm, mode of inscription—intervallic, differentiated histories" (quoted by Wood, 1989, p. 372), might be applied to our concept of the future. However, he argues, this does not eradicate the risk of its conceptualization solely in terms of the "future past", that is, constituted by multiple projections from the past, as in Winnicott's fear of the breakdown which has already happened (see Chapter Four).

Wood claims that Derrida's contemplation of the verb "venir" (to come, included in the French for the future: "l'avenir") and Levinas's analysis of the ethical relation to the otherness of the Other, which is rooted in the notion of the discontinuity of time, point to the emergence of a postmetaphysical concept of the future. Consequently, for philosophy, this would "rest ultimately on the invitation that we extend to the other to open ourselves to the (ad-venture) of thinking, without the prospect of completion, and without aiming at some prescribed destination" (Wood, 1989, p. 382). Wood's words in relation to philosophy vividly characterise a psychoanalytic relationship which is committed to the struggle for an openness to the unknown and, intrinsically, to the surprise of the future. Hoffman crystallizes the experience of a shift in the direction of such an openness to future possibilities:

> For quite a while I've woken up tensed, coiled against the next disaster, right up against the wall of a possible end. But now, a succession of tomorrows begins to exfoliate like a faith ... once time uncoils and regains its forward dimension, the present moment becomes a fulcrum on which I can stand more lightly, balanced between the past and the future, balanced in time". [Hoffman, 1998, *Lost In Translation*, p. 280]

# REFERENCES

Aaron, J. (1994). Finding a voice in two tongues: gender and colonization. In: J. Aaron, Teresa Rees, Sandra Betts, and M. Vincentelli (Eds.), *Our Sisters' Land, The Changing Identities of Women in Wales*. Cardiff: University of Wales Press.

Aitken, K. J. and Trevarthen, C. (1997). Self/other organization in human psychological development. *Development and Psychopathology, 9:* pp. 653–677. Cambridge: Cambridge University Press.

Aristotle. Physics. *The Complete Works of Aristototle, Vol. 1,* ed. Jonathan Barnes, Princeton, US and Chichester, UK: Princeton/Bollingen, 1984.

Benjamin, J. (1990). *The Bonds of Love, Psychoanalysis, Feminism, and the Problem of Domination.* London: Virago.

Benjamin, J. (2006). The analyst's fear of doing harm and learning through enactment. Conference paper presented at Confer, London: 9th October 2006.

Bion, W. (1970). *Attention and Interpretation.* London: Karnac, 1984.

Binswanger, L. (1946). The case of Ellen West, trans. W. Mendel and J. Lyons. In: R. May, E. Angel, H. Ellenberger (Eds.), *Existence.* New York: Basic Books, 1958, pp. 237–364.

Binswanger, L. (1946). The existential analysis school of thought, trans. E. Angel. In: R. May, E. Angel, H. Ellenberger (Eds.), *Existence.* New York: Basic Books, 1958, pp. 191–213.

Binswanger, L. (1949). The case of Lola Voss. In: J. Needleman (Ed. and trans.), *Being-In-the-World, Selected Papers of Ludwig Binswanger.* New York and and Evanston: Harper and Row, 1967, pp. 266–341.

Birksted-Breen, D. (2003). Time and the *après-coup. International Journal of Psychoanalysis, 84*: 1501–1515.

Borch-Jacobsen, M. (1991). *Lacan, the Absolute Master.* Stanford, CA: Stanford University Press.

Boschan, P. (1990). Temporality and narcissism. *International Review of Psycho-Analysis, 17*: 337–349.

Boss, M. (1979). *Existential Foundations of Medicine and Psychology,* trans. S. Conway and A. Cleaves.Northvale, NJ and London: Jason Aronson, 1994.

Bourke, J. (2005). *Fear, A Cultural History.* London: Virago, 2006.

Butler, J. (1990). *Gender Trouble.* London: Routledge.

Cavell, M. (2000). Keeping time: Freud on the temporality of mind. In: M. Levine (Ed.), *The Analytic Freud, Philosophy and Psychoanalysis.* London and New York: Routledge.

Chodorow, N. (1978). *The Reproduction of Mothering.* Berkeley and Los Angeles, CA: University of California Press.

Cohn, H. (1997). *Existential Thought and Therapeutic Practice.* London: Sage.

Dalal, F. (2002). *Race, Colour and the Processes of Racialization.* Hove, E. Sussex: Brunner-Routledge.

De Beauvoir, S. (1949). *The Second Sex.* Harmondsworth: Penguin, 1974.

Derrida, J. (1975). Le Facteur de la vérité. In: *The Postcard: From Socrates to Freud and Beyond,* trans. Alan Bass. Chicago and London: University of Chicago Press, 1987.

Derrida, J. (1981). Positions: interview with Jean Louis-Houdebine and Guy Scarpetta. In: *Positions,* trans. A. Bass. Chicago and London: University of Chicago Press.

Dinnerstein, D. (1976). *The Rocking of the Cradle and the Ruling of the World.* London: Souvenir Press, 1978.

Dosse, F. (2006). Travail et devoir de mémoire chez Paul Ricoeur. In: F. Dosse, A. Finkelkraut, J-C. Guillebaud (Eds.) *La Mémoire, Pour Quoi Faire?* Paris: Les Éditions de l'Atelier.

Eichenbaum, L. and Orbach, S. (1983). *Understanding Women.* Harmondsworth: Penguin 1985.

Ellis, K. S. (1973). *Prediction and Prophecy.* London: Wayland.

Ellis, M. L. (2000). Shifting the ego towards a body subject. In: B. Seu (Ed.), *Who am I? The Ego and the Self in Psychoanalysis.* London: Rebus Press, pp.156–180.

Ellis, M. L. (2005). Sexual languages/cultural bodies: transforming psychoanalysis. *Psychodynamic Practice 11*, No. 4: 405–415.

Ellis, M. L. (1997). Who speaks? Who listens? Different voices, different sexualities. In: J. Schaverien (Ed.), *Gender, Countertransference and the Erotic Transference*. Hove, E. Sussex: Routledge, 2006, pp. 123–142.

Fanon, F. (1952). *Black Skin, White Masks*. London: Pluto Press, 1986.

Flax, J. (1993). *Disputed Subjects, Essays on Psychoanalysis, Politics and Philosophy*. New York and London: Routledge.

Fletchman-Smith, B. (2002). Unpublished paper. Presented at Women's Therapy Conference, London, June 2002.

Foucault, M. (1969). *The Archeology of Knowledge,* trans. A. Sheridan Smith. London: Routledge, 1995.

Foucault, M. (1976). *The History of Sexuality*, trans. R. Hurley. Harmondsworth: Peregrine, 1984.

Freud, S. (1899a). Screen Memories. *S.E.* 3, 301.

Freud, S. (1900a). *The Interpretation of Dreams*. *S.E.* 4–5.

Freud, S. (1905[1904]). On Psychotherapy. *S.E.* 7, 255.

Freud, S. (1905d). Three Essays on the Theory of Sexuality. *S.E.* 7, 125.

Freud, S. (1912e). Recommendations to Physicians Practising Psycho-Analysis. *S.E.* 12, 111.

Freud, S. (1912b). The Dynamics of Transference. *S.E.* 12, 99.

Freud, S. (1914g). Remembering, Repeating and Working-Through. *S.E.* 12, 147.

Freud, S. (1915b). Thoughts for the Times in War and Death. *S.E.* 14, 275.

Freud, S. (1915c). Instincts and Their Vicissitudes. *S.E.* 14, 111.

Freud, S. (1918b [1914]). From the History of an Infantile Neurosis. *S.E.* 17, 3.

Freud, S. (1920g]). Beyond the Pleasure Principle. *S.E.* 18, 3.

Freud, S. (1925a [1924]). A Note Upon the 'Mystic Writing-Pad'. *S.E.* 19, 27.

Freud, S. (1920). Aspects of development and regression. Aetiology, trans. J. Riviere. In: *A General Introduction to Psychoanalysis*, New York: Garden City Books, 1952.

Freud, S. (1923b). The Ego and the Id. *S.E.* 19, 3.

Freud, S. (1924c). The Economic Problem of Masochism. *S.E.* 19, 157.

Freud, S. (1926d [1925]). Inhibitions, Symptoms and Anxiety. *S.E.* 20, 77.

Freud, S. (1933a [1932]). New Introductory Lectures on Psychoanalysis. *S.E.* 22, 3.

Freud, S. (1937c). Analysis Terminable and Interminable. *S.E.* 23, 211.

Freud, S. (1937d). Constructions in Analysis. *S.E.* 23, 257.

Fromm, E. (1970). *The Crisis of Psychoanalysis*. Harmondsworth: Penguin, 1978.

Gardiner, M. (1989). *The Wolf-Man and Sigmund Freud,* London: Karnac Books.

Green, A. (2002). *Time in Psychoanalysis,* trans. A. Weller, London: Free Association Books.

Grosz, E. (1994). Refiguring lesbian desire. In: L. Doan (Ed.), *The Lesbian Postmodern*. New York and Chichester, Columbia University Press.

Heidegger, M. (1927). *Being and Time,* trans. J. Macquarrie and E. Robinson, Oxford: Blackwell, 1990.

Hinze, E. (1967). Transference and counter-transference in the psychoanalytic treatment of older patients. *International Review of Psychoanalysis, 14:* 465–474. Referred to by Junckers, G. (2006). Editor's preface. In: Junckers (Ed.) *Is It Too Late? Key Papers on Psychoanalysis and Ageing.* London: Karnac.

Hoffman, E. (1989). *Lost In Translation*. London: Vintage.

Hoffman, I. (1983). The patient as interpreter of the analyst's experience. In: S. Mitchell (Ed.), *Relational Psychoanalysis*. Hillsdale, NJ: The Analytic Press, pp. 39–76.

Hoffman, E. (2004). Between worlds, between words: some thoughts on self-translation. In: J. Szekacs-Weisz and I. Ward (Eds.). *Lost Childhood and the Language of Exile*. London: Imago MLPC and Freud Museum Publications.

Huet, V. (1997). Ageing: another tyranny? Art therapy with older women. In: S. Hogan (Ed.), *Feminist Approaches to Art Therapy,* London and New York: Routledge.

Irigaray, L. (1977). *This Sex Which Is Not One,* trans. C. Porter. Ithaca, NY: Cornell University Press, 1985.

Junckers, G. (2006). Editor's preface. In: G. Junckers (Ed.) *Is It Too Late? Key Papers on Psychoanalysis and Ageing.* London: Karnac.

Jung, C. G. (1912). Symbols of Transformation. *C.W.* Vol. 5, trans. R. F. C. Hull. London and Henley: Routledge and Kegan Paul, 1981.

Jung, C. G. (1913). The Theory of Psychoanalysis. *C.W.* Vol. 4, trans. R. F. C. Hull. London and Henley: Routledge and Kegan Paul, 1961.

Jung, C. G, (1916). Psychoanalysis and Neurosis. *C.W.* Vol. 4, trans. R. F. C. Hull. London and Henley: Routledge and Kegan Paul, 1961.

Jung, C. G. (1917). On the Psychology of the Unconscious. *C.W.* Vol. 7, trans. R. F. C. Hull. London and Henley: Routledge and Kegan Paul, 1970.

Jung, C. G. (1928). On Psychic Energy. *C.W.* Vol. 8, trans. R. F. C. Hull. London and Henley: Routledge and Kegan Paul, 1969.

Jung, C. G. (1930). Some Aspects of Modern Psychotherapy. *C.W.* Vol.16, trans. R. F. C. Hull. London and Henley: Routledge and Kegan Paul, 1981.

Jung, C. G. (1931). The Stages of Life. *C.W.* Vol. 8, trans. R. F. C. Hull. London and Henley: Routledge and Kegan Paul, 1969.

Jung, C. G. (1934). The Practical Use of Dream Analysis. *C.W.* Vol. 16, trans. R. F. C. Hull. London and Henley: Routledge and Kegan Paul, 1981.

Jung, C. G. (1935). What is Psychotherapy? *C.W.* Vol. 16, trans. R. F. C. Hull. London and Henley: Routledge and Kegan Paul, 1981.

Jung, C. G. (1936). The Concept of the Collective Unconscious. *C.W.* Vol. 9, trans. R. F. C. Hull. London and Henley: Routledge and Kegan Paul, 1968.

Jung, C. G. (1939). Conscious, Unconscious and Individuation. *C.W.* Vol. 9, trans. R. F. C. Hull. London and Henley: Routledge and Kegan Paul, 1968.

Jung, C. G. (1941). The Psychological Aspects of the Kore. *C.W.* Vol. 9, trans. R. F. C. Hull. London and Henley: Routledge and Kegan Paul, 1968.

Jung, C. G. (1946). The Psychology of the Transference. *C.W.* Vol.16, trans. R. F. C. Hull. London and Henley: Routledge and Kegan Paul, 1981.

Jung, C. G. (1949). The Significance of the Father in the Destiny of the Individual. *C.W.* Vol. 4, trans. R. F. C. Hull. London and Henley: Routledge and Kegan Paul, 1961.

Jung, C. G. (1952). Synchronicity. An Acausal Connecting Principle. *C.W.* Vol. 8, trans. R. F. C. Hull. London and Henley: Routledge and Kegan Paul, 1969.

Jung, C. G. (1955).The Theory of Psychoanalysis. *C.W.* Vol. 4, trans. R. F. C. Hull. London and Henley: Routledge and Kegan Paul, 1961.

Jung, C. G. (1955). The Stephen Black interview. In: W. McGuire and R. F. C. Hull (Ed.), *C. G. Jung Speaking, Interviews and Encounters* (pp. 243–256). London: Pan Books, 1980.

Jung, C. G. (1957). The Houston films. In: W. McGuire and R. F. C. Hull (Ed.), *C. G. Jung Speaking, Interviews and Encounters* (pp. 264–339). London: Pan Books, 1980.

Jung, C. G. (1959). *The* face to face *Interview.* In: W. McGuire and R. F. C. Hull (Ed.), *C. G. Jung Speaking, Interviews and Encounters* (pp. 380–393). London: Pan Books, 1980.

Jung, C. G. (1960). The art of living. In: W. McGuire and R. F. C. Hull (Ed.), *C. G. Jung Speaking, Interviews and Encounters* (pp. 397–405). London: Pan Books, 1980.

Jung, C. G. (1961). *Memories, Dreams, Reflections,* trans. R and C. Winston. London: Collins 1974.

Jung, C. G., von Franz, M-L., Henderson, J. L., Jacobi, J., Joffe, A. (1964). *Man and His Symbols,* London: Pan, 1978.

Kant, I. (1929[1787]). *Immanuel Kant's Critique of Pure Reason,* trans. Norman Kemp Smith. Basingstoke: Macmillan Press, 1993.

Klein, M. (1921). The development of a child. In: *Contributions to Psychoanalysis, 1921–1945* (pp. 13–67). London: Hogarth Press (1948).

Klein, M. (1923). Infant analysis. In: *Contributions to Psychoanalysis, 1921–1945.* (pp. 87–116). London: Hogarth Press (1948).

Klein, M. (1929). Infantile anxiety-situations reflected in a work of art and in the creative impulse. In: *Contributions to Psychoanalysis, 1921–1945* (pp. 227–235). London: Hogarth Press (1948).

Klein, M. (1932). *The Psychoanalysis of Chidren.* London: Virago (1989).

Klein, M. (1946). Notes on some schizoid mechanisms. In: *Envy and Gratitude and Other Works 1946–1963* (pp.1–24). London: Hogarth (1984).

Klein, M. (1948). On the theory of anxiety and guilt. In: *Envy and Gratitude and Other Works 1946–1963* (pp. 25–42). London: Hogarth (1984).

Klein, M. (1950). On the criteria for the termination of a psychoanalysis. In: *Envy and Gratitude and Other Works 1946–1963* (pp. 43–47). London: Hogarth (1984).

Klein, M. (1952a). The origins of transference. In: *Envy and Gratitude and Other Works 1946–1963* (pp. 48–56). London: Hogarth (1984).

Klein, M. (1952b). The mutual influences in the development of ego and id. In: *Envy and Gratitude and Other Works 1946–1963* (pp. 57–60). London: Hogarth (1984).

Klein, M. (1952d). On observing the behaviour of young infants. In: *Envy and Gratitude and Other Works 1946–1963* (pp. 94–121). London: Hogarth (1984).

Klein, M. (1957). Envy and gratitude. In: *Envy and Gratitude and Other Works 1946–1963* (pp. 176–235). London: Hogarth (1984).

Klein, M. (1961). Narrative of a Child Analysis. London: Virago (1989).

Kristeva, J. (1974a). *Revolution in Poetic Language.* New York and Guilford, Surrey: Columbia University Press, 1984.

Kristeva, J. (1974b). *About Chinese Women.* London: Marion Boyars, 1977

Kristeva, J. (1979). Women's time. In: T. Moi (Ed.). *The Kristeva Reader.* Oxford: Basil Blackwell, 1986, pp. 187–213.

Kristeva, J. (1980). *Powers of Horror, An Essay On Abjection.* New York: Columbia University.

Lacan, J. (1953–1954a). *The Seminar of Jacques Lacan, Book 1, Freud's Papers on Technique, 1953–1954,* trans. J. A. Miller. Cambridge: Cambridge University Press, 1988.

Lacan, J. (1954b–1955). *The Seminar of Jacques Lacan Book 2, 1954–1955,* trans. J. A. Miller. Cambridge: Cambridge University Press, 1988.

Lacan, J. (1993). *The Seminar of Jacques Lacan Book 3, 1955–1956,* trans. J. A. Miller. London: Routledge.

Lacan, J. (1966a). *Écrits.* Paris: Seuil.

Lacan, J. (1966b). *Écrits, A Selection,* trans. A. Sheridan. London: Tavistock Publications, 1982.

Lacan, J. (1964). *The Seminar. Book XI. The Four Fundamental Concepts of Psychoanalysis,* trans. A. Sheridan, London: Hogarth Press, 1977.

Laing, R. D. (1959). *The Divided Self,* Harmondsworth: Penguin, 1965.

Laing, R. D. (1961). *Self and Others.* Harmondsworth: Penguin, 1976.

Laplanche, J. (1992). In: J. Fletcher, and M. Stanton (Eds.), *Jean Laplanche, Seduction, Translation, Drives,* London: Institute of Contemporary Arts.

Lessing, G. (1766). *Laokoön : An Essay on the Limits of Paintings and Poetry,* trans. E. McCormick. Baltimore: John Hopkins University Press, 1984.

Levinas, E. (1947a). *Existence and Existents,* trans. A. Lingis. The Hague: Martinus Nijhoff, 1978.

Levinas, E. (1947b). *The Time of the Other,* trans. R. Cohen. Pittsburgh, PA: Duquesne University Press, 1987.

Mann, T. (1924). *The Magic Mountain.* London, Vintage, 1999.

Merleau-Ponty, M. (1945). *The Phenomenology of Perception,* trans. C. Smith. Routledge and Kegan Paul, 1986.

Merleau-Ponty, M. (1960). Phenomenology and psychoanalysis: preface to Hesnard's *L'Oeuvre de Freud,* trans. A. L. Fisher. In: K. Hoeller (Ed.), *Merleau-Ponty and Psychology.* NJ: Humanities Press International, 1994.

Merleau-Ponty, M. (1964). *Signs,* trans. R. McCleary. Evanston, IL: Northwestern University Press.

Minkowski, E. (1923). Findings in a case of schizophrenic depression, trans. B. Bliss. In: R. May, E. Angel, H. Ellenberger (Eds.), *Existence.* New York: Basic Books, 1958, pp. 127–138.

Mitchell, J. (1974). *Psychoanalysis and Feminism.* Harmondsworth: Pelican Books, 1975.

Mitchell, J. (2006). Memory and psychoanalysis. In: P. Fara and K. Patterson (Ed.), *Memory.* Cambridge: Cambridge University Press, pp. 95–112.

Needleman, J. (1967). On a critical introduction to Ludwig Binswanger's Existential Analysis. In: J. Needleman (Ed. and trans.), *Being-In-the-World, Selected Papers of Ludwig Binswanger*. New York and and Evanston: Harper and Row, 1967, pp. 7–145.

Nunez, R. and Sweester, E. (2006). With the future behind them: convergent evidence from Aymara language and gesture in the crosslinguistic comparison of spatial construals of time. *Cognitive Science: A Multidisciplinary Journal. 30, 3:* pp. 401–450.

O'Connor, N. (1988). The personal is political: discursive practice of the face-to-face. In: R. Bernasconi and D. Wood (Eds.), *The Provocation of Levinas, Rethinkning the Other*. London and New York: Routledge.

O'Connor, N. (1990). Is Melanie Klein the one who knows who you really are? *Women, A Cultural Review, 1, 2:* pp. 180–188.

O'Connor, N. and Ryan, J. (1993). *Wild Desires and Mistaken Identities, Lesbianism and Psychoanalysis*. London: Karnac 2003.

Osborne, P. (1995). *The Politics of Time*. London and New York: Verso.

Parker, R. and Pollock, G. (1981). *Old Mistresses, Women, Art and Ideology*. London: Routledge and Kegan Paul.

Parker, R. (1995). *Torn In Two, The Experience of Maternal Ambivalence*. London: Virago.

Plotkin, F. (2000). Treatment of the older adult: The impact on the psychoanalyst. *Journal of the American* Psychoanalytic *Association, 63,* pp. 275–281.

Pollock, G. (2006). On ageing and psychopathology—discussion of Dr. Norman Cohen's paper, "On loneliness and the ageing process". In: Junckers (Ed.) *Is It Too Late? Key Papers on Psychoanalysis and Ageing*. London: Karnac.

Proust, M. (1913). *Swann's Way*, trans. C. K. Scott Moncrieff. London: Penguin, 2000.

Rack, P. (1982). *Race, Culture and Mental Disorder*, London and New York: Tavistock Publications.

Rée, J. (1998). *Heidegger, History and Truth In Being and Time*. London: Phoenix.

Rée, J. (1999). *I See a Voice, Language, Deafness and the Senses—A Philosophical History*. London: HarperCollins.

Reggiori, J. (2004). Individual psychotherapy in the second half of life. In: S. Evans and J. Garner (Eds.), *Talking Over the Years*. Hove, E. Sussex: Brunner-Routledge, pp. 131–145.

Rickman, H. P. (1964). *Preface to Philosophy*. London: Routledge and Kegan Paul.

Ricoeur, P. (1983a). *Time and Narrative, Vol. 1*, trans. K. McLaughlin and D. Pellauer. Chicago and London: University of Chicago Press, 1985.

Ricoeur, P. (1983b). On interpretation. In: R. Kearney and M. Rainwater (Eds.), *The Continental Philosophy Reader*. London and New York.

Ricoeur, P. (2004). *Memory, History, Forgetting*, trans. K. Blamey and D. Pellauer. Chicago and London: University of Chicago Press.

Rose, J. (1982). Introduction II. In: J. Mitchell and J. Rose (Eds.), *Feminine Sexuality, Jacques Lacan and the école freudienne*, trans. J. Rose. London and Basingstoke: Macmillan, pp. 27–57.

Roustang, F. (1976). Towards a theory of psychosis. In: *Dire Mastery*. Baltimore and London: The John Hopkins University Press, 1982.

Ryan, T. (2000). The search for 'self' and 'other' in therapeutic communities. In: B. Seu (Ed.), *Who am I? The Ego and the Self in Psychoanalysis*. London: Rebus Press, pp. 143–155

Sabbadini, A. (1989). Boundaries of timelessness. Some thoughts about the temporal dimension of the psychoanalytic space. *International Journal of Psychoanalysis, 70*: 305–313.

Scarfone, D. (2005). Laplanche and Winnicott meet … and survive. In: L. Caldwell (Ed.), *Sex and Sexuality, Winnicottian Perspectives*, London: Karnac.

Said, E. (2000). *Reflections on Exile and Other Essays*. Cambridge, MA: Harvard University Press.

Said, E, (2003). *Freud and the non-European*. London: Verso.

Samuels, A. (1993). *The Political Psyche*. London and New York: Routledge.

Sass, L. (1992). *Madness and Modernism*. Cambridge, MA and London: Harvard University Press, 1994.

Sass, L. (1994). The *Paradoxes of Delusion*. Ithaca, NY: Cornell Univiersity Press.

Schafer, R. (1983). *The Analytic Attitude*, London: The Hogarth Press.

Schaverien, J. (2002). *The Dying Patient in Psychotherapy*. Basingstoke and New York: Palgrave Macmillan.

Stacey, J. and Biblarz, T. J. (2001). (How) does the sexual orientation of parents matter? *American Sociological Review*, Vol. 66 (April): pp. 159–183.

Stern, D. (1998). *The Interpersonal World of the Infant*. London: Karnac.

Walton, J. (1997). Re-placing race in white psychoanalytic discourse: founding narratives of feminism. In: E. Abel, B. Christian, H. Moglen (Eds.), *Female Subjects in Black and White* (pp. 223–251). Berkeley, Los Angeles and London: University of Californai Press.

Webster, R. (1995). *Why Freud Was Wrong,* London: HarperCollins 1996.

Winnicott, D. W. (1958c). Child analysis in the latency period. In: J. D. Sutherland (Ed.), *The Maturational Processes and the Facilitating Environment.* London: The Hogarth Press, 1985.

Winnicott, D. W. (1959–1964). Classification: Is there a psycho-analytic contribution to psychiatric classification? In: J. D. Sutherland (Ed.), *The Maturational Processes and the Facilitating Environment.* London: The Hogarth Press, 1985.

Winnicott, D. W. (1960a). The theory of the parent-infant relationship. In: J. D. Sutherland (Ed.), *The Maturational Processes and the Facilitating Environment.* London: The Hogarth Press, 1985.

Winnicott, D. W. (1960b). Ego distortion in terms of true and false self. In: J. D. Sutherland (Ed.), *The Maturational Processes and the Facilitating Environment.* London: The Hogarth Press, 1985.

Winnicott, D. W. (1962). The aims of psycho-analytic treatment. In: J. D. Sutherland (Ed.), *The Maturational Processes and the Facilitating Environment.* London: The Hogarth Press, 1985.

Winnicott, D. W. (1963a). The development of the capacity for concern. In: J. D. Sutherland (Ed.), *The Maturational Processes and the Facilitating Environment.* London: The Hogarth Press, 1985.

Winnicott, D. W. (1963h). Psychiatric disorder in terms of infantile maturational processes. In: J. D. Sutherland (Ed.), *The Maturational Processes and the Facilitating Environment.* London: The Hogarth Press, 1985.

Winnicott, D. W. (1963j). Dependence in infant-care, in child-care, and in the psycho-analytic setting. In: J. D. Sutherland (Ed.), *The Maturational Processes and the Facilitating Environment.* London: The Hogarth Press, 1985.

Winnicott, D. W. (1971). *Playing and Reality.* London: Tavistock.

Winnicott, D. W. (1988). *Human Nature,* ed. C. Bollas, M. Dais, and R. Shepherd. London: Free Association Books.

Wittgenstein, L. (1953). *Philosophical Investigations,* trans. G. Anscombe. Oxford: Basil Blackwell, 1986.

Wittgenstein, L. (1967). *Lectures and Conversations.* Ed. C. Barrett. Oxford: Basil Blackwell.

Wood, D. (1989). *The Deconstruction of Time.* Atlantic Highlands, NJ: Humanities Press, 1991.

# INDEX